Leisure & Community Services

D1098710

Please return this item by the last date st.
it was borrowed.

Renewals
Any item may be renewed twice by telephone or post, provided it is not
required by another customer. Please quote the barcode number.

Overdue Charges
Please see library notices for the current rate of charges levied on overdue
items. Please note that the overdue charges are made on junior books borrowed
on adult tickets.

Postage 7 8 5 . 4 3
Postage on overdue notices is payable.

03/02	27 OCT 2003	7 MAR 2007
-9 APR 2002	23 JUN 2004	
27 APR 2002		- 4 MAY 2007
	18 AUG 2004 28 FEB 2005	14 AUG 2007
-3 SEP 2002	BEC	
24 SEP 2002		23 MAY 2008
	2 5 NOV 2005	
25 NOV 2002	16 SEP 2006	- 2 APR 2024
22 FEB 2003	24 FEB 2007	

THE LONDON BOROUGH

238.00

publishing

Helter Skelter Publishing, London

BROMLEY LIBRARIES

3 0128 02398 5610

This edition published in 2001 by Helter Skelter Publishing,
4 Denmark Street, London WC2H 8LL

First published in the United States of America by E.P. Dutton, 1974
under the title *S. T.P. A Journey Through America with The Rolling Stones*

First published in Great Britain by Michael Joseph Ltd under the title
Stones Touring Party Paperback edition Panther Books Ltd, 1975
First Helter Skelter edition, 1997

Grateful acknowledgement is made for permission to reprint from the
following: *A Moveable Feast* by Ernest Hemingway. Copyright 1964
by Ernest Hemingway. Reprinted by permission of Charles Scribner's
& Sons.
Steppenwolf by Herman Hesse. Translated by Basil Creighton.
Copyright 1929, 1957 by Holt, Rhinehart and Winston, Inc.
Reprinted by permission of Holt, Rhinehart and Winston, Inc.

A CIP record for this book is available from the British Library

ISBN 1-900924-24-2

The publishers would like to thank the following for their help with
this edition: Robert Greenfield himself and Sue Bradbury at Michael
Joseph. Helter Skelter would also like to give a special thanks to Karin
Bird and to the wonderful Mr. Rankin for his foreword.

Cover design by Bold.
Typesetting by SAF.

"In May 1972, the Rolling Stones began a tour of the States, and Robert Greenfield, the rock journalist, went with them to record it. He's an enterprising writer, often deserting the circus itself to follow the progress of individuals brushed by its passage. He's clever too at analysing the comings and goings of the beautiful people, Mrs. Jagger among them, and his portrait of Truman Capote is as malicious as its subject. There is also a riveting section on the Stones' sojourn chez Hefner where what every ageing Playboy Club member dreams of really happens. Drama abounds. Jagger gets gaoled in Providence while, 50 miles away in Boston, the audience boils up to near riot. There's lashings of dope 'n' sex, as they used to call it in the Underground press, all described with that obligatory air of deadpan detachment... a theatrical experience."

George Melly, *The Guardian*

"Accustomed as we are to rock revelry, I doubt if anything before, or since, can match the spectacular high links of that [1972] Stones tour which straddled America."

Donald Zec, *Daily Mirror*

"Greenfield has done his work well, talking to almost everyone involved with the tour. His view is panoramic and rich with impressions."

Lloyd Grossman, *Time Out*

"...exceptionally well-written and highly readable."

Jerry Hopkins, *Los Angeles Times*

"Unsparing in its picture of the calculation and lyrical decadence behind the tour."

John Rockwell, *New York Times*

"Skip this review and rush right down to you local bookstore and get a copy... reads like the best fiction."

Ed Ward, *Creem*

Foreword

1972 was the year of the flexi-disc. They came free with your copy of *Sounds, New Musical Express* and *Melody Maker*. 1972 was also the year of *Exile on Main Street*, which many Stones fans regard as the band's greatest album - maybe even the best rock album ever made. Extracts from it appeared on a free flexi-disc (*NME* cover-mounted, I think). I remember my local newsagent had sold out before I could get down there. Not that I was disheartened. I was twelve years old and not a big fan of the group. My big sister's boyfriend was. He'd let me hear *Let It Bleed* (I think the thing that most impressed me was the free poster of Mick Jagger as Ned Kelly). I'd argued with him, told him Alice Cooper and Hawkwind could stiff the Stones any day. Shows how much I knew...

May 1972 saw the Stones set out on a North American tour. Post-Altamont, the band had a lot of work to do. Groups like The Who and Led Zeppelin were out there, aiming at the tag 'Greatest Rock 'n' Roll Band on Earth'. As Jagger, Richard and the rest set off to reconquer America, a Rolling Stone journalist called Robert Greenfield accompanied them. He caught the whole act, and survived to bring back the story.

And what a story it is.

Greenfield is an exceptional writer. We don't just get the salacious stuff (though there's enough of it to satisfy!), but are also presented with needle-sharp images of the cities on the tour and, with them, the state of America's psyche. Greenfield takes us to Los Angeles, where the US makes the world's 'fantasy food'. He delineates a San Francisco rapidly undergoing a change for the worse as the counter-culture turns respectable. Chicago, meat capital of the nation, is here, too, and so is New York. Along the way, the tour gathers momentum, attracting more and more celebrities, sleaze-balls and groupies into its maelstrom. At one point, the entourage takes over Hugh Hefner's Playboy mansion for what has to be the wildest party ever seen there.

Yet Greenfield is also very good on the tedium of touring, the relentless and ruthless grind of it all. Toughness is required to service such an undertaking, and there are great portraits of the men behind the scenes, especially Marshall Chess and the redoubtable Chip Monck. Greenfield also finds time for sympathetic descriptions of the quiet Stones - Watts, Taylor, Wyman - and pays overdue attention to the more minor players, Stones 'members' such as Nicky Hopkins and Bobby Keys - we get their stories, too. Ian Stewart pops up from time to time, remaining, as in other books about the band, a shadowy figure, yet his presence is palpable throughout, sane and rather sad and, for me, the group's talisman.

A Journey Through America is just that. Greenfield notes the growing violence and paranoia in US society, counterpointing the grandeur of the tour (Lee Radziwill and Truman Capote were among the hangers-on) with the mess in Vietnam and the growing ugliness of the prevailing youth culture. Riots and gate-crashings, clashes with police and authority… while aloof from reality, Greenfield reminds us that back then the Stones acted as a perfect barometer of the times.

He wasn't alone, of course. Other journalists and photographers followed the tour. Among them, the film-maker Robert Franks, intent on capturing scandal on celluloid for his infamous record of the tour's excesses, *Cocksucker Blues*. In one episode, Greenfield both trumps all these other commentators and shows his basic humanity by recording the events surrounding the film, but from the point of view of the sad groupie on the actual airplane.

By the time the Stones get themselves arrested in Rhode Island, and head on to the final triumphant shows in New York, even sceptics will find themselves feeling some sympathy for the old devils, as a weary Mick Jagger celebrates his twenty-ninth birthday and Chip Monck finds the owners of Madison Square Garden strangely reluctant to let him drop five hundred live chickens onto the final night's audience.

This is one of the greatest rock books ever written, an objective and sometimes moving account of the madness surrounding the Stones and the madness of a nation at war with itself. That Greenfield emerged alive and with a semblance of sanity is a major achievement. That he also gifted us this account is a goddamned blessing.

Ian Rankin
Edinburgh, 2001

Preface to the 1997 edition

Where to begin? Having labored without cease (and with no success whatsoever) for the past twenty-five years to get this book republished, I should have quite a lot to say about it now. In actual fact, the exact opposite seems to be true.

Having written *A Journey Through America with the Rolling Stones* at the fairly tender age of twenty-five, I now seem to be twice as old. (Not to mention sixteen times as tired.) In the quarter of a century which just whizzed by my head like a shot, the world itself has entirely changed. Not once but a hundred times. Nothing now is as it once was. Or so all those cyberpunks playing their cyberpunk music much too loud down the cyberpunk hallway would lead you to believe.

And yet even as I write this preface, word has come down from on high that once more this summer, those self-same Rolling Stones will again journey through America in the name of sex, drugs, and rock 'n' roll, not to mention the occasional cheeseburger with fries to go. No matter how madly the world spins, some things never do seem to change, at least not in the oh so fickle world of rock.

Still, all is not now as it was back then. Although Mick and Keith and Charlie remain Rolling Stones (and without any one of them, the band itself would no longer be the Stones), Mick Taylor and Bill Wyman are no longer up there playing with them. Having left of their own accord, both are still around. Sadly, the same cannot be said for those who have been lost along the way.

Had anyone told me twenty-five years ago that Ian Stewart, the Stones' original piano player, whose drugs of choice (in order of preference) were red meat, single malt whiskey, and golf would be long dead while Keith Richard, he of the lifestyle that challengeth human endurance, would not only be alive and well but living much like Uncle Wiggily in Connecticut, I would have laughed myself sick and then gone out looking for yet another party after the show in some multi-tiered Hyatt along the road.

I may have just come to my first substantive point.

Since whenever the Rolling Stones' names come up in conversation these days, it's only the fact of their surviving that seems to count, perhaps what's most remarkable is that so few of those portrayed in this book have actually met their maker in the ensuing years. Among those who were close to the Stones back then, only Ian Stewart and Nicky Hopkins, a gentle soul who was never all that healthy but whom the Stones regularly brought in to replace Stew on piano in the studio and on tour, are dead. Truman Capote, the well known American author, has also shuffled off his mortal coil. But then he was the reason I found myself leaving the tour in Nashville at five in the morning. The awful truth was that this was the last thing in the world I wanted to do.

Having been assigned to cover the entire tour by *Rolling Stone* magazine, I had been informed over the phone that after I filed one last story, my services would no longer be needed. "Truman, baby" (as Stones insiders on the tour called Capote) would be taking over for me. My job was to make my last article an utter masterpiece, one suitable for framing, no doubt on the front cover of the magazine. Accepting the challenge, I flew home and got to work.

What no one knew back then was that although Truman Capote partied heartily with the Stones, he would never write a single word about any of it for anyone. Instead, he preferred to talk about his adventures to Johnny Carson on late night television. Even now, it's hard to find a more fitting metaphor for what this tour was really all about. Not sex or drugs or rock 'n' roll but both overwhelming stardom and the initial acceptance of rock 'n' roll in America by mainstream culture, not to mention a large segment of the jet set as well. In terms of celebrities using one another amidst a feeding frenzy of massed media, this tour began the modern era in rock.

How was it that I found myself along for the ride in the first place? You well may ask.

I got the job because I'd accompanied the Stones on their "farewell tour" of England in the spring of 1971. I'd then spent two never-to-be-forgotten weeks in Keith Richard's bungalow-by-the-sea in the south of France, waiting for him to finish having fun so we could complete an interview which then ran on the cover of *Rolling Stone*. I was someone the band's management trusted.

My fondest memories of the tour remain entirely personal and so did not make their way into the book. Rocking and rolling in the back of the bus and in various hotels until all hours of the night with Gary Stromberg, Chip Monck, and the Pisces Apple Lady herself, Chris O'Dell. The never ending kindness extended to me by Georgia Bergman, Alan Dunn, Peter Rudge, and the late Ian Stewart. Clearly, I remember drinking dark beer with Charlie Watts and photographer Annie Leibovitz in some very collegiate pizza parlor in Dallas where all anyone on the tour really wanted to do was see Dealey Plaza and the grassy knoll from which the shots were supposedly fired that really killed JFK.

Just as clearly, I remember sitting before a show in Houston in the boxy little house trailer used to whisk the Stones out of arenas after every show. At a fold-up dining table, I was wailing away like Art Tatum on an acoustic typewriter (a writing device not attached to any serial port) to make my deadline. I looked up to see a bemused Charlie Watts peering at me through one of the trailer's open windows. "Doin' yer homework then, are ya?" he asked, drumsticks spinning like helicopter rotors in his hands as he went on to play.

Perhaps the strongest memory I have of the tour is how I felt when I finally saw what the editors at the magazine had done to all the copy I'd filed from my home in LA. Without informing me, they'd edited my masterpiece down into no more than elaborate captions for some terrific photographs by Annie. Having already been unceremoniously yanked off the tour, I now felt twice betrayed. From a payphone at the back of some pseudo-French cafe on Melrose Avenue in LA, I told the man in charge what he could do with his magazine and resigned. So much for my burgeoning career in rock journalism. Stuck in Topanga Canyon, I watched helplessly as the Stones played cities I never got to see. It was quite a shock to the old rock 'n' roll ego.

Once all the tremors subsided, I knew I was done. The time had come for me to return to graduate school, earn my Phd., and begin teaching. Then from out of the proverbial blue, I received a phone call from a publishing house which has been out of business longer than either of my children has been alive. Having seen what I'd written in the magazine, they were interested in my doing a book.

Accepting the princely sum of four thousand dollars (in later years, I would come to refer to this as my first mid-four figure advance) while wondering if there could actually be this much money in the world, I flew to New York to pick up the tour as it reached its calamitous conclusion in Madison Square Garden. Thankfully, I still had my plastic photo laminate identifying me as a full fledged member of the Stones' touring party. (In fact, I still have it now. All bids to be faxed to the publisher.) Amazingly, I had not missed all that many shows. What I hadn't seen personally, I was able to reconstruct from interviews I did later on.

Once the final shows were over, I embarked on a personal odyssey, going from LA to San Francisco to New York to London and then Kingston, Jamaica where the Stones were recording *Goat's Head Soup* before returning once more to California. Taking up residence in a damp two room cabin that overlooked the blue Pacific, I wrote this book in about three months.

As it turned out, the book itself appeared long before its time. Though it may well be the first book length journalistic account of a rock tour, there was no audience for it then. In America, only fifteen hundred hardback copies and thirty five hundred trade paperback copies were printed. As the years went by, the book acquired a kind of status of its own. Hard to find, it became a collector's item on both sides of the Atlantic.

Not until I went out to publicize *Bill Graham Presents: My Life Inside Rock and Out* in 1992 (I'd had my first real conversation with Bill while interviewing him for this book) did I begin meeting people who told me how much this book had meant to them during their teenage years. From what I could gather, no volume without explicit sex scenes on every other page had ever been stolen from more public libraries. For a more sincere tribute, no author can ask. I only wish that some of the friends to whom I gave signed first editions hadn't lost them in the divorce, when the commune split up, man, or when the earthquake struck.

In terms of my relationship with the Stones themselves, it is to their great credit that from them, I never heard a single discouraging word about the book. (But then how could I, mate, when every last word in it is true?) Not that I spent much time hanging out with them once the tour was over. With the Stones both then and now, you were either on the bus or off the bus. After the book was done, I had no more business with them, nor them with me.

Always, my central connection to the band was Keith. We'd first met on the farewell tour to England when without saying a word to one another, we both took the hinges off a dressing room door in Brighton so the band could get inside. After interviewing Keith in Jamaica, nearly twenty years went by before I saw him again. In an office in New York City in the middle of the afternoon, he put away half a bottle of Wild Turkey while talking to me about Bill Graham. Although his drug of choice had changed, he was still Keith in almost every way. In terms of life's rich pageant and where it often leads us, that's about as much as you can ask of anyone.

In any event, twenty five years on, here's *A Journey Through America with the Rolling Stones* coming at you once more with all stops out just like the Stones themselves. As I did back then, I hope you enjoy reading it as much as I did putting it together. Settle back, put up your feet, and get ready to roll with the Stones.

As Mister Jagger himself once wrote, "It's only rock 'n' roll/But I like it." And I do. Still. For that more than anything else, with the possible exception of my family, I truly am grateful.

Robert Greenfield
Carmel, California.
June, 1997

For Michael H., who was the child of us all.

This is to thank Jerry in San Francisco, Joel in the Canyon, Mollie and Manny in Brooklyn, and Jeff and Sammy in London for letting me live in their homes when I didn't have one of my own. This is to acknowledge the folks who told the truth when you asked them a question.

Closer to home, I'd like to congratulate the Pacific Grove All-Stars and all their ladies for their on-the-court attitude and Don and Margo in particular, for theirs off. Finally, I'd like to thank Janice for keeping me dry through the wettest winter in eighty-three years.

'Music does not depend on being right, on having good taste and education and all that.'

'Indeed, then what does it depend on?"

On making music Herr Haller, on making music as well and as much as possible and with all the intensity of which one is capable. That is the point, Monsieur.'

Hermann Hesse, Steppenwolf

Tales from Rock and Roll Heaven

MY MAN ERNIE

Maybe my man Ernie has nothing to do with any of this. But I can still see that bus pulling out from the corner in Brooklyn with the bank and the clock on it on a murky November day in 1963, with Ernie sitting where he always sits, last seat on the right, all the way in the back, high up over the engine so he can lean out and spit at passers-by when the bus gets slowed in traffic and there's not much flowing by on the streets.

As the bus pulls out, green and whalelike from the corner, spouting white fumes from the exhaust, Ernie has his head stuck out of the window, and he's hunched up and squinting forward. With the palm of one hand he is pounding out this rhythm against the side of the bus... 'Hey... you... getawf... a... my cloud' and again, 'Hey... you... getawf... a... my cloud' and kicking it out in time with his black, high-top Converse sneakers on the green, poured-plastic seat in front of him. Slap, bang, pam, wow... 'Getawf... a... my cloud...' so that the whole bus is vibrating slightly from side to side and the old ladies are beginning to peer from around their brown-paper shopping bags at this newest outrage on a system of public transport regularly ridden by madmen.

For some reason Ernie suddenly looks back, toward the corner with the bank and the clock on it, and sees me coming to the stop. I'm loaded with books and late for classes, a miserable freshman at a municipal college, and Ernie is the first dropout, from everything, but he digs me and wants to explain so out the bus window he sticks his right hand in which a tiny Japanese transistor blares. I catch one faint 'getawf' and know it is the Stones and then Ernie laughs his deep crazy belly laugh and points to the

radio as if to say... YOU DON'T NEED TO KNOW MORE...
HERE! THIS IS IT!!

And as the bus picks up speed and disappears into traffic, Ernie
sits with his hand out of the window, holding an imitation Sony
aloft to a gray and threatening November sky, as some kind of
final offering, as if to say, 'Don't rain on it, Lord, it's only rock
and roll.'

It is possible that Ernie might even have gone to see the Rolling Stones on one of their early tours across America, but I doubt
it. The Apollo Theater on Wednesday nights was where he saw
his music—James Brown, Wilson Pickett and Otis, B.B., Spoon,
and T-Bone, the Temptations, the Orlons, and Major Lance—
with a bottle of Thunderbird in his coat pocket, if he could afford
it.

I am sure he did not see them in 1969 because he spent that
year and a good part of the next in a federal prison for draft eva-
sion, a crime which fit those times, and that tour, far better than
the one in 1972.

It is now five or six years since I have seen Ernie but I can say
with a fair degree of accuracy that he was not among the 500
thousand people who sent postcards to Madison Square Garden
asking to attend one of the four Rolling Stones' concerts there
July 1972. Postcards were never part of his style.

So maybe all of this is irrelevant. Ernie is married now, someone tells me, and he paints houses for a living. He still lives in
Brooklyn but rarely plays the mouth harp on basketball courts at
three in the morning anymore. It seems he's developed this whole
new way of speaking, too, so that you can hardly tell that he came
from the projects and the schoolyard and the night center.

And all this is completely understandable to me. In a few years
Ernie will be thirty. We all will. And congratulations are not necessarily in order.

Prologue

MAY

During the final week in May 1972 the weather in Los Angeles was unseasonably warm. In a place where there are no seasons and the days pass in neat succession, one late-night weather report being exactly like the six that preceded it, extremes in temperature are always welcome. The blazing desert heat of a selected week in July gives Angelenos a chance to complain about summer and run to the beach. The no-breathing-possible hours when the Santa Ana blows in late August and September are a prelude to autumn. The cloudy, temperate days that pass for the rainy season in January are an attempt to portray winter in a town where there is no winter. The fluctuations in the fever chart of L.A.'s temperatures are like old friends, come round to remind you of the passing of time, of another piece of a year gone away somewhere, unnoticed.

So the week of ninety-five-degree days that ended May, days that piled the brown gray smog layer upon layer over Beverly Hills and Hollywood, and crowded the white sand at State Beach with browned bodies, that had the cars parked three deep and at angles on the coast at Sunset and Chatauqua boulevards, brought the message that it was about to be summer again.

America, a country that Los Angeles is sometimes said to be part of, was entering its one hundred and ninety-sixth year of Constitution. In Vietnam, there was a war going on, and we were losing. Four hundred miles up the California coast from L.A. a black woman named Angela Davis was on trial for her life. The charges were murder and conspiracy and we (the citizens of California, as represented by the state's attorney) were losing. Ronald Reagan had been the governor of California for over six years. Richard Nixon had been president of America for nearly four years. No one knew if they were winning or losing. It took too much effort to find out.

Few, if any, of these things, however, concerned one entire segment of the L.A. catalogue of subcultures: genus, music business; species, rock and roll; hereinafter referred to as the rockbiz. That week, rockbiz people had more important things on their minds, hearts, and checking accounts.

In England, where some tradition still exists, a royal coronation is a signal event, a moment in time that people date their own lives around. They bundle up their children in scarves and woolies and take them out to see the parade so they may tell *their* children about it. They buy plates and cups and silver spoons with the date and portraits of the royal family on them to commemorate an event they know will not soon come again.

No one thought to merchandise china with the faces of the Rolling Stones on it as they toured America during the summer of 1972. It was one of the few business oversights made.

For, in the rockbiz, bands spring full blown from hypester's heads, do one tour and an album and return to the obscurity from which they came. Unlike the Broadway stage, the rockbiz does not bestow commercial favor on revivals of great old bands. Comebacks are usually unsuccessful and no band that has ever been number one has slipped and then made it all the way back to the top. The rockbiz is perfectly L.A., totally American, *transitory*, hard, cruel, full of paranoia, with all of it going on in the monstrous present only, the great now, and with such *extreme* rewards for those willing to accept its challenge and go out on the edge to make it.

No, what the rockbiz cared about in May was not Angela Davis or the state of the nation or the blazing sunshine on the Strip, but a tour that was about to become the event of the season, and of the decade. And what the rockbiz buzzed about today, the youth of America would be listening to in four weeks, buying in five, and growing sick of in seven.

But the Rolling Stones' 1972 tour was bigger even than the youth of America, if such a market can be transcended in the space of a single sentence. After ten years of playing together, the Stones had somehow become the number one attraction in the world. Absolutely. The only great band of the sixties still around in original form playing original rock and roll. Finally at the top of the sickening heap of hype and promotion that makes the music industry rank right up there with politics and used cars as a future career for your child to avoid.

The Stones had been together for *ten years*. In the rockbiz, this is unheard of. Completely. They were royalty. No, even better, they were kings. Undeniably. By acclamation.

And it was to America they came to receive their crowns.

Each previous time the Rolling Stones had gone on the road in America for money, and to spread the gospel of good ole rock'n'roll, they had managed to crystallize whatever rampant energy was about in the country at the time. So it was that in 1969, their tour was a mad, chaotic adventure run by show-business hustlers and out-and-out grifters, with planes leaving empty in the middle of the night and landing at strange airports, and concerts getting underway five and six hours late. Still, throughout the chaos ran a motif of celebration, celebration for a counterculture that was finally getting to see a band they had long revered as heroes, fabulous cats who pissed where and when they wanted, who smoked dope and got busted but managed to always get their bail, who didn't accept medals from the Queen of England like the Beatles but went to Morocco and hung out in the hills with tribesmen. Because of all their changes, the Stones had not worked regularly for more than two years, so in 1969 they came back to find a new America, where people didn't scream or throw jelly babies at concerts, but smoked dope, listened, and got off on what they heard.

In the end, though, the chaos won out and what that tour is remembered for is Altamont, more by other people than by the Stones themselves, who were around for all the celebration too. But, with Altamont in mind, and with the knowledge that the 1972 tour would be twice as long as the previous one (two full months) in thirty major cities, with a tour party twice as large as that of 1969, the intent was to make this tour *professional*. A key word. And respectable. No more late concerts or multi-thousand-dollar unpaid tabs run up by the boys at the Plaza. This time everything, but everything, down to the smallest detail, would be done right.

Beginning with the sale of tickets. Tickets will cost six dollars and fifty cents each. A reasonable price. They will go on sale by mail in some cities and in California by Ticketron, an LA.-based computer firm. There will be a limit of two per customer. In theory, therefore, anyone who wants to go will be able to both afford a ticket and obtain one. In theory. No theory yet evolved has ever managed to stand up to Rolling Stones' Action Karma.

Jeffrey is from Encino. If you know Encino you already know a lot about Jeffrey. Encino is in the San Fernando Valley, on the other side of the Santa Monica Mountains from the sea.

There's always lots of smog in the valley and kids grow up straight and tall from drinking all that vitamin C-enriched O.J. and high-in-calcium milk. A lot of times life here is like a TV series. The kids drive Porsches and Peugeots because their fathers hold down executive jobs or own stereo distributorships, and a lot of 'em are Jewish and a lot of 'em are not, and they hang out at the Copper Penny and walk out on the check and throw lettuce around. They drop reds now and then and smoke dope but essentially they are just L.A. kids, full of the na vete a New Yorker might call dumbness, but they are kind clear through, and *sweet*. Anyway, Encino is a better place to be from than a lot of places in the valley because the kids there are for sure a little sharper than the ones from Chatsworth or San Fernando, which are places no one ever goes to.

Jeffrey, then, is from Encino and he knows he is being ripped off. Has to be. He has spent the night sleeping out in the Topanga Plaza shopping center along with about two hundred other kids, bundled in sleeping bags and blankets, with an occasional wine bottle rolling away on the concrete toward one of the cement, potted-tree boxes. Now with the sun climbing to a point high above the Century Broadway, a mammoth Southern California department store, and beating down on the white concrete, he has a half hour before the doors open. It is still so early that the day's smog layer hasn't begun to collect. Jeffrey changes into a white shirt he's brought along for the purpose and smoothes out the wrinkles in his pants and puts on a tie he hasn't worn since he dropped out of junior college and went to work at the Ford place. He smoothes his hair on both sides, and marches through a door on the side of the building marked 'Employees.' 'I'm in personnel,' he airily informs the guard there and he's actually three steps into the store before some pinched-face old biddy at a desk whimpers, 'Young man, *I* am in personnel and I've never seen *you* before.' The guard puts the collar on Jeffrey and shows him the door. The crowd outside is rattling around in its sleeping bags and newspapers, wondering how long before the doors open and tickets go on sale, and they see a fellow Stones fan being pushed out a door by a guard. 'Bitchin,' someone yells out. 'Way to *go*, man.' A few girls cheer.

'Mao? Mao! You are yes... the Mao Tse-tung of rock and roll. Sure you are. The people's promoter. Only now you're a film star too... like Jackie Gleason or Bob Eubanks. Only you're different, Bill... you made your million before you won your Oscar.'

Peter Rudge, manager of the Rolling Stones' 1972 tour of America is on the phone to Bill Graham, the grand old man of rock promoters, who founded the Fillmores, East and West, and will be responsible for the concerts in San Francisco, Los Angeles, San Diego, and Tucson. Rudge is in a room in the Beverly Rodeo (pronounce it Ro-day-o) Hotel in Beverly Hills with a phone receiver tucked in the ridge of his shoulder and a cigarette burning down between the second and third fingers of his right hand.

Both fingers are stained yellow with nicotine. Hot sun outside the windows is ignored. Lamp by the bed switched on. Ashtrays full of butts. Cigarette to mouth, puff-puff. Snap-snap go the fingers, plumes of smoke jetstream out of the nostrils, punctuating the sentences, 'Just checkin is all, Bill,' Rudge says, in this way he has of saying completely offensive things to people that make them smile. 'Just checking you remember the dates. The Rolling Stones? Yes... I know you're busy linin up your concessions for the night, but can I have a minute of your time?'

Rudge is a beefy, hawk-nosed, twenty-five-year-old Englishman with hair nearly down to his shoulders who spins off sentences like a rugby player breaking away from the field for the far touchline. Over the phone he has perfected this lethal, rapid-fire, David Frost-type delivery. Both he and Frost attended Fitzwilliam College at Cambridge. Rudge played rugby there, but an injury to his left leg ended his sports career and led him to find his true place, in the arts.

'The thing is, Bill, we've got to find out why they're charging the kids seven dollars a ticket at Long Beach. Naughty that is, naugh'y. Where's that extra half-dollar going?'

Everything that concerns the Stones on this tour concerns Peter Rudge. It pains him that the demand for tickets is so great at Ticketron outlets that the computer overloads and it takes twenty minutes to punch in a request. People who have waited up all night for tickets are told to go home, because teletype operators, unused to this kind of pressure, are in a state of battle fatigue and shock.

Peter Rudge does not want any fuckups on this tour. He does not want anyone killed at any time. He does not want anyone to call the Stones capitalist rip-off pigs. Goddamnit, and right now, he wants to know why they're daring to charge fifty cents extra at the arena in Long Beach.

'You've got it now, have you, Bill? The thing is, Bill, you're like an old man... no, it's nothing personal. It's just that you'll be booking Lawrence Welk soon'.

As luck would have it, Jeffrey sees Tod and Lee, two other guys from Encino in the crowd. He's down but not out. Out but not through. The three of them go around the far side of the building and Tod and Lee pull up this heavy iron grating, heave and grunt until they get it far enough off the floor for Jeffrey to wiggle under. He gets inside and pushes it up and they both slip underneath it. They go down a back stairway and it looks like they've got it made this time, until the stairway brings them out right by the desk where the same old biddy from Personnel is sitting. She sees Jeffrey and whimpers for a guard who throws them all out the same door.

'Hey, it's that dude *again*,' someone in the crowd shouts. 'Far *out*, brother.' There are more cheers.

Jo Bergman, a lady with a small, white, fine-boned face that looks almost pinched beneath her great corona of frizzy black hair is afloat on a bed covered with crew manifests, flight plans, promoter's schedules, and tour itineraries. She has the room a few doors down from Rudge in the Rodeo but all the doors on their floor have been thrown open and all the rooms have become one carpeted, airconditioned asylum populated by wired, babbling Rolling Stones' tour planners.

Miss Bergman is biting a pencil and looking desolate. She has misplaced something. For the past five years of her life she has been finding misplaced items for various Rolling Stones, Mick Jagger in particular, arranging for their cars, their weddings, their nannies, finding flights when there are no flights, doing things no civilised person should ever call upon another to do. Before that she worked for a firm called Nems, which handled the Beatles.

'SMERSH,' Jo says suddenly giggling away like the wicked witch in the *Wizard of Oz*. 'The SMERSH passes. That's what I'm looking for.' She burrows through two mounds of paper and emerges with a handful of red laminated passes with black letters on them and room for a photo, beneath a printed version of Peter Rudge's name and a line for his countersignature. 'His *counter-signature*,' Jo says. 'Do you understand? No one goes anywhere without these.'

'What's the S.T.P. stand for?' she is asked.

'Well, Chip Monck says it's "Stop Teasing Polacks." Somebody else says "Start Tripping Please" or an advertisement for the drug of the same name. Or that stuff you put in your engine to go faster? Vroom-vrooom? It started out as "Stones Touring Party".'

'What did?' Alan Dunn asks, coming through a side door to the room no one has noticed as yet: Dunn is an island of calm in a sea of crazies. Born almost within the sound of Bow Bells in Streatham, London, and therefore an official Cockney, he began with the Stones as a driver. He holds a pilot's license, was a road-cycling champion, rode horses as an extra in *Ned Kelly*, has permits to drive London Transport tube trains and double-decker buses, and earth-moving vehicles. Logically enough, he is in charge of transportation.

'I've just remembered I haven't had my breakfast today yet, Jo,' he says quietly. 'What is it, four o'clock? I called down to room service hours ago for some Eggs Benedict.'

Peter Rudge sticks his head in the room. A room-service waiter bustles in past him and begins setting up a table. 'Hello Alan,' Rudge grins. 'What's this? Champagne dinners in the middle of the afternoon? Burning up the per diem, boy? Throwing caution to the winds, eh?'

Dunn laughs and says, 'How we doing?'

'Pre'ey bad,' Rudge says. 'Right now we're walkin to Vancouver. After workin on it since January, it's a bit worryin not havin a plane to the first gig.'

Rudge exits and Chris O'Dell sweeps in. She is a straw-thin

lady with wide surprised eyes and blond, stuck-out Orphan Annie
hair who is secretary to Marshall Chess, president of Rolling
Stones Records. In actual practice she does all the things Jo Bergman used to do for the Stones in London while they are in L.A.
'Oh,' she says to Alan, who is smiling the contented smile of a
man about to finally dig into a long overdue meal. 'What are all
those black things on your eggs?'

'Benedicts,' he says, calmly slopping brown sauce over a good-
sized portion of his plate.

Jeffrey knows that somebody is in there already, cutting a corner,
and waiting on line for tickets *ahead* of him. Even as he stands
outside the store, he is being ripped off. Hot already and it's
only nine-thirty. The unsmogged sunshine makes everything look
dead and worn, glints off the great fountain-type things that pass
for sculpture on the second-floor mall that is replete with over-
hanging lights for night strolling and shopping. The plaza is truly
one of the valley's architectural wonders. Jeffrey, Lee, and Tod
leave the crowd and keep walking, casually, up the mall steps,
around to the building's other side where they locate another
entrance with a moveable grating. Up it goes and Jeffrey's in and
under and down a back stairway that opens out into the Boy's
Department.

The Boy's Department. Jeffrey ducks into a dressing room to
think this one out for a second. No telling what that heat-crazed
biddy downstairs will do if she gets him this time. But they aren't
selling tickets in the dressing room. He walks on to the floor, and
over to a pile of Levis where he straightens his tie and makes like
one of those floorwalkers you see in Macy's or Burdine's, who
are all the time straightening up piles of things to make themselves look official. Farther down the counter is a cash register
next to which lays—and right here it is bonus time, without a
doubt—the nameplate of some poor salesman or clerk who left
it there at closing time, figuring to pick it up in the morning.
Jeffrey clips the nameplate onto his pocket and takes the escala-
tor down to the Ticketron booth. For the first time all day, he is
legal.

And already eight people are in line there. Bitchin. All sus-
picions confirmed. The company's got the fix in for its own
employees. All these poor kids who have been outside for any-

where from ten to sixteen hours, on the pavement, with nothing but a bottle of Boone's Farm apple wine and an unlimited supply of grass to keep them going are being... ripped off. Precisely. It's got to where you have to be a criminal in America these days just to stay even.

'Who is that?' the lady in front of Jeffrey says suddenly to the lady in front of her, pointing. 'I've never seen him before.' Two old darlings standing in line for tickets for their grandnieces or something and Jeffrey can feel the bust coming. 'Oh,' he says, charming as you please, lying through his teeth, 'I work in the Boy's Department I started last week.'

Well, the ladies are hemming and hawing over that one and about to go for the guard when a longhair in front of them says, 'Hey. He's okay. I know the guy. He works in shirts.' The two ladies relax, the bust is postponed and Jeffrey smiles gratefully to the fellow freak who pulled him out.

Ian Stewart comes into the room at the Rodeo where Dunn is trying to eat. Stew is a short square Scot with black hair and a prognathous jaw who has been with the Rolling Stones longer than anyone. He *is* a Rolling Stone, having been their original piano player when Jagger, Keith Richard, and Brian Jones were looking for a drummer who could find the offbeat and a bass player who would show up for gigs. When Andrew Oldham took over managing the band, it was decided that Stew, who had always looked solidly respectable, did not fit the image. Since he had been driving them to gigs anyway, he kept on doing it. He still does this now, ten years later, driving gig to gig to check out the amps and the stage set, sitting down on stage occasionally to play piano on 'Brown Sugar' or 'Honky Tonk Women.'

'Brown sauce on Eggs Benedict?' he says to no one in particular. 'How disgustin.'

'How we doin on the plane to Vancouver?' he asks Rudge. The plane to Vancouver is non-existent. Rudge has just hung up after a ten-minute phone conversation in which he battered a man from the company contracted to supply the Stones with their own Lockheed-Electra. Rudge explained to the man that the jet must be ready by nine Friday night, so that the band can do a sound test in the hall because the Vancouver police have required them to open the doors to the hall at three on Saturday afternoon

to prevent trouble on the streets. In the conversation, Rudge has
used the word 'need' in every other sentence, interspersed with
an occasional 'Yes, I understand,' then immediately following it
again with another sentence of 'need.'

'We're walkin is all,' he says now, rapid fire and double quick.
'Nothin serious though.'

'Well,' Stew says, 'we can always do Vancouver on July 17...
between Toronto and Montreal.' Both Rudge and Dunn blanch
visibly at the thought. 'Serve the bloody Canadian government
right.'

'We own it, don't we?' Rudge says, meaning Canada, ' 'E says
we do.' He points to Dunn. 'If we own it, we don't have to go
through Customs.'

'Rhubarb,' Stew scowls. 'It was all a lot simpler when they were
being driven to gigs in the transit. Just get in and go. None of this
international foolishness.' He gets up and leaves the room. After
he's gone, Rudge says, 'How's he going to Canada?'

'With the crew,' Dunn says, from around his eggs, 'Western
Airlines.'

'Does he approve of that airline?'

'No,' Dunn says, without changing expression or breaking the
rhythm of the fork to his mouth. 'He might drive his old red
transit up yet. Across Lake Erie. Like the old days.'

'Did he tell you that?' Rudge says, pretending to be worried.
'Did he? You're his friend, Alan, I know. He wouldn't be caught
dead telling young Rudge his plans, that's for sure.'

As soon as it's ten o'clock the Century-Broadway opens officially.
Buzzers go off and the doors pop open and Jeffrey feels it as much
as hears it. Thundering... from across the building... toward him
and the Ticketron counter. Then he sees them. The horde of
freaks who will not be denied, hauling ass through the furniture
department, pounding past shelves of cut-glass decanters and
wooden salad bowls, running up the down escalators, tearing
away the rope from in front of the Ticketron booth and obliterat-
ing the line. For the first time all day, Jeffrey feels fear.

Dunn and Rudge go off to confer about the plane-to-Vancouver
crisis. They're in a room for a very long time with the doors
locked.

They must be hammering out something in there. Some kind of deal. Jo Bergman is stapling away at the itineraries when she hears a scream from the roof of the building next door. She looks up and there is Dunn, with one leg hooked over the pipe railing and both hands waving free, crying, 'I've got it. I've got it. We'll fly the Playboy plane to Seattle, then bring them around through some logging port by boat and there'll be no Customs. None.'

'Things are getting a little weird around here,' Jo giggles, squeezing down hard on the word 'weird' and stapling everything on the left side of the bed together.

By the time the thundering stops and the crowd starts milling around and shouting at the Ticketron lady, Jeffrey has the situation in hand. In his palm to be exact. Four tickets for the Stones at the Los Angeles Forum. Two of the tickets he sells immediately for thirty dollars apiece. The other two he pockets. He pulls off his tie, throws away the nameplate and gets back to the Ford place where he works in time to clock in a full day.

Everyone who wants a ticket is not as resourceful as Encino Jeffrey. In the San Francisco area, for instance, eighteen thousand tickets are available at two hundred Ticketron outlets, with a limit of four per customer. Roughly this breaks down to the first twenty-two and a half people on line at each place getting satisfaction. And so concert promoters begin receiving letters.

Dear Sir,
My son stood in line for many hours on Monday in hopes of buying tickets to see the Rolling Stones but they sold out before he could get to the window. He wanted to take his only sister to this great perform-ance. My daughter, who lost her leg last year from bone cancer, now has lung cancer. There is no cure. She does not know this. If you can find it in your hearts to send us tickets... with the help of God she will be able to attend. It is just a matter of time before she will leave us and go to Heaven. Please help me give her some pleasure....

In Detroit, 30 thousand letters are received, with 120 thou-sand requests for the 12 thousand available seats. In Chicago, 34 thousand tickets sell-out in five and a half hours. In Los Angeles, when a second show is added at the Forum, 50 thousand pieces of mail arrive, pleading for a chance to watch. That week in L.A., a ticket to a Stones' concert was better than a negotiable bond. You could get anything you needed for it.

Seven grams of hash and a twenty-dollar lid was not considered an unreasonable asking price. Nor were offers of fifty dollars and over. With the Stones playing three places in the L.A. area, the Forum, the Long Beach Arena, and the Hollywood Palladium, the Palladium immediately became the hottest ticket, the Panama Red of admission slips. One kid spent a day on the phone looking for a way into the Palladium, making offers, raising and raising the ante with each call until he finally got one... in exchange for two tickets to Jethro Tull and Led Zeppelin at the Forum and the Grateful Dead at the Hollywood Bowl and twelve new albums. All he had to do then was wait in line outside the Palladium for eight hours and he was home free.

They couldn't sell the 1969 tour to the media. Life, Look, *the* Saturday Evening Post, *they all turned it down. Why all the interest now? It could have been Mick that got it at Altamont... and that's why they all want to be around this time.*

Ethan Russell, *the Stones' photographer*

A few months before the tour begins, in late spring, Michael Philip Jagger, called Mick, and Keith Richard, n e Richards (Andrew Oldham suggested he drop the final 's' of his given name to make it more sibilant or more teeny-market acceptable or something) are on their way to the L.A. studio where the final mix on an album to be called 'Exile on Main Street' is going on. Both Jagger and Richard have been in Los Angeles since just after Christmas, doing this one thing—mixing, that is, arranging the separately recorded tracks so as to give each song its peak overall sound and feel.

Like most music work, mixing goes on at night. It's early evening as the two roll down the Strip in Mick's car. Word has just got out in the music papers that there will be a Stones' tour in the summer. Jagger pulls into a parking lot across from the studio and they sit there for a moment, with the car radio on, talking and listening to the music. Four young girls come up to the car and Mick rolls his window down. The girls recognize him and giggle. One, braver than the rest, a fifteen-year-old California hardbelly, with nothing more on her mind than tomorrow's surf conditions and the exciting presence of Jagger, comes forward and breathes, 'Oh, Mick. We heard today you're gonna tour. That's... great!'

'Yeah,' Mick says.

She takes another step forward and leans toward the car. 'Mick,' she says, all twinkling and breathy, 'aren't you afraid of being shot?' Jagger has to look twice and very carefully at the girl's face to make sure he's not being put on. But she is just looking at him innocently, sincerely interested, having asked the first natural question that popped into her head when she heard her favorite band and rock's greatest superstar were going to take it out on the road again.

'Yeah,' Jagger says slowly, 'yeah. I am.'

All during May, as the tour gets closer and George Wallace gets gunned down in a suburban Maryland shopping center, Mick's out-of-the-business friends somehow manage to subtly bring the sobering subject into conversation, without actually getting down to saying *it*, but hinting that perhaps it is.... ah, unwise to... cross such a dangerous place as America, in the summertime too, and perhaps... ah but surely Mick, there is no real need for you to go out again, what with movie offers and your own album so long overdue?

Each time, Jagger would inevitably drop the mask of bored inattention and quiet politeness he uses to get through most social situations, and bring forth that total schoolboy sincerity and honesty which is such a contrast that it can be heartrending and say, 'Well... ai mean... it's more or less wha ai do, inn't it? So I've *got* to do it. Ai mean, either I do it or... I don't do it. If I don't do it... wha am I going to do? Do ya know wha ai mean? I'm not going to do it forever anyway... so....'

Each person who heard him say it would say oh yes, well, if you feel that way, certainly, I can understand that, and go away realizing what a *hero* Mick really was, what a true champion, and how brave.

As he himself would say after the tour, 'Don't say I wasn't scared, man. I was scared shitless.'

On this tour, security was to be of the essence. Two black security guards would be along, one (Stan Moore) to oversee general hall and backstage operations, the other (Leroy Leonard) to body-

guard Mick and Keith, to be in the room next to them in hotels
and Holiday Inns, to sit on stage and hand Jagger the silver bowl
of rose petals that get strewn in the air during 'Street Fighting
Man,' to watch out for their asses in all danger-possible circumstances.

Still Rudge worried. He worried like a campaign manager with
a candidate to protect. He worried like a Secret Service man,
assigned to guard the president. The week before the tour, his
worries centered on the Palladium gig in L.A.. The Hollywood
Palladium is the home of Lawrence Welk and his Champagne
Music Makers, a-one and a-two, a low, conventional-looking,
L.A. stucco building that accommodates about forty-five hundred
people for a rock concert. Over fifteen thousand letters requesting sixty thousand tickets to the Palladium concert were received.
The Stones specified they wanted to play the hall because it is a
smaller place, with some feeling to it, a welcome break from the
antiseptic hockey arenas and sports stadiums they would be playing in most cities.

But the Palladium has a history of easy access, of broken-in
doors for Alice Cooper concerts, and bikers cruising on the street.
It is a place kids can get next to and hang out around, and even
a little girl I pick up hitchhiking on Ventura Boulevard tells me,
'The Palladium, man? I know there's going to be a riot there.
That's a walk-in concert. Everyone's goin to that one, ticket or no
ticket.'

So, with the tour five days away, Peter Rudge has the full-
blown Palladium horrors. He knows what is going to happen
there. Every kid in L.A. with nothing to do on Friday night will
come down to check out the action and then they'll start grabbing bricks from the construction site across the street and the
windows will go and every biker-Hells-Angel-brute-greaser from
Sepulveda Boulevard and San Berdoo will roar up in a cloud of
Harley smoke and it will be on. A full-scale riot. In his mind,
Peter Rudge can see how the newspapers will treat it, the headlines, big and black, and the tour he has worked on non-stop for
the past six months will go poof and vanish quietly in a puff of
smoke.

So he calls a meeting to talk about security. The Palladium
promoter, his second, and the hall manager attend. Rudge brings
along *his* second, Stan Moore, a powerfully built black man who

is on leave from his job as a government security officer to do the same for the Stones. Moore is in his forties, has spent twelve years as a policeman and detective in Baltimore, and worked for Bill Graham in the early days of the original Fillmore. Rudge arrives at the meeting very late and is ushered up a stairway, through a suite of offices to a polished wooden table strewn with maps, diagrams, and blueprints. A star-burst lamp and a burnt orange carpet and a secretary scurrying for Cokes. A Japanese-American policeman sits at the head of the table. He has sergeant's stripes on his sleeve and a tired look on his face. 'Can we begin?' he asks. 'They left two bombs today at the Lebanese Embassy. No one knows who. They're blaming everyone. Even the Japanese.'

The promoter begins to detail his plan of action. Two men at the gate and one at the back door, the marquee with no indication that the Stones are inside, merely a 'Sorry, Sold Out' notice. Five of his men on the street in the morning, ten in the afternoon, twenty as darkness approaches.

'And,' he says, concluding triumphantly, 'at 4:30, the L.A.P.D. come on.' He stops and smiles. 'And they're *crack*.'

The Japanese-American sergeant accepts the compliment with a weary smile. 'And there'll be no parking on El Centro, none at all,' the promoter goes on.

'How about on Sunset?' Peter asks nervously, puff-puffing another cigarette into extinction.

'Well, you've got to understand, the normal flow of traffic out there on a Friday night is unbelievable anyway....'

'What if say, one hundred motorcycles come down Sunset in the normal flow of traffic,' Peter says, 'and choose to stop in front of the Palladium with their motors running?...'

'*Nothing* stops on Sunset,' the sergeant says quietly. 'If one hundred motorcycles come down that block, they go back up it. If they stop, we give 'em tickets. The city can use the money.'

'Ex-cellent, sergeant, ex-cellent,' Peter says, talking to him as though he were a small child showing off some new toy. 'But what about this perimeter?' His finger darts to a place on one of the maps on the table. Smoke streams out into the lamplight. Heads crane to see what he is referring to. 'I'll have ten bikes,' the sergeant says quietly, 'forty men on foot... and if I need 'em, five thousand men to back me up.'

'Don't mess with the L.A.P.D.,' the promoter says proudly.

'We'll be okay,' his partner says: 'We've got our vents wired, our windows boarded up, and three men on the roof. All the trash cans are gone and our men will be out in the street, attacking the kids, asking for tickets. Now what I wanna know is what happens when the Rolling Stones don't show up on time?'

Rudge is being challenged 'The Rolling Stones will be there,' he says, not bothering to even acknowledge the question with a look.

'That's what you say now but when that night comes around and it's time for them to go on, all the security in the world isn't gonna do us a bit of good, if they aren't here.'

'The Stones will be *there,*' Peter repeats. 'Now what about this catch basin out in the parking lot. I hear kids are planning to sneak in through the drainpipe.'

Drainpipe. What drainpipe? Who is this crazy Englishman? How does he know about drainpipes in the parking lot of the Hollywood Palladium? The hall manager scurries for the blueprints. Rustling of paper and clearing of throats. Confusion.

'Here.....'

'Ah, no... there, no, gimme a minute.' Hands in the lamplight. Blueprints. 'A minute. I'll find it.'

'There... here it is.... No, no way, Peter. It's a one inch pipe. Rest assured no one will get in that way.... Peter, trust us, we'll have dog handlers out there....'

The meeting goes on for another fifteen minutes, then the sergeant leaves. He forgets his hat and has to come back for it, then leaves again. As the meeting breaks up, there's another flurry of reassurances. 'Look, Peter, it's gonna be taken care of...'

'The L.A.P.D. regard this place as a sacred house. They police the shit out of it.'

'Peter, just leave it to us. We'll do it right, you'll see.'

'Yes, well,' Rudge says, 'Stan? We'll be goin now.' They come down the staircase into a crowded Palladium ballroom. Cocktails sparkling and dance music lilting in the air. Women with blue-rinsed hair in washed-out taffeta gowns and men who look like they play a lot of tennis to keep their gray muscular sideburns in trim. Rudge looks across the room at a great banner that's strung across the stage and it says 'YORTY FOR PRESIDENT' in large letters. 'Mayor Sam?' Rudge says wonderingly to himself, 'Mayor Sam?'

For a second he stands there and just stares, this long-haired, English freak businessman from working-class Wolverhampton, in a black velvet jacket and jeans, the quintessential rockbiz outfit, glamor and poverty all at the same time, accompanied by a very together-looking black man with a definite Afro. Why, they are everything Mayor Sam stands foursquare against, they're the soft white underbelly that undermines America, they're crazies, and they've just come from a meeting that would delight the heart and win the vote of every manjack and silly old dear in the place who are convinced that law and order is the eleventh command-ment, right up there with 'Thou shalt not kill.'

Rudge and Stan Moore leave the hall and get into one of the boat-like airconditioned limousines they're using to get around. Rudge sinks exhaustedly into the front seat while Stan gets behind the wheel and eases her out of the lot.

'All this just to put that band on stage,' Peter sighs. 'Dog han-dlers, cops, wired vents... it's not exactly what rock and roll's all about, is it, Stan?'

'Sure are proud of their cops, ain't they?' Stan says.

'Too proud,' Rudge says, sitting suddenly bolt upright, '*too* confident. I don't trust them. They sound like they wouldn't mind a few kids getting their heads broken. We'll just have to get here early that night and go through it all again, by ourselves.' And so saying he sinks back in his seat and relaxes, a totally para-noid man at home in a business where there's no one he can trust.

While all this went on in their name, the Rolling Stones them-selves were to be found in a small back-room rehearsal hall on Santa Monica Boulevard. On the door to the room hung a small sign that said 'Extra-Terrestrial Funk 4-11p.m.' and outside it sat blond Chris O'Dell and a stunning looking coffee-coloured girl with eyes like blue jade. 'We're security here,' Chris giggled. 'How do you like us?' In actual fact the precise location of the hall was an absolute secret, so tightly kept that when you inquired after the band's whereabouts in the instrument store out front, people would look through you blankly and say, 'Stones? What are you talking about?'

Rehearsals for the tour had begun some weeks earlier in Montreux, Switzerland, near Keith Richard's residence of the month. Since leaving England for tax purposes, Keith and his lady, the actress Anita Pallenberg, had been involved in a European odyssey. Since Anita had just given birth to their first daughter, Belle Starr, the rehearsals came to him in Montreux, at a cost of about ten thousand dollars. Playing from six at night until six in the morning in a small movie house, the Stones roughed out a list of about thirty-five songs from which they would choose the basic set for the tour. Once the show was set, they would be playing it night after night with virtually no changes.

From 1963 until 1966, the Stones were a touring band, working almost non-stop, constantly gigging. They rarely rehearsed for a live performance. If a promoter offered them the use of a hall on the morning of a gig to do a sound test they'd as likely as not get mad, curse into the phone, and go back to sleep. Now that they had become the premier band of an era, with a lead singer who represented as much and more than Frank Sinatra ever did to millions of people, they felt the need to make totally sure of what they did. The band itself was no longer as close as it once had been, with all of its members around the age of thirty, each having his own home and family, and separate world. So rehearsals served to bring the group feeling back again.

Walking into a small room to hear the Stones playing at full tilt is somewhat like going into a friend's house, only to discover eight of the greatest pool hustlers in the world hunkered over a table you've played a million times and never beaten, and they're running balls by the hundred. Maybe you've seen these guys on TV somewhere but for the very first time you realise how really good they are. So, too, with the Stones. Seeing them in huge sweat-smoked arenas is to view them through an ordinary focus. When you see them in a plain old back room playing through tiny amps that let you hear every note, you realise they haven't made it as far as they have solely on their personalities.

But they have become personalities, in their ten years of kicking around near the top, where the real madness is. On vocals, Mr. Mick Jagger, who always seems smaller and quieter at first meeting than he really is. On lead and rhythm guitars, Mr. Keith Richard, a person you would look twice at in any crowd, once described by a lady who seemed quite taken with him as 'absolutely the most physically foreboding person I have ever seen.' Keith has added a golden rooster track of frosting to one side of his thatched artichoke-cut hair, and around his neck he wears a turquoise necklace. On lead and rhythm guitars, Mr. Mick Taylor, the youngest in the band, still nearly a kid, a beautiful soloist and pure blues musician. On drums, twirling the sticks in his hands forever, Mr. Charlie Watts, with a pile of empty beer cans growing around his feet. On bass, Mr. Bill Wyman, who *is* the oldest person in the band but not in rock and roll, and, along with Watts, the possessor of one of the great Buster Keaton stone-faces. Supporting the Stones, on piano, Mr. Nicky Hopkins, a gaunt lad, for a long time the most prolific and talented session man in England. Mr. Bobby Keys on sax, from the great state of Texas, girls; he makes every stereotype about musicians on the road true. On trumpet, Mr. Jim Price, also from Texas; he smokes cigars and likes to laugh. Ladies and gentlemen... the band.

It is Jagger's theory that if the band is going to play in large halls once on tour they should rehearse in one. So after a few sessions in the back room, they move to an awesomely empty sound stage at Warner Brothers' studio in Burbank which is designed to give the band the feel of an auditorium. The stage also allows the Stones' production manager, Edward Herbert Beresford Monck, called Chip by his friends, to begin assembling the theatrical environment that will surround the Stones during two months of concerts.

Paint and wrenches and ratchets and resin dust and tape (gaffer's and double-edged, and 3M double hazard for the edges of the steps that lead on stage), sockets and screwdrivers and rubber cement—the real world of things that Chip Monck operates in. These are his considerations, the tools that allow him to construct the environment necessary for the principal, that is Michael Philip Jagger, to distort himself on stage nightly.

The actual stage the Stones will play on lays on one side of the airplane hangar-sized sound stage. It is made of six plywood pieces that have been painted white and coated with Duralon. Two great, painted, fire-breathing sea serpents intertwine on a sea of white, a representation of a drawing in a Donald Duck comic book that Mr. Monck bought as a child in 1945 and still carries around in his briefcase. The deck is washed in warm water and Seven-Up to make it danceable.

Two huge theatrical transfer vans, which will cart the environment from city to city, travelling some fifteen thousand miles before the tour is over, are parked in the centre of the hall. Out of the trucks come two hydraulic tractor-like forklifts, each with a platform holding six speakers. Both of the forklifts crank up to a height of eighteen feet from where it is hoped the sound will spread evenly in big arenas from both sides of the stage. Behind and above the Stones' amps rides a forty-foot-long metal bridge that supports fifty lamps with different colored gels on them. The truss cranks up and down, too. Ten yellow shipping carts with numbers and letters stenciled on the sides stand scattered on the hangar floor. Each carries the cable that links the lights to the two dimmer boards that control their intensity.

Up by the ceiling is Chip Monk's crowning achievement for the tour, his pride and joy, a mirror, sixteen-feet wide by forty-feet long, made up of ten lightweight Mylar-covered panels. Monck got the idea for the mirror from a very bright college student who wrote him a letter suggesting that the spotlights, in this case six 1500-watt Super Troopers, be placed in *back* of the band and aimed up and into the mirror. The angle of incidence, as it always did in high-school physics, equalling the angle of reflection, and presto the Stones are backlit as well as frontlit, with great intensity and sharpness.

Monck has gone to these extremes because Michael Philip Jagger is the only performer he's ever worked with who overshadows the technical stuff around him. Whatever Chip gives Mick to play with, he uses it to its fullest extent and makes his own. Chip can see it, night after night. Mick *digests* things, and the weirder the stage stuff you can find for him, the more amazing his performance will be. Anyway, that's how Monck feels. There are rumours in the rockbiz that Chip Monck has finally blown it this time, gone too far and extravagant and expensive and the mirror will last three shows and be discarded, a seven thousand-dollar folly.

As Monck directs the unloading operations, the Stones begin rehearsing. Outside, the sun has sunk behind the mountains and the freeway into the Pacific and a slight breeze is beginning to eddy around the taco stand down the street. Inside, people are starting to eddy around the sides of the sound stage.

No way to keep it a secret anymore. The Stones are in town. Gram Parsons of the Byrds and the Flying Burrito Brothers is about, as is Dallas Taylor, Crosby, Stills, and Nash's original drummer. Also present are people who hold music business jobs, but only as some sort of excuse, since most of their time seems to be spent introducing famous musicians to one another, scoring good coke for them, and hanging out. Someone comes in with a metal box with locks and hinges all over it and the warning 'Desiccated—Do Not Open Except for Use and Inspection.'

'It's a gift,' someone explains, in a hushed and reverent tone, going on to name the San Francisco band that sent it.

'If it's a gift from them,' Mick Taylor smiles, 'it must be some evil, mind expanding drug.'

Keith Richard is called over to examine the problem. Pausing occasionally to adjust his red-tinted sunglasses and knotted-at-the-neck yellow aviator's scarf he finally pries open the box to find a plastic bag that holds at least a kilo of green plant matter and cigarette papers to roll it up in. The gift is passed around for inspection and everyone looks at it approvingly. Then it is given to Keith for safe-keeping. 'Why me?' he asks plaintively. 'Why am I always the bagman?'

With the rehearsals in a semi-public place and the days to countdown growing fewer, the pressure increases. People are talking about the Stones' tour, wondering if it's too late to get tickets anymore, reading about it in *Rolling Stone*. 'Exile on Main Street' is out and everywhere at once. You can't turn on the radio without being swept under by a tidal wave of Rolling Stones' records, old and new. One of the prime movers behind the earthquake is Wolfman Jack.

Wolfman Jack is more than a mere disc-jockey. He is the last of the great AM radio screamers, a man whose voice became the voice of the American night on 'XERB, outta Tijuana, Mexico, bay-beee,' a station with God knows how many watts of power, that could be heard with equal clarity in Big Sur, Kansas, the entire South, and, on a good night, all points north. The Wolf-man left XERB for KDAY, a Los Angeles AM station that is probably the most progressive in the country. In L.A. he could do no wrong.

When you ask someone in Los Angeles how far one place is from another, they are likely to say, 'Oh, by the freeway, twenty minutes.' Yes, but the question was, how far? You can go twenty-five miles on a freeway in twenty minutes if the wind is right. So one of the first lessons one learns in Los Angeles is that every-

thing is... very... far... away... from everything else. You are constantly in your car. But always. With the radio on to break the
dull rhythm of flowing asphalt and pebbled green-and-white exit
signs. In such a situation, it is only normal to develop an inti-
mate relationship with that voice coming out of your dashboard.
It is symptom one of the L.A. syndrome to chuckle quietly and
feel warm all over when a favorite disc jockey comes on. It's like
seeing an old lover. Hell, most people in L.A. spend more time in
their cars than they do with their lovers, new or old.

Consider the Wolfman, in Ear City, where they got to dig him
all the way down the line, and for the week before the tour he
is a ductless gland, pouring Stones' adrenalin directly into L.A.'s
carbon monoxide bloodstream. He is playing six, eight Stones'
cuts an hour, two solid hours of golden Stones' oldies at the
drop of a forty-five, all of it finally climaxing the night Wolfman
gets to be the first jock in America to preview 'Exile on Main
Street' and have his listeners rate it, cut by cut. Outta sight. Wolfman is on top. He's heard on fifteen hundred stations around the
world, four hundred and twenty of them scattered through forty-
two countries in Europe, Asia, and Africa. He's heard on Armed
Forces Radio, on college stations, on tapes, on discs; he's a commodity. As his agent-manager so aptly puts it, 'I got a computer
print-out yards long. Look at the demographics. He's in every
market.'

On the day after the Stones begin rehearsing at Warner Brothers, Wolfman Jack is going to lunch just one block down from the
number one billboard on the Strip (which this week is advertising 'Exile on Main Street,' of course). The Strip is America's main
street of hype and promotion, where Dick Clark and Phil Spector
are across-the-street neighbors, and Tower Records, which bills
itself as 'the largest record store in the known world,' the closest
thing to a true community center L.A. has. Down the Strip aways
stands a tall skinny hotel that is unremarkable save for the fact
that its rooms are perpetually occupied by visiting rock stars, their
producers and arrangers, saxophone players, showbiz lawyers, and
personnel management specialists. Its coffee shop, which stays
open 24 hours a day, has people wondering which mirror Fellini
is crouched behind with his Arriflex. Drag queens, transvestites,
and groupies, too bizarre to handle, hop from table to table at
5.00a.m. awaiting the arrival of whoever is *hot*.

The Wolfman, or Jack to those who prefer to be more formal, is, being shown to a table in the hotel's Mafia-dark, red-plush dining-room bar. He is a burly goateed man in a fringed shirt, high-heel boots, with a gold bracelet around one wrist and a diamond ring on his pinky finger. He is accompanied by his agent-manager, who carries a briefcase.

'The Stones, bay-bee,' Wolfman says, as a waitress wants to take his order, 'I play dem and people rush into de station and wanna kiss my hands. Dey da heaviest act in da bizness. In the world.

'I been through the sixties and part of the fifties and now the seventies and the Stones are heavier than de Beatles ever were. If Jesus Christ came to town, he couldn't sell more tickets. Do ya understan?'

'I'm playin six Stones' cuts an hour. Dey call-me up and ask for more. After three in a row, dey call me up for more. When we got that album in, our station manager said, "Track it." Somebody said, "How bout that song with the word 'shit' in it?" He said "I don't care if they say motherfucker in it. Track that album." Do ya understan?'

'Wolfman loves the Stones,' his agent-manager explains, 'because his roots are in the blues.'

'Dey bring people together,' Wolfman says, pushing on, ''cause they're whites makin' black music. Everybody black digs the Stones. Everybody white. And dey got the Chinese and the Mexicans, too. Do you understan what I'm talkin about?'

'Do you understan' is a Wolfman trademark, a guttural interjection he uses to puncture remarks that flow in machine-gun bursts. He slumps back a little in the booth and cuts into his steak.

'You know what's funny?' his agent-manager asks. 'As long as the Wolfman's been around, he's gotten to talk to almost everyone in the business. God, he's even had six songs written about him. But the one person he wants to meet, he can't. Mick Jagger.'

'Do you know them, hah?' Wolfman asks me. 'What's Jagger doin?'

'Would you like to come on the air one night and tell us about him?' asks the agent-manager.

'Yeah. Like anythin. What's he like? What's he do? Go and buy a paper at night like everyone else? Do ya understan? Their life

style... dey ain't gods no more, dey're immortals.... He's got to
want to talk to me. Me and him are the same kind of people.'
Wolfman cuts a chunk off his steak and sulks at the thought of
all the good work he's been doing for the Stones without any
acknowledgment.

'You tell dem the Wolfman would love to talk to Mick,' he
says. 'Any time. You tell 'em what a Stones enthusiast I am, and
that I been pushin' 'em all the way. They're the greatest and I'm
wit 'em all the way. So you get him to make that phone call. But
gimme a week to promote it first.'

When the band starts playing on the sound stage at Warner's, the
only people who do not tiptoe around and fade into the walls
and try to be inconspicuous is the crew. And on this tour even
the crew is a production.

Rock and roll shows are traditionally taken out by long-haired,
technical geniuses who can wire up entire cities, bang stages
together, go for long hours without food and sleep and still score
a chick during the show. Freak crews are motivated by one of the
logical extensions of the Woodstock spirit which is, 'we may have
long hair but we are more together than any forty-hour-a-week
union man. Right now I may be sitting here smoking this joint,
but when I start working I don't have to stop for coffee breaks.'

This time, they do. Chip Monck has insisted on taking out the
first yellow-card rock and roll show in history. Union, all the way,
with half the men longhairs holding new union cards they would
rather not have.

When Rudge was first looking around for someone to run the
tour in January of 1972, his first consideration was the Madison
Square Garden Corporation, an organisation so staid that it considers the New York Rangers to be authentic longhairs and wonders if the Moody Blues are a man or a woman. The Garden
packages Holiday on Ice and what they don't know about rock
and roll is counterbalanced by their connections and resources
(read: money). MSG is so conservative, however, that they were
unwilling to come up with money in front that would have provided Rudge with operating expenses while the tour was getting
underway and so they lost the tour to selected individual promoters throughout the country. But, because of the Garden's early
interest in the tour, and because of Chip Monck's desire to have

his own men on the lights when they work New York—for him, the most prestigious gig of the tour—the decision was made to take out a union crew.

As the band kicks into 'Brown Sugar' with Charlie's bass drum booming and the horns punching holes in the melody, the mix of people on the sound stage is decidedly strange. Pony-tailed carpenters and bearded electricians working side by side with reasonable-looking, positively midwestern family men. Jack Casady, bass player for the Jefferson Airplane, considered by many to be one of the absolute premier musicians in rock, materializes out of an iron pipe, literally from nowhere, then vanishes again. Mick Taylor is snaking leads and Keith is pumping up and down, driving rhythm. The Stones do 'You Can't Always Get What You Want' which unfurls slowly, like a carpet being unrolled, then leap into 'Jumpin' Jack Flash.' But the acoustics are terrible. The sound stage is empty and it rings like a bell, and no one can properly hear what they're playing through the monitors. During a break Keith sits on one of the yellow carts, talking about his new daughter. 'She's back home in Switzerland with Anita, man,' he says, 'and they're gonna stay there. I don't want to have to be looking after anybody else. Not on this tour.'

'I *must* be getting old,' sax player Bobby Keys insists, in a Texas accent seventeen years on the road has done nothing to diminish. 'I don't ever remember bein kept awake by the people next door in a hotel.'

'Well,' someone asks, 'who's next door to you?'

'Everyone,' Keys says sorrowfully. 'Everyone in the goddamn hotel. And it's party all the time.'

Meanwhile, back on the Strip, things are fulminating. Gibson-Stromberg, a public relations firm with a sign in its hallway that says 'Twelve Press Agents—No Waiting' is sorting through last-minute letters, hanging up on long-distance callers who insist they're John Lennon, and being petitioned by legions of writers who have suddenly made the transition and become rock writers... and therefore eligible for tickets to the Stones' concerts.

Mr. Bob Gibson and Mr. Gary Stromberg, two very interesting gentlemen who are birds of distinctly different plumage, maintain offices on (where else?) Sunset Strip. Kids standing by their front door, across from Tower Records and next to the Old World

restaurant, are as likely as not to come over to people going in to
see them to ask if they'd like to hear a cassette of original songs.
One time a guy in a full wet-suit, flippers, snorkel, weighted
belt, rubber feet, and goggles on his head, the *works,* walked
in the front door and asked if they knew of any bands looking
for underwater drummers. Gibson, who is blond, bearded, and
rotund, is reported to have put down his phone long enough to
say 'Tell the schmuck not this week.'

A year before the Stones' tour, while Peter Rudge was in America shepherding The Who through a tour, he began making
inquiries about rock and roll PR firms. Everywhere he went, he
heard the name Gibson-Stromberg. Rock writers in countless
cities proudly pulled up their shirts to reveal Gibson-Stromberg
T-shirts. Rock moguls like Denny Cordell (Shelter Records),
David Geffen (Asylum Records), who at one point was going
to handle the tour by himself, and Peter Asher (James Taylor's
manager) sung the praises of Gibson-Stromberg. As did Chris
O'Dell. So when Rudge brought The Who to L.A., he decided to
check their operation out, something which made both Gibson
and Stromberg happy. Far out, they thought, we're gonna get The
Who. Another group to add to their bulging stable of the top
seventy rock acts.

Rudge got into it with them as only Rudge can—three-hour
rap sessions and meetings with the entire staff—and then he
disappeared. Far out, thought Gary Stromberg, who is dark,
bearded, and wasting away—another English flake. Unbeknown
to Gibson and Stromberg, Rudge was doing CIA-like advance
work for the Stones' tour. Three months later they were contacted
and Stromberg was invited to meet Jo Bergman over breakfast.

There is an inevitable pattern for people who want to be sucked
into the Stones' vortex. First, you meet Jo, or someone else in the
command squad, and are scrutinized: then, sooner or later, you
meet Jagger. Having passed the first test, Stromberg reported to
the Beverly Hills mansion where Mick was residing while 'Exile'
was being mixed. The mansion had once belonged to Marion
Davies and the good Gothic touch of Hearst was still all around.
Paths choked with vines leading to a mammoth free-form swimming pool where boats used to float but now only dead leaves
and broken branches lay. Jagger had just awakened, it being two
or three in the afternoon, and what Stromberg remembers about

that meeting was how alone he looked, sitting at a great table beneath the huge portraits, how very *frail* Mick, the number one superstar in the world, was.

Mick, sitting there yawning and trying to make his head work, finally told Gary that all he wanted was for the press to be taken care of properly. But for Gibson-Stromberg, the Stones' account is an absolute plum, the number one ego-feeding piece of business in the world, one that Gibson would have done for nothing, well virtually nothing, money being the lifeblood of the game, but the Stones... the Stones are more than money. To be with the Stones means you are the best. So Gibson and Stromberg work out a campaign for the Stones' tour, one that is designed to sustain the public's interest over a two-month period and make it build in every city toward the concerts in New York. They decide to *blitz*. Now, the best example of a blitz in recent rock and roll publicity is James Taylor on the cover of *Time*. Sweet Baby James is one honey of a singer and guitar-picker to he sure, but only twenty-two years old, and what the hell is he doing on the cover of *Time*? The reason he is there is that James' manager Peter Asher and Gibson-Stromberg have decided to blitz. James is going to disappear into Martha's Vineyard for a year or so and Asher decides to go for all the marbles. They're going to have to live off the publicity for a long time... so Gibson-Stromberg go to it... by placing phone calls to editors, to people in the record biz who talk to their friends on newspapers and magazines. By setting up a very high-level circle of people who do not normally talk about rock and roll singers to hype James, they convince *Time* that they've got to jump on this because James Taylor is more than just one person who sings, he is the embodiment of a whole new musical movement which *Time* dubs 'The New Rock: Bittersweet and Low' or something equally hideous. What the hell. It doesn't matter. *Time* is not going to get it right anyway. They're not rock and rollers, What they will do is put James' face on a million news-stands and help move a lot of albums to people who might not buy them if they saw him on the cover of *Rolling Stone*. This way everyone will make more money and James can take his year off and get his head together.

Similarly, the Stones do not tour every year. They are five gentlemen who are too complicated to get together more often. Their tours take a long time to organize, and they've been around so long this might even be the last one. Might be. Anyway it's an angle. Plus, there is no need, and no way to hype this band, no way you can oversell them. So... you blitz. This means going for features and/or covers in five major magazines—*Life, Time, Newsweek, Esquire,* and *Rolling Stone*. If you do that, you've done your job. Of course, in doing it, you've got to make sure they send writers who aren't out to make a name for themselves. You want people you can trust. Someone like Albert Goldman of *Life* (who has written trenchantly about the death of rock several times and come down on individual performers) is someone Gibson might not want along. A Tommy Thompson or Tony Scaduto, who bio'ed Dylan so successfully, is infinitely preferable. Another factor is that the Stones, and Jagger in particular, have been answering questions for ten years. If some writer should insist on a structured interview rather than be content to hang out, and get it and then *blow* it, it's a minor disaster, because on this tour no publicity is better than bad publicity.

Bob Gibson gets his publicity machine rolling and lines up his five big ones, *Life, Time, Newsweek, Esquire,* and *Rolling Stone,* and the magazine tangos being danced are ferocious. The jockeying is brutal. Writers are suggested, then dropped. Editors are on the phone trying to find out who's in charge of the tour—Gibson-Stromberg, Rudge, or Marshall Chess. Names are bid on like in a stock auction. Writers who one week find themselves unable to get through to editors they have worked with for years are suddenly called person to person and long distance at home, and flown up for story conferences. And the key word is *access.* It's all who do you know, how well do you know them? Can you get a piece of the action? Yeah? If so, then far out, you're our boy.

It's a terrible world all right, the rockbiz and the rock PR biz, and the magazine world, and things are going so fast and furiously that when *Saturday Review* phones wanting to send along William Burroughs, it's an idea that gasses everybody. With the five major publications taken care of; Gibson figures it's okay to fuck around a little, and Bill Burroughs is such a crazy sonofabitch anyway. God he could be great for the film they are going to make of the tour. The whole thing is an upper. When Burroughs drops out and *Saturday Review* substitutes Terry Southern, well, that's okay too. At least he's famous.

Truman Capote's name is being bandied about for *Rolling Stone* and even though Jagger's not so anxious for him, Bob Gibson figures, hell, Truman is atmosphere, theater. Let it happen, he figures. As incongruous and silly as it can get. For, as Gibson would say after it was all over, 'I would have liked to have seen Teddy Kennedy come along to write about the Stones. It's just as ludicrous.'

By now, the stage is pretty well set. Peter Rudge and his boys have done all they can in L.A. All those red passes with the black cryptic letters have photos pasted on them and they've been countersigned and distributed. Everything that can be worried about is still being worried about, but there's no time left anymore.

At a quarter to twelve on Friday night, the very night before the plane leaves for Vancouver and the road begins, Wolfman Jack plays 'Sweet Virginia' off the 'Exile' album, with its 'Got to scrape that shit right off your shoes' chorus. Then in a hushed, reverent voice, he says, 'Just a minute. After this record, in a minute, we actually gonna be talkin... to... Mick Jagga.' And there is a pause to let the name shimmer through the airwaves, and sink in, and then the Wolfman rasps, 'Be right back.' All over L.A., in GTOs and Vettes cruising down Sunset and speeding past White Oaks and Tujunga Wash, and in darkened bedrooms where kids have to keep the radio down so as not to wake their parents, people lean forward and wait for the Wolfman and Mick Jagger to converse.

In the house up in the Hollywood Hills that belongs to Michael Butler, scion of the Butler Aviation fortune and the man who bankrolled and produced *Hair*, blond Chris O'Dell has to keep running from one room to the other to tell Mick she's still working on it. Chris has been trying to get through to the Wolfman for hours, but the station switchboard is jammed and Chris doesn't know the Wolfman's private number. She keeps on trying, though, because Wolfman is her favorite disc jockey ever, and more than once she's told Mick, 'Oh Mick, I want to meet the Wolfman so bad. You know what he looks like so introduce me if we see him.' And there are not many people in the business that Chris has not already met, much less have their private number. After working at Apple and for Peter Asher and having been Leon Russell's Pisces Apple lady, and the subject of the song of the same title, she knows just about everyone.

'I'm still tryin, Mick,' Chris says, sticking her head into the room where Mick, Keith, and a few other people are just lying back, listening to music and watching how the floor relates to the walls.

'Aw, Chris, cawm awn, sit down wi us...'

'Ooh, here he is. I've got him. Talk to him, Mick...' A man is about to realize his dream.

'Mick?' the Wolfman says. 'Ah Mick... everybody here is nervous 'cause you're on the phone, bay-bee. I'm nervous, too. Whatta you think a that, hah?'

Mick laughs. Then there is silence.

'How's it feel to be number one, bay-bee? All this Stones mania, it's like 1966 all over again, huh?'

'Well, it's noice,' Mick says ever so politely. 'We've been at it now for eight years. Nine since our first record. It's gratifyin.'

'Yeah. Lissen, the vibrations you give off on records are just unreal. Y'know wha I'm talkin about?'

'Tha's noice, Jack.' More silence.

'And ah'm gonna go on playin Stones' cuts till they pull me off the air. Do you believe me, bay-bee?'

'I believe it, Jack.' Silence a third time.

'It must be nice to be alive and be a creator like you. Lissen, Mick babe, I love you bay-bee, how 'bout you introduce this next record for me....'

And in a small polite voice, doing his best not to laugh out loud, Mick Jagger goes into a short and solemn dedication, as though it were still 1966 and people were walking around with transistors to their ears listening to Murray the K. 'From Mick Taylor and Bill and Charlie and Keith, here's one from all of us...' as the music from 'Sympathy for the Devil,' a song the Stones would almost certainly never play live again in America after Altamont, comes up in the background and Jagger's voice begins hawking and honking.

It was time for the tour to start.

Book One

Chapter One — JUNE

At least the heat has broken. With the temperature clicking at sixty seven degrees the next day and the time 10:31, the S.T.P. bus is rolling through cool, foggy L.A. toward the airport and the first concert.

A small man in the back of the bus is halfway out of his seat and talking. His fist is balled up and he's whamming it into his thigh. He's passing a joint along to the guy in back of him who's all sleepy-eyed and trying to make his face work. 'Ah, good mornin,' Bobby Keys says to the joint. 'And good mornin to you, Marshall. Now, what ah wanna know is what do ah do with this?' Keys reaches into his pocket and twirls a small plastic bag around.

'Get rid of it,' Marshall Chess says. 'Definitely... get rid of it. Remember that time we played Helsinki on the European tour? They had dogs waiting for us when we went into Finland...'

'Ah doan know... it's such a *little* thang...'

'Then don't go through Customs on the same line as me,' Marshall laughs.

All of the tension of the past few weeks has been building to this... the moment the show gets on the road. Marshall feels it. He's wired, excited, there's a gig tonight, the first one... and the feeling is catching. A bus full of crazies, headed off to who knows what kind of adventure... jiminee... it's like that day in June when your mother finishes sewing name tapes on everything you own and packs you down to the station where the bus for Camp Cula-Monga stands waiting, jammed with hundreds of jittering kids you don't know at all but will be sharing life secrets with in a few days.

It's peak experience time, with grownups getting to act like

kids, with the Stones as an excuse and a reason and an avenue
to bizarre encounters. Peter Rudge is ratcheting in and out of
his seat, saying, 'We're about to hit the beaches. We're about to
hit the beaches,' and there's that definite going-off-to-war excitement in the air.

Certainly, to wear an S.T.P. badge is to be a part of a small army.
All of the technical assistance, all the innovation in stage technique and rehearsing, the twenty-seven people along to work...
there could be no doubt that a lot of it was motivated by the basic
insecurity that must plague all performers—the knowledge that
one day they will go out on stage and play to an audience that
just *sits* there, resembling nothing so much as a still-life portrait
of the House of Lords, and that will be *it*. Time to hang it up and
start living in the country.

For the Stones were taking a definite chance. Despite the overwhelming ticket demand and the avalanche of media interest in
them, they were going on the road with essentially the same kind
of show they had done in 1969. What nobody could forecast was
how the kids would react to it. The Stones would do a classic
rock and roll set, composed of twelve or fifteen separate and distinct numbers, each with a beginning, middle, and an end, starting out hard and fast, calming in the middle, then all-out rocking
at the end designed to leave the audience up and dancing when
it was over.

When the set ended, so did the show. The Stones rarely did
encores. They worked like *stars*... come out, hit 'em hard, zonk
'em, then run to the limos before the cheering stops, out of the
building and on to the plane. Strictly 1966 Beatles-type stuff
that made the distance between the musician and the customer
unbridgeable. In the spirit of P. T. Barnum, the Stones always left
'em wanting more.

But would they want more? Probably, but the Stones this time
around were about to be thirty or older and the audiences would
be fourteen, fifteen, sixteen, some younger. Would they dance?
Did they know who Chuck Berry was? That he'd come to Phil
Chess, Marshall's father, in the early fifties with a tune called
'Ida Red' and that Chess had told him to rewrite the lyrics, and
two weeks later it was called 'Maybelline.' Chess recorded it and
drove to New York to lay some acetates, and some bread, on Alan
Freed and by the time he'd gotten back to Chicago, people were

screaming to buy it. They'd made it number one and Phil Chess didn't know a damn thing about it because he'd been busy driving back home in his car, selling forty-fives out of his trunk to record stores along the way.

It was no accident that Marshall Chess was on this tour, or that he ran the Rolling Stones' recording operations. He was a blood link to the music the Stones are all about... Muddy Waters and Bo Diddley, and Chuck Berry... 'Rolling Stone Blues,' 'Mona,' and 'Johnny B. Goode.'

By the summer of 1972, though, all of it had already become very tame, ancient history. Rock singers were working half-naked with snakes twined around their midriffs. Their hair was dyed burnt sienna and they were flaunting their omnisexuality as helicopters dive-bombed their audiences with skyloads of paper panties. The Stones played straight, English, white, second-generation rock. There was the slim, but very real, possibility that this time around in the American rockbiz drugstore, where new, amphetamine-charged inputs were plentiful, the Stones would prove to be no more than a placebo.

As the tour bus pulls out, none of this troubles Marshall Chess. A small, pretty man with a Jewish hooked nose, shirred henna hair, and penetrating eyes, who was in the habit of muttering nonsense Spanish-sounding syllables to himself when he felt impatient or exasperated or both, 'Ai ya hela Maria Santo hayzoos....' Marshall knows, absolutely *knows* that the tour will be a bitch, a mother, absolutely the last big blowout for a long time. The party to end all parties. The biggest charge around.

Marshall figures to be present to dig all of it, one way or another. Ostensibly he is along to promote 'Exile on Main Street.' But before the tour is a week old, the album will skyrocket to number one, selling some 800,000 copies and 200,000 tapes. Promotion work will become unnecessary, as will the buzz of calling Mick long distance and saying, 'Hey, babe... Yeah... we did it, man... number one...' There will be no congratulatory cables to send, no warm rush of accomplishment for a year of effort and the half-million dollars that went into making the album.

Marshall, a very proud man, who has been in the business ever since he began sweeping out the Chess studios at 2120 Michigan Avenue in Chicago when he was fourteen and who has been through all the changes that come when you start as the son of a hard-driving, self-made Jewish businessman and go through primal therapy to get your head straight, will have to find something to *do*, some concrete reason to be on tour, a *project*. He will slip completely into his role as executive producer of the tour film, which is going to be shot by the small, compact man standing in the aisle of the bus with an Eclair 16 obscuring his face and a just-passed joint in his hand. In one smooth motion, the man takes the joint, hits on it, puts it in front of the camera lens, films it, then passes it on.

With this simple act, Robert Frank immediately establishes his S.T.P. credentials, the ability to get loaded and go on functioning. Frank, who at forty-seven is the oldest person on tour, has a patient Middle European face and the demeanor one usually finds among men who spend the day sipping coffee and reading the papers in sunny Swiss or Austrian caf s.

He comes to the Stones through his book of black-and-white photographs entitled The Americans. In his introduction to the book, Jack Kerouac described him as, '...Swiss, unobtrusive, nice, with that little camera that he raises and snaps with one hand, he sucked a sad poem right out of America and on to film.... To Robert Frank, I now give this message: You got eyes.'

Although Jagger has never seen any of the films Frank has made featuring people like Allen Ginsberg and Gregory Corso (*Pull My Daisy, Me and My Brother*), he hires him to film the tour. Frank knows little about rock and roll, less about the Stones. It is not a world that interests him. He is part of an earlier, more artistic, Beat sensibility. Still, he feels a great affection for Jagger, great sympathy for a man who can talk to him on his terms and then deal with rooms full of showbiz sharks and lawyers.

As the joint goes down the aisle of the bus and back up again, it's like the opening scene of a World War II movie, where the light of the last cigarette is used to illuminate the faces and introduce the members of the platoon. The S.T.P. platoon consists of the press agent (redoubtable Bob Gibson), the makeup man (who Jagger hired eight hours before the tour bus is scheduled to leave), the guitar-maker (a pipestem thin, blond-haired version of Jimmy Stewart in *Mr. Smith Goes to Washington*, who wears a triple-X Stetson hat at all times and takes care of the twenty-seven guitars along for the ride), the accountant (not an accountant at all, but a twenty-year-old College student who, before the tour ends, will handle and pay out $192,000 in cash), the baggage man, Willie (who talks like Wallace Beery and has the face of a New York City cop), and the doctor (whose speciality is emergency medicine and who is equipped to maintain all life systems in the event that everyone's worst fantasy comes real).

The supporting cast are minor players in the tour movie, names that no one knows, faces that the audience never gets to see. They are the people who will go through the cruelest and most drastic life changes on the tour, whooshed up from the relative normality of their everyday lives into the eye of the rock hurricane, close enough to the sick center to share in all the adulation and worship that gets directed at the Stones. As Marshall Chess puts it, 'When thirty-five chicks come to fuck the Stones, and there are only five Stones, that leaves thirty chicks, so anyone close to the tour gets one... it's part of the ritual, and it's easy to get sucked in so that soon all you're doing is talking, thinking, and worrying about the Stones... they're nice cats, the Stones, I work for them, but they are not my life I am my life... But sometimes I get sucked in too.'

Peak experience. It's all out there, waiting, as the bus dumps the tour party out into a sickly green bus terminal waiting room filled with floral old ladies with Paradise 1000 Travel Club patches on their bulging breasts and handbags, and men discussing Vida Blue's continuing and amazing holdout with the Oakland A's.

'Saw in the paper where he's going into cabinet-making,' one says to a buddy. 'Fifty grand a year.... who needs baseball?'

The tour party stands around, waiting to be told where to go. Peter Rudge goes into an office and comes out with a distressed look on his face. 'Jo,' he says, in the tone of a man having a large tooth extracted, 'the plane can't land in Vancouver.'

'Why can't it land in Vancouver?' she asks calmly.

'I can't seem to get a straight answer.'

There are answers all over the front page of the morning's *Los Angeles Times*. There have been two hijackings the night before, one by a black man wearing a U.S. Army captain's uniform and chain smoking hashish. He demanded, and received, five hundred thousand dollars, changed planes in New York and wound up in Algiers, where he was met by four persons identified as 'Black Panthers.'

The Tac Squad quickly circles up, like a wagon train in times of Indian attack. 'Is it the hijackings?' Alan Dunn asks.

'I can't find out,' Rudge says. 'The pilot's failed to file some papers, I think....'

'Maybe we can...'

'Hold on...,' Marshall Chess says, and the next thing anyone knows he is hanging off a pay phone saying, 'Yes, operator... in Ottawa... Pi-erre Tru-deau. The prime minister, yes. And my credit card number is...'

Might as well go right to the top. All it takes is a credit card and some rock and roll chutzpah and you can talk to the national leader of your choice.

'Yes,' Marshall says into the phone. 'This is Marshall Chess. Of the Rolling Stones. We have a concert scheduled tonight in Vancouver. Eighteen thousand people are waiting for us and our plane has been denied permission to land in Canada. If we don't show up, those kids are going to be... *aroused.'* Good word there. No sense in alarming the prime minister unduly by predicting that if the Stones don't show, hordes of angry kids will burn the city and then sweep eastward toward his personal estate.

'Yessir, I'll hold,' Marshall cups one hand over the phone receiver and tells Rudge that he's on with one of Trudeau's press secretaries. They've patched him into the guy's home from the capitol building in Ottawa and now the guy's gone to *his* other phone to talk to Trudeau himself. It's well known that Pierre is both a right guy and a very deep cat, who more than once has been seen wearing a fringed jacket and rocking out to the sounds of some loud and funky Canadian band. So he is the obvious man to set this straight.

But as Marshall re-explains the situation on the long-distance wire, Rudge is finding out that there's little the P.M. can do. The pilot simply has failed to file flight plans early enough to receive international clearance. It's become a matter for the Tac Squad. As one, Rudge, Jo, and Alan move to the pay phones and begin dialing. Mouths moving, brows furrowing and unfurrowing, eyes opening and shutting, receivers jammed into their ears, they look like a Larry Rivers construction of people trying to get a last bet down before the sixth comes in from Aqueduct.

They arrange for the plane to land at a small suburban airport in northern Washington state and for six limousines to be waiting there to drive everyone into Vancouver. Which means that the Stones and friends will have to pass through normal, everyday roadside Customs, a prospect that does not make Rudge very happy.

Half an hour later, after the chaos has subsided to a normal level and the tour party has dispersed itself through the terminal like particles in solution, the Stones arrive. Flanked by Leroy and Stan, their two black bodyguards, surrounded by a shimmering circle of blond, brown-skinned, blue jade- and copper-colored ladies. In silk and corduroy and studded jeans, they come walking toward the plane like a great splash of watercolor on the dull and empty waiting room canvas.

Primarily, it's their clothing. How the hell?... Do they look like that all the time?... I say, Martha... are they some sort of band? Keith is wearing a black and white striped suit made out of silvered sailcloth that must glow in the dark. Huge silver shades hide his eyes. Wound around his neck as a scarf is a three-and-a-half-foot bright yellow Tibetan prayer flag covered with red ink mantras which used to hang as a windowshade somewhere. In his hand he carries a small black doctor's bag. Not long after they arrive, the plane taxis into position and takes off.

The plane ride is quiet, nervous, expectant, and when the plane touches down in Bellingham, Washington, two hours later, Mick and Keith are the last people off. They come out into bright sunlight, fertile green farm and timberland stretching away to distant purple mountains. They both begin laughing... Jagger grabs Keith's arm and they go tearing ass down the runway, like schoolboys set free for the summer holiday, with the breeze whipping Keith's scarf around his head and their hair falling into their eyes.

When Jagger comes back, he does one of his I-am-a-child routines, peering intently into the turbo jet, toying with the prop, finally allowing them to point him to the limo before he starts chinning himself on the wing. The local folk, already open-mouthed at the presence of a school of black, shiny polished limos, just gape.

At the Canadian border, a hapless Customs man in a log cabin with a Canadian flag on top struggles with manifests, crew lists, and baggage numbers. He has never, never seen people who look and act like this. Polite, co-operative, smiling, but defiant, as though to say, we are playing your little game here but it does not really apply to us. People spill out of cars and Robert Frank has the Eclair screwed into his face and rolling, as Bill Wyman tracks him with a Super 8. A pushy TV camera crew materializes and tries to shove microphones into people's faces.

'Where are you from?' someone asks one of the boys with a sound pack and a shoulder harness.

'Channel 8,' he says proudly, 'Vancouver. Where you from?'

'Estonia,' Keith says loftily, stalking away before he can reply. The Customs man marks everything okay and the trunk lids get slammed shut. The limos speed off, the drivers pushing down on the accelerators until the cars reach that perfect cruising speed where the road disappears and there are no bumps to remind you you're still in contact with the earth.

Vancouver, Canada's fourth largest city, has been chosen for the debut concert because it is geographically perfect... located on the West Coast where the tour is to begin, yet far enough away from the rock establishment in L.A. and San Francisco to give the band a chance to break in the set and pick up some road rhythm. On the day the Stones come to town, Vancouver has all its flags at half-staff, marking the death of the Duke of Windsor, and Howard Hughes is said to be in residence on a floor at the Bayshore Inn. The local police are still walking softly when it comes to dealing with large groups of kids. Some months earlier, at a peaceful marijuana smoke-in in the Gastown area of the city, police on horses got out of hand and the ensuing bad publicity has caused the force to maintain a low profile ever since.

The downtown area of the city seems quiet and deserted as the black limousines flash through, save for a young, pretty couple mooning down an avenue of stores, looking in windows. 'Hey,' Marshall Chess shouts out his window, 'wanna see the Stones tonight? Stop the car, driver.' Chess peels two tickets off a thick wad of freebies that he's got and hands them over. 'Ohhh wowww,' the girl breathes and her face goes all soft, as if to say... hey, what's the angle, man? I mean just 'cause we wanna go, is that why you're giving them to us? And there is no angle, save for Robert Frank twisting down on the fine focus knob of his camera and getting all their innocent bewilderment on film for the movie.

When Marshall and Robert get to Pacific Coliseum, a large

sweaty ice-hockey arena where the gig is going to be, Marshall doesn't think twice about going out the back door to get rid of the rest of his tickets. They aren't doing him any good... of course he takes Robert along with him, just in case anything interesting happens. The kids out back are really young, guys with shaggy blond hair and faded jeans and football shirts and gee-whiz faces, the girls all tanned and smiley in those wraparound halters that leave their backs all brown and naked.

'Who wants to see the show?' Marshall asks.

'Hey,' a kid says.

'Hey... for free?' another says. 'Hey, hey, ... this guy's givin away tickets. C'MON.'

Marshall Chess is decimated by a wave of pretty blond kids who rip at his hair and tear at his eyes, a spinning brawling whirl-pool of kids clawing for free tickets. A cop jumps in and wrestles Marshall out, and he comes up blinking and gasping. He limps a few steps off to one side, shouts 'Have a ball,' and flings the whole handful of tickets up in the air. They separate and flutter down and begin tumbling end over end on the concrete. The kids are right on top of them, not making much noise, just fight-ing for each one very intently, like peasants scrapping for the last few crusts of bread left on the manor. Marshall watches for a second, then retreats backstage where it's safer. Hell, the tickets don't mean a thing to him. He can get as many as he wants or needs. All he wanted to do was turn some young kids on to the show.

It's no more than a few minutes later when a kid hits the back door with everything he's got, bursts into the backstage area and is punched and thrown back out. Bang, the door is slammed shut. Wham, it opens again, two more kids trying to fight their way in. Then it's slammed shut again, as someone screams, 'Chain for the door, chain for the door!' No sooner do they padlock the doorway, cursing, than do thirty or forty kids hit the roll-up cor-rugated metal door. The metal buckles and starts to fold, like an old fighter going down from a hard right to the gut. Peter Rudge is out of the dressing room and running, and by the time he gets near the door it is actually three or four feet off the ground and rising. What Rudge does is leap like a football tackle, and slam into the door with his shoulder, then grab on and hang there, shouting for help. The Stones' bodyguard jumps up there with

him and then they're joined by two rather weighty, visiting promoters who have come to Vancouver to get some idea of what to
expect when the Stones play their cities.

'We're isolated,' Rudge cries. 'We're blind 'ere. Get us some
police round the back.' Bangabangbang, the doors are being
kicked rapidly, in succession, the tattoo of boots against metal
like small-arms fire. The promoters and the bodyguard are shoving huge metal garbage disposal units against the outer wall, and
it's like an authentic battle situation at some beleaguered outlying
post.

What no one knows is that a sea of kids, some two thousand or
so, have hit the front of the building, smashing plate-glass windows, flinging rocks and bottles and bringing down seven policemen. The Mounties have been called out, and they'll eventually
subdue the rioters and move them away from the building. But
the whole anarchy-filled moment is like a Zen slap in Rudge's
face. For the first time it dawns on him that he's in this one
alone, that while the building is crumbling, half his people sit in
the dressing room discussing when the limos are going to leave
and sampling the food. No rock and rollers on this tour, Rudge
thinks, and the only way he's going to get them through the next
two months is to kick asses and scream and scream and never let
up for a second.

Inside the hall, the good kids, the ones who have paid their way
in, have sat fairly docilely through Stevie Wonder's set. Wonder,
both black and blind, is a piano and harmonica-playing singer-
songwriter who will precede the Stones every night they work.

'Thank you for your attention,' Chip Monck tells the crowd.
'If you find it a bit crowded there on the floor, I should like to
remind you that it is not nearly as comfortable for the people
outside as it is for you.'

An empty bottle of Lamb's Navy Rum comes cartwheeling out
of the stands and crashes into splinters on the concrete floor just
in front of the stage.

'We will be on in about five minutes, so if you could be patient
and give us your total attention....'

A brown beer bottle explodes into shards on the stage apron
itself. The good kids? They've come to fight and kick, and immediately after the Stones go on, two young boys come walking
toward the stage fifteen rows up, in the stands, cursing as they

come. 'Chicken shit cops,' one says. 'Chickenshit motherfucking cops.' They come right to the rear of the stage, uproot a heavy section of iron pipe railing and heave it to the concrete some twenty feet below, with enough force to kill anyone who might have been unlucky enough to be standing underneath it.

Two ushers wrestle one of the kids down and go to work on him, beating him as he lays struggling on the steps. His friend takes three steps and delivers a roundhouse kick that wastes one of the ushers, opening up the side of his face with a welling great smear of blood. The other kid springs up and runs away. Ten minutes later, they're both circling the arena, cursing and triumphant, Clockwork Orange Alex and a pal, having pulled off a satisfying bit of the old ultra-violence.

The Stones themselves on stage are, as always, oblivious to what's going down in the house. They play for nearly two hours and do seventeen songs, but it's not much of a concert. The kids who aren't fighting sit quietly and watch, as though shocked to discover that the Stones are really mortals, mere men who need microphones to he heard, like everyone else.

Keith Richard blows two guitars and is disgusted. Marshall doesn't like Chip's lighting, and he says so. He's sure the physics is all wrong, that the beams focus the eye away from Mick who is, after all, the reason for the show, and the price of admission. The band stays up until four in the morning making changes in the set, discussing which songs to drop, and which to keep, and what order to play them in.

Peter Rudge wakes up the next morning to a three-column, bold-type headline in the Vancouver paper, 'STONES' FANS BATTLE POLICE'. The wire services pick up the story and one changes the number of rioters from 2,000 to 22,000 and, of course, that's the version *The New York Times* runs so the phone calls begin whizzing cross-country.

Namely, what the hell is going on up there, Peter? Jeez, that's only Vancouver and already the damn thing is out of control and on the front page.

As Sunday dawns gray and foggy in British Columbia's number one street-fighting city, an AM radio deejay shouts enthusiastically in a voice that could peel the paper off the ceiling, 'Last night, the Stones were INCREDIBLE. And if you missed 'em, gang, you missed... a GREAT ONE.'

The next day, the Stones fly into Seattle. In one of those neat intermeshings of art and legal procedure, the jury in San Mateo, California, returns a verdict of not guilty on the murder-conspiracy charge facing Angela Davis just as the Stones go on stage for the third show of the tour, and the second of the day. The first show has been a red-hot rocker, a distinct change from the night before in Vancouver, and the second is even better, the first real knock'em-down-drag-out set of the tour. Halfway through it, Jagger steps forward to the mike and asks the crowd, 'Who got free today?' Like a patient schoolmaster, he waits for a reply and when there is none, he says, 'Angela Davis got free today. Fuckin great...'

The song that Jagger wrote for and about Angela Davis, 'Sweet Black Angel,' is one of the better tracks on the just-released 'Exile On Main Street' album. It is well-worded, witty, with sardonic Jamaican steel drums in the middle, and a squawking and rolling harmonica in the background. In contrast with the very complexly played, essentially simply rock and roll that makes up the rest of the album, 'Sweet Black Angel' comes across as a sophisticated art song, and another example of what Jagger can do when he puts his hand to something.

For as Jagger himself will say, 'One half of me wants to make a lot of money and like spend it all, but the other half is jivey enough to really want to see it all happen. I do, you know. Because one revolution in American history isn't enough.' Even though he and his Nicaraguan-born wife, Bianca, are one of the great pop couples (whatever that means), whose whereabouts can be traced in the fashion and gossip columns of the popular papers, they still have their hearts in the right place; they have that sense of a world divided into the oppressors and the oppressed. And some months before the tour begins, in Paris, they both march in support of Angela at a rally that begins in the Place de la Bastille.

But when Jagger realises that many of those marching alongside him are carrying the hammer and sickle, he freaks. 'What the fuck?' he says to one of them. 'You walking for Angela and carrying a Russian flag? You've got to be out of your mind. Go back to the thirties, man, forget it ..., the twenties. 'Cause the hammer and sickle has cut down more fucking people in Russia who are Angela Davis than it ever has in America....'

Radical politics, yet another of Jagger's games, is one with certainly as many perils as his flirtation with Satanism during the
'Beggar's Banquet' and 'Let It Bleed' album days. Yet it is one
that he seems unable to resist. Angela is such a perfect symbol
for everything that is wrong with America: she is black, she is a
woman, she is beautiful, brilliant, she is oppressed. More than
once, Jagger has contributed his time and money to righteous
radical defense funds in Great Britain. Should someone ask him
to do something that he considers politically valid on this tour, he
will. That's what he says. Since America is not his home, merely
the place he comes to work in, his adopted second country, one
that buys more Stones' albums and fill more concert halls than
England ever could, it's doubly difficult to know what to do.
That stage is no place to find out what's going on in the street.
The mix of rock and roll and politics, dogma and doo-wop, has
always been a strange one.

So as Stevie Wonder, who performs in African tribal robes and
wears his hair braided into corn rows, comes off and the Stones
go on, the Seattle police slap the cuffs on a frizzy-haired black kid
who can be no more than twenty and looks totally wasted. Four
cops bend his arms behind his back, slap another pair of cuffs
around his ankles and then lift him, like a dead tiger at the end
of a hunt, carrying him backstage.

As soon as they get the kid out of the sight of the general
public, they drop him and drag him for thirty feet or so across a
marble floor out a back door where a plainclothesman in a white
jacket delivers a gratuitous kick to his chest. Face down, the kid
is then dragged across 150 feet of open parking lot until he is
in the lee of the police van, in deep shadow. There, they begin
working him over, using cuffs, fists, and knees, coming down on
the kid's face and groin, one cop frozen in the half-light swinging
his doubled fists over his head like an ax-handle before coming
down on top of the kid with piledriver force.

But neither Jagger nor the Stones see any of this. There are
thousands of kids out front who have not insulted policemen and
are screaming and dancing. Most of them are white. Dripping
and delighted after the first killer show of the tour, the Stones
leap into limos and are whisked back to their hotel.

For them, the rock and roll merry-go-round of the tour is just
getting into gear. Even the hotel they're staying in is semi-legend-

ary. Located directly on the Puget Sound, it affords a marvellous
view of the harbour and an opportunity for guests to fish directly
from their windows. Delightful. Especially for the jaded sensibilities of a stoned-out band on the road. The legend began one
night when the band that pioneered barbiturate rock got bored.
Bored as only a band with a room full of groupies so stoned they
were dissolving into the carpet, having already performed every
perverse act everyone could think of; can be. Bored. So that when
one of the boys in the band pulled in a mud shark, and it lay
there, cold, wet, murky, and dying on the carpet, it took but a
few minutes of persuasion to convince this one chick to find out
what it was like... to get juked... with a just-dead fish. When
Frank Zappa wrote a suite based on the incident and word got
around the biz, bands couldn't wait to play Seattle. One top English band used four-dollar New York steaks for bait, pulled in a
room's worth of sharks, then passed out on a couch, smelling like
the Fulton Fish Market on a very hot day in July.

And if the Stones are truly the meanest, dirtiest, angriest rock
outlaws of them all, there's no saying what degeneracy they're
going to come up with in this palace on the Sound.

As the first postgig party of the tour commences back in the
hotel, most of the Stones are there as well as whatever ladies have
managed to crack through security by waiting in the lobby or hitting on some S.T.P. dude at the hall. There's a bit of smoking, a
little music from the cassette player, and a lot of people watching
each other, waiting for something to happen.

Marshall Chess is there, and he literally bounces off the bed
to tell Keith, 'It was a *bitch*, man. I went all the way in the back
for the second show. Just by myself? With the kids? And I got off
like everyone else. A *motherfucker.*' Keith smiles and sinks wearily
into a chair. Marshall slides back down on the bed. There are
some young kids at the party and one pulls an envelope out of
his pocket and snorts out of it and passes it down. The next kid
snorts out of it, too, and hands it to Marshall. Now Marshall
has been around dope all his life. Ever since he began going to
recording sessions at the age of ten, he has seen people getting
high, so he asks the kid next to him what's in the envelope and
the kid says, 'Smack,' and goes on snuffling and inhaling to make
sure he's copped a solid hit.

Marshall passes the envelope to a blond girl with a shiny face who looks maybe seventeen and he tells her what it is and she smiles and nods her head and hits on it before passing it along.

Marshall is blown out. Musician's have always gotten high in some way, pills or smoke or booze. Musicians are high people. But the casual way these kids take hits off an envelope someone *tells* them is full of heroin freaks Chess out. They're like the kids who rushed him for tickets outside the stage door in Vancouver. These are the people he makes records for and he flashes that he doesn't know them any better than anyone else. Even though he's hipper than their parents will ever be and doing something they all think is so far out and very groovy, he is already definitely of another generation.

And when the Stones' bodyguard vaults into the room and says 'Let's go,' to Mick and Keith, Marshall doesn't have much more of a chance to think about it. The hotel manager, disturbed at the noise emanating from the room, has called upon the local police to investigate and right this minute they are on their way up in the elevator.

The next day everyone speculates on what those cops would have done if they'd found famous names in that room instead of kids who'd just flushed and hidden and thrown away their stashes. And how the Stones, totally innocent this time around, positively clean, would have been right back there in the headlines again, with the tour over almost before it began.

Still, the Stones got away with it, and the story gets better with every retelling. The entire S.T.P. caravan is high off the two good shows in Seattle. San Francisco is next and, as the plane taxis down the runway, Charlie Watts is up behind the stewardess, shadowing her as she demonstrates the use of the lifejacket and the location of the emergency exit. 'You cahn't feel good today, can you?' Charlie asks Bobby Keys. 'Not after awl that drinkin you did las night.'

'Hell,' Keys drawls, 'it wasn't the drankin. When ah got back to mah room ah found a gayng-bayng goin on. In *mah bed.* Chick looked like Joe Palooka.'

'Like who?' Charlie inquires politely.

'Lahk a bus mechanic,' Keys clarifies, shaking his head sorrowfully at the memory of it all.

Champagne and orange juice make the rounds and the feeling on the plane is that the tryouts are over. In San Francisco, the big time starts... magazine writers, the rock establishment, Bill Graham, and more of these young kids who are strangers in their own land. It's been nearly three years since the Stones were last in Northern California, performing at an outdoor concert on a cold December day at a speedway called Altamont.

Tales from Rock and Roll Heaven

WARM SAN FRANCISCO NIGHTS

There was still magic at the edge of the Western world then and a good concert at the Family Dog or the Avalon or even Winterland would bring them out of their rabbit warrens and little cubbies where they had been holed up, high for days, watching that record go round, getting off on Love or the Airplane or the Dead, so very high that it took a full day to get it together enough to actually venture out into the street where you had to deal with (giggle-giggle) concrete realities like traffic lights and telephone poles.

People would hitch and drive two hundred miles up the coast from where they'd been living clean in the country, with lots of home-grown, a wood fire, and maybe just one album to get them through the night. Freaks didn't own TVs then, they collected albums. If you closed your eyes behind Stevie Winwood singing 'Forty Thousand Headmen' or David Crosby's 'Guinevere,' you could see all the pictures you wanted... so it was worth all the paranoia associated with going into the city on the off chance that it would come together at the concert.

Because if it did, and the band was right, and the floor wasn't too crowded, there was room inside the music for everyone, enough space between each bending, soaring electric note for the whole audience to get together. Even though you were doing no more than dancing in front of the amps or passing a joint to a guy next to you whom you'd never seen before, you were a part of the feeling. No one was there just to see the band. The stage was merely a convenience for those who were interested in watching. Everyone was there to be with everyone else, the great *us*, all right there, just hanging out.

So incredible things happened as a matter of course. With that

many people walking around in a state of psychic charge, the
flashes were inescapable, sparks jumped across people's lives and
ignited life situations that went on for months. And all of it had
to do with the mystical electric energy that the band on stage was
pouring out, and that the audience was feeding back.

There was a small but definite number of *magic* bands, who
were known to have the power to levitate a hall and start the
energy flowing. One of them was the Quicksilver Messenger Service, San Francisco-based, who would play 'Who Do You Love?'
for nearly an hour and transport crowds to other dimensions.

By 1969 though, most of the magic was gone. It had seeped
out of the cities to the country and been burned out of people by
methedrine and heroin. Perversely, the audiences for rock concerts had increased, as more and more people discovered how it
felt to hear electric music under the influence of drugs that were
quickly becoming available to everyone, regardless of age or eco-
nomic persuasion.

In need of a new musician, the Quicksilver Messenger Service
picked up Nicky Hopkins, an English-born pianist who had just
left the Jeff Beck Group. Hopkins, who was in San Francisco to
record with someone else, had heard vaguely of Quicksilver, but
didn't really know much about their music, or their following.
What began as a few days of session work stretched into four
months of recording and then a tour.

'Quicksilver is back on the road, man,' people whispered to
each other, 'and they're *far out*... just like '67... and they'll get
you *off*.' Monterey Pop *angst*, that nostalgic longing for the clean
purity of bygone flower-power days, had already begun to flood
the minds of those just starting to get high.

Out they came, the ones who were still alive, out from their
rabbit warrens and little cubbies, speeding their brains out or getting stoned into palsied stupors on angel dust and animal tran-
quilizer. The people who drove up the coast had to deal with
the burn artists and red freaks on the streets outside Winterland,
but once they got inside... sure enough... it happened again. The
magic was there, and people looked at each other wide-eyed as
the music poured out of the amps and Nicky Hopkins played
a riff that was water, pure water; it flowed off his fingertips.
People danced and whirled and Winterland became a spaceship,

an actual astral spaceship of good feelings, headed for some distant star.

And three years later, at a Rolling Stones' recording session in Jamaica, Nicky Hopkins would close his eyes, remembering, and shake his head and say, 'Yeah, I recall all tha stuff. People comin backstage at Winterland to tell us how great we all were. And everybody in the band so wiped out, they were a semitone off; either way, through the whole set. It was so awful… God, it made me want to puke.'

So much for spaceships.

Chapter Two

Winterland was perfect. It was what the age demanded. No pretence of communal feelings like the old Family Dog, where gypsy families of flute-playing women and children whirled circles on the dance floor, where apples were free for the taking in barrels out by the fireplace and no one bothered to introduce the acts. Not even the basic-human hospitality of the old Fillmore West, where there were chairs to sit in if you wanted and a restaurant that served brown rice and vegetables.

Winterland was a barn, where five thousand people could be crowded in, and the cardboard-container Cokes were filled with shaved ice to cut down on the overhead, water being cheaper than Coke syrup. The iced sugar doughnuts were perfect when you were stoned and had those junkie cravings for something sweet. The concessionaires had short hair and treated the kids the way carnival barkers treat sideshow crowds, like suckers.

Still, for all its shortcomings, Winterland was a place a band could play-in. It had *some* feeling to it, and it was a palace when compared to a soulless, antiseptic arena like the Oakland Coliseum. By choosing to play in Winterland rather than Oakland, the Stones lost money in order to say, look, we are determined to finally do this city right. Finally. For San Francisco had always been one place where they had fucked up, and royally.

On the previous American tour, they'd headlined a show featuring Terry Reid, B. B. King, and Ike and Tina Turner at the Coliseum. When the Stones finally took the stage, they were forty minutes late. A power surge blew out their amps and left them standing there, helpless and silent, until repairs could be made. Midway through the set, Bill Graham, who was promoting the concert, and a Stones' roadie disagreed on the finer points of crowd control. The two began rolling around under the piano, discussing the matter. Between shows, the Stones' hyper-Jewish tour management demanded they be paid their share of the gate receipts immediately or the band would not go on. Never one to shirk from melodrama, Graham grandly wrote out a check, cornered Jagger in back of the stage and told him to go back to England, clean·up his act, forget it all, we'll cancel the second show. 'DO YOU KNOW WHAT GOES ON AROUND YOU?' he shouted, irate that, as he put it, the greatest performer in the world was surrounded by a bunch of yo-yos.

So that when the second show ended, the three-hundred-dollar buffet dinner that had been laid out in the dressing room, the English beers and imported cheese, the shrimp and liver pat , were all over the floor and smeared in a circle around a poster of Graham that hung on one wall. Someone drew a balloon coming out of Graham's mouth that said, 'This is where my head is at,' and in the picture, he is throwing the finger to the world.

The next time the Stones work the Bay Area is at Altamont, at the free concert that is to be their way of saying thank you to America, and their chance to generate some of that San Francisco magic they'd heard so much about but never experienced. Originally scheduled for Golden Gate Park, the concert site is moved and moved again and a plethora of people, including attorney Melvin Belli, get in on the proceedings until it is finally set in the only place that will accept it—a bare sloping piece of land near Livermore with a natural bowl at the bottom where a stage can be built.

Upon the advice of the Grateful Dead, the Stones' managers arrange for the Hell's Angels to provide security in return for five hundred dollars' worth of beer. Some six months earlier, the Stones had used the British Angels as security for their Hyde Park free concert and that had worked out fine. Of course, some British Angels do not even own motorcycles, but still... Angels are Angels, and San Francisco people assure the Stones' managers that they can be trusted. If there really is a counterculture, then it must have its very own police force too.

But on the day of the concert, the Angels get as loaded as anyone and use sawed-off pool cues to enforce their law. Mick Jagger gets punched in the face as soon as he gets out of the helicopter that drops him backstage and the very first thing Jo Bergman sees is a group of very stoned people standing around watching someone writhe around on the ground with the full-blown acid horrors. One of the Stones' bodyguards gets his arm broken and Marty Balin of the Jefferson Airplane is knocked unconscious in a fist fight right in front of the stage. At one point in the afternoon, all of the roadies of the bands scheduled to play huddle inside one of the equipment vans to confer about getting clubs and clearing the Angels out, vigilante fashion. They decide it will only bring about more bloodshed.

By the time the Stones go on, it's dark. The crush of people in front of the three-foot stage is terrifying. Their eyes are crazed, they're pushing, trying to get forward, closer, trying to reach up and touch the magic source. Sporadically, Angels leap into the crowd, beating anyone who gets in their way. Jagger pleads with the crowd, 'Brothers an sisters... brothers an sisters... who's fightin and what for? A-who's fightin, and a-what for?'

But it's hopeless. There are Angels sitting on drum cases and freaks going mad by the amplifiers, literally foaming and clawing at their faces as though they're possessed by the gods in some classic Greek tragedy. The Stones are loaded too; it's their last gig, they want to go home; all they can do is play. Someone has led Jo Bergman up the hill in back of the stage and she hears the music stop, then start again, and wonders what that means. There is only one helicopter available for the ride out, and it has room for only nine people and gas enough for just one trip. Eighteen people, the Stones among them, jam the copter and just before it takes off, Jo sees this young white girl crying bitterly. An eighteen-year-old black man has been stabbed to death by a Hell's Angel who saw him rushing toward the stage with a revolver in his hand. The gun was later found to be unloaded.

The copter takes off at a forty-five-degree angle and limps away, motor fluttering and coughing for life, like the very last flight out of Vietnam. It is only when they get back to the relative sanity of their hotel rooms that the awful horror of the day dawns on the Stones. Only then does it all become real. By the next morning, they are all on planes headed out of the country.

At Altamont, the day is not yet over. Chip Monck gets knocked when he tries to regain possession of the purple starburst carpet the Stones have worked on. The Angels have it, and they insist that the stage lights be kept on so they can party, drink off the rest of the beer and get loose. With the very white lights of 'Street Fighting Man' shining down upon them, they do just that until the generator runs out of fuel, taking time out only for one blindly stoned kid who accidentally wobbles into one of their

bikes. Him they chase up a hill and stomp into bloody uncon-
sciousness.

Until now San Francisco had not opened up its Golden Gate
to the Stones, and it would be an early test of the shiny red
S.T.P. machine Peter Rudge had put together, and of the Stones'
new professionalism, if they got through their four days there
unscathed. Hell, it would be a miracle if they got through it without battling Bill Graham, who would once again be promoting
their concerts.

Graham is a San Francisco fixture. Much like the Stones, he
has outlasted everyone who once was a threat to him, and continued, through good times and bad, until there is hardly anything
more to say about him that matters, save that he exists, and is
in total control. Graham himself is *total*, a man who has always
insisted on nothing more than his absolute right to be just himself to the exclusion of all else.

A tired-faced, hollow-eyed man who can still remember the
days when he was a 'mambo nigger' in New York City, staring
hungrily through a store window at a pair of thirty-four-dollar
dancing shoes he could not possibly afford, Graham now lives in
a tree-surrounded Marin County home with a private basketball
court out back. His life is very much a realization of the American Dream, showbiz style.

He began as a performer-manager with the San Francisco
Mime-Troupe, then got in early on the commercial end of one
Ken Kesey's first Acid Test celebrations at Longshoreman's Hall.
Soon after, he began promoting shows in an old theatre on Fillmore Street in the gut of San Francisco's ghetto. From there he
moved to the Carousel Ballroom, renamed it the Fillmore West;
bought the old Village Theater on Second Avenue in New York
City, named it the Fillmore East, and a rock and roll empire was
born. From 1968 to 1972, the Fillmores were the showcases for
a whole era of popular music.

Through it all, even in the haziest of communal San Francisco,
Graham would not hesitate to inform anyone who asked that
the hall was *his* house and his alone, and if you didn't act the
way you're supposed to, you could get your ass right back on the
street where you belonged. If you chose to pursue the dialectic,
Graham would more often than not accommodate you by chas-
ing you out onto the asphalt himself, or, if the case warranted

it, run you halfway to Golden Gate Park with a security guard behind him trying to keep up.

Graham fought with the light show unions. He fought with the Grateful Dead. He brought Otis Redding, Aretha Franklin, and B. B. King to white audiences and treated them the way no white man ever had. He managed the Jefferson Airplane. He stopped managing them, and fought with them. He fought with the Hell's Angels, finally refusing them admission to his shows after a long and continuing series of incidents. For this he received the first of seven bullets, indicating he was a marked man. He began a record label for San Francisco-based talent and gave Lenny Bruce work in his last, sick, crazy, paranoid days. He fought with the Motherfuckers, New York's tough Lower East Side street gang. For his trouble, he was beaten with a chain outside the front door of the Fillmore East. He gave a lot of people a lot of music and made a lot of money. Finally he closed both Fillmores, allowed himself to be the subject of a not-so-documentary documentary about it, and 'retired.' Then he bought Winterland and went on promoting more shows than ever before.

Graham no longer needed the money, nor did he get as much pleasure from it all as he had in the early days. Still he kept on, cause he loved it, loved the give-and-take involved in bringing an act like the Stones to San Francisco, loved the business of the business, and the satisfaction that a well-promoted concert gave him. He kept on, because like the Stones, there wasn't anything else in the world at which he was number one.

'An actor can sit in his cold-water flat,' Graham would say, 'and say, "I'm not leavin till they give me *Hamlet*." And nineteen years later, he's still there, shaving. Sometimes you got to go out and do shoe commercials. I did shoe commercials enough. After seven years, what's it going to say on the billboard, "Zasu Pitts presents the Rolling Stones in San Francisco"? No... this can't be...'

What it has to say is 'Bill Graham presents...' because even for Graham, who is as hard and professional as they come, the Stones are a special rush. Even the dangers of putting them on a stage are more extreme.

Graham has a fantasy about the San Francisco concerts that is as full blown and horrible as Peter Rudge's Palladium nightmare. Just as one of the shows breaks and the Stones come rushing out the back door, on the run, a truck that had been circling the block will come to a dead stop and the tailgate will drop open and out will roll four Hell's Angels who'll put the snatch on Mick Jagger and whoever else is near and then roll back into the truck. The truck will pull away and HIJACK! The Angels will have kidnapped Mick Jagger for ransom. Like a perfectly planned bank job in some foreign suspense movie.

Graham doesn't talk much about this to anyone. Not even to Peter who is as fully wired and totally immersed in the horrendous possibilities as Bill. It is certain that no bikers will be allowed in the hall. That is Bill Graham policy. What has to linger in the back of Graham's mind is an incident that receives almost no publicity at all. Only a few weeks before the Stones play San Francisco, at an outdoor concert in a medium-sized California city, twenty-one thousand people pay their way in to see an English band perform. All bikers with tickets are made to take off their colours to avoid interclub warfare inside the gates, and they comply. Halfway through the set, one biker goes over to another and puts two bullets through his head with a pistol. The murderer is arrested on the spot and the concert continues without further incident.

Nine thirty in the morning and this guy on television is admitting he knows nothing about ballet, then he goes on to review a performance by the Joffrey. Jeez-us. Then his face changes shape, the color balloons out around his head and he begins talking about, 'Some kids who are first in line to see the Rolling Stones... they were there twenty-three hours before anyone else had the same idea, and to tell you the truth, folks, I just can't see it myself.' The color is now puddling in streams around his eyes, and gray morning light is coming in through the hotel window. 'I think Mick Jagger is one of the most repulsive performers I've ever seen. Of course, people who've seen him tell me he's fantastic... I've never actually seen him *live*...'

Of course not. The livest you've ever been is on tape with a six-second delay. Turn on the television to find out what kind of day it is outside and you're subjected to this kind of punishment. It's for sure that the ravages of time have done nothing to help San Francisco. Two more years and it's going to be Detroit, with a few charming eccentricities. Take the social note in the morning's *Chronicle*.

'Wendy Weir, sister of the Grateful Dead's rhythm guitarist, Bob, will hold a reception for the band as soon as they return from their current tour...' Used to be the only place you could read about the Dead in a regular newspaper was in the section where they detailed Ken Kesey's legal activities and kept an eye on musicians arrested for possession. It all certainly has become respectable.

The Stones are sequestered in a Japanese-style hotel replete with green tile, sit-in bath-tubs and packets of crystals that turn the water a special color. The place is supposed to be a definite up after the so-so accommodations in Vancouver and Seattle, so naturally when the Stones get in, there's all this confusion and milling about and the suitcases, each with its own special yellow tape number on the side, stay on the baggage truck.

The man with suitcase number one, Michael Philip Jagger, looking tired, frail, and disappointed, addresses the Tac Squad. 'It's dreary,' he says, rolling his eyes up in his head and doing that world-weary little Chaplinesque shrug with his shoulders. 'You cahn't open a window. It's like suffocatin.' And, of course, the Tac Squad knows just what he means. The Stones are stashed in their own building, one that houses the Japanese consulate on the second floor and has all kinds of separate entrances that lock. The place is a pillbox, perfect for security, but lacking that essential view of the pastel skyline sweeping down to the blue bay filled with puffed white sails and the graceful arch of the bridge. Out of the windows in this place you can't see a thing.

The Tac Squad starts going around in circles, making phone calls to Marin County real estate agents and taking quick inspection tours of the more regal downtown hotels. Through it all, Bill Graham is shuffling around in his purple nylon Woodstock jacket, making sure that things are being taken care of. Right from the moment Jagger first sees him, comes over and says, 'Hi, Bill,' and gives him the firm handshake, Graham has this sense that the past has been erased. Oakland 1969 never happened. Mick has matured, as has Bill. For, as Graham himself will tell you, it's not as if he was super-nice last time and the Stones were assholes. At times, Bill Graham will be the first to admit, there is no bigger asshole than Bill Graham.

'Bill,' Mick says, 'wha's doin in town? Is there some good black music on somewhere?' Bill makes a few phone calls and finds out that it is dead. Nothing. Monday night.

'Come *on*, Bill, 'Jagger teases. 'Ai mean really... this is your town. Let's go out and *do* something.'

Graham gets on the phone, pleased because it's not Mick the star and Bill the Jewish merchant, but an equality, a meeting of professionals. He gets in touch with the man who runs the Trident, Frank Werber. Werber, a bearded, very slow-talking, centered man, directed the fortunes of America's folksinging favorites, the Kingston Trio, throughout the sixties. Now he runs the Sausalito restaurant that is the meeting place for the divergent cultural strains that make up the hip segment of San Francisco in the seventies. Bill explains that he is in this bind... he has the Rolling Stones on his hands and nowhere to take them.

Frank understands. But he also has a little problem. The Trident is traditionally closed on Monday nights and he himself still serving a six-month sentence for the possession and cultivation of marijuana. The case was long fought and much appealed, with Frank insisting that marijuana was a sacrament and therefore legal, but to no avail. Right now they have him on work furlough, which means they let him out in the morning on the condition he gets back in by ten at night.

Since it's for Bill, and the Stones, and since desire can move mountains, Frank says he'll try and get it together. When Bill hangs up the phone, he comes over to Mick like a caterer who has just arranged the big wedding of all time, in the Grand Canyon, for four hundred couples with a full symphony orchestra. 'We're goin to dinner,' Bill says and the statement kind of puts an end to the room crisis. Mick is getting bored with it all anyway. As so often happens when he merely expresses a whim, he's realised how much weight it carries with the rest of the band, and how whole sections of the S.T.P. party are out trying to make his whim a reality. So he just sighs and says, 'Let's stay... it's not so bad as that.'

In Sausalito, they're getting ready. The young and perishable waitress-ladies who are one of the restaurant's main attractions are being gathered to push tables together. It's hard to describe the kind of tremor that runs through the hip demimonde when they actually get a chance to come into contact with the Stones. It's like getting to see God and fuck your favorite movie star at the same time, a melange of nervous emotions both sacred and profane. Out at the restaurant, they're getting loose with a vengeance, so that when the Stones arrive it'll all be really mellow.

Getting 'loose' so that things will be 'mellow' are key concepts in Marin County. Hip Marin County is full of ex-New Yorkers, dope dealers, coke runners, waterbed salesmen, pop musicians, organic juice drinkers, staunch Republicans, long-distance joggers, houseboat dwellers, and suburban families headed by insurance men who've sold more than a million bucks' worth of policies in the preceding fiscal year. It's the best place in the country to catch an authentic glance at one suggestion as to what the future of America might be. Nowhere else have soft drugs been integrated as successfully into normal, everyday life and as soon as the federal government completes its first marijuana consumption census, they're going to find that the per capita dope-inhalation rate in Marin is right up there with the kif farmers of Morocco and the bhang sellers of southern India.

As the night wears on and people get looser and looser, and stoneder and stoneder, they start wondering, 'Wow. Are they really coming? Will they show? I wonder, wow, could they, d'ya think...' and other such ramblings so that by the time the lights of the small fleet of limos comes on to Bridgeway and down the hill into Sausalito, the expectation in the room is nigh on manic, and when a voice cries out, 'It's THEM Oh... THEY'RE COMING,' everyone freezes right where they are, thinking, 'Oh, God, gee, gotta be sure and be mellow, whew, wish I hadn't smoked that last one, uh... I...'

The guy who's running it all looks across the room at these human statues, all of whom are locked in and gazing at the front door, waiting, and his stomach sags because he knows it's a sure thing that the Stones will do one of their lightning exits on this crowd, there being nothing they like less than being gaped and clutched at, even on the most astral stoned level. 'Let's go, let's go,' the guy begins chattering, like a catcher calling encouragement to his fading pitcher. 'Move some of these chairs. Bring that table over here.' People start to jerk out of it and by the time the Stones come in, everybody is moving, working, and it looks like a party already in progress. Jagger grins and the guy running it knows it's all going to be all right. It's going to be one of those nights San Francisco has a reputation for. Loose. Laid back. Mellow.

The next day the streets around Winterland are filled with kids sitting on sidewalks, waiting patiently in line, their boots off and copies of *Good Times* scattered around them, with sleeping bags and wool ponchos under their heads. One guy is safe and secure in a lean-to he's built against the building's back wall.

Graham has nearly seventy-five private cops on the street, some ten thousand dollars' worth of security. While they do a competent job of keeping the peace, the streets around Winterland are no ones vision of the new world. They are inner city and confrontations are common. Two guys, who look like they get their t-shirts tie-dyed at a winery, challenge a black cop to tell them where they can and can't walk and they're quickly hustled into a city police car. A heavy-looking brother in black leather gets chased off the street by a white security man, stops, then says in a very clear and solemn voice, 'You white bastard I'm gonna shoot you, motherfuck. You dead!' Then he runs off down an alley. The private cops go back to work.

At 4:15 in the afternoon, the Stones troop down a concrete passageway out of the bright sun with Nicky Hopkins bringing up the rear, carrying for some reason a tray set with tea service for two.

Hopkins is an arrow-thin young man. All the thin adjectives ever invented apply to him. He has what was once the prescribed British rock star hairstyle that has now grown overlong. An Addams family face peeks out from among floppy hanks of black hair and thick Edwardian sideburns. God, is he thin. There isn't a Jewish or Italian mother in America who wouldn't be thrilled to the soles of her Stride-Rite shoes to sit him down at a table and stuff him full of food, especially because he has these great sorrel eyes that transform what could be a ghoulish face into something kind.

Of all the boys in the band, he has the closest ties to San Francisco, having lived out in Marin County for nearly five years. He's worked on enough local albums to qualify as a member of the local musicians' collective. Nearly every major city has its own circle of successful and semi-successful rock musicians these days, but only San Francisco, New York, and L.A. have an industry based on the music and a press and cultural establishment to go along with it.

One of the premier members of that establishment is backstage and working. Jim Marshall, a small, dark, bird-like man, has spent the last twelve years of his life in dressing rooms or to one side of the stage following pop music as it went from jazz to folk to rock. When Keith Richard swung his guitar on to a shorted-out mike stand on a wet stage in Sacramento in 1964 and nearly frizzed the ends of his hair permanently, Jim Marshall was there. When Brian Jones walked the incense-filled stadium grounds of the Monterey Pop Festival in 1967, with a head full of DMT, Jim Marshall was right there. 'We're good, y'know,' he can remember Brian saying back then, 'and Mick's great. But bloody 'ell, I wouldn't want to go up after him,' as he pointed to a sweating, performing Otis Redding.

Jim Marshall even saw the Beatles, *ten times.* He is more or less the history of the rockbiz behind the lens of a Nikon and this time around be has reached the absolute top. The pinnacle, the one that every photographer dreams about as a young and freckled kid growing up somewhere in the Midwest... Jim is shooting a cover for *Life* magazine. Fat City. *Life* is one of those magazines that didn't want to be bothered even to hear that there was a tour going in 1969, but now, thanks to Gibson-Stromberg and changing times, they've sent along Tommy Thompson, one of their top writers, and hired Jim to do the cover.

Jim is getting no co-operation from anyone. None. Jim, who is widely known as an aggressive photographer, is being treated courteously but at arm's length. No one's sure what kind of article *Life* wants to run on the Stones, nor do they completely trust Jim to take the kind of picture that won't embarrass the principal. Besides, for the S.T.P. crowd, Jim is a bit abrasive—he doesn't fit precisely with the genteel civilized flow that goes on around the band.

This infuriates Jim. As he says, 'In a given situation under pressure like that I can shoot better than anyone. I'm not sayin I'm a super big name, but it's a matter of fucking trust. Someone should tell these fucking cats I'm not going to rip them off. I would fight with *Life* for a good photo against anything that would compromise the Stones. To try and justify myself at this stage of the game is... fucking ridiculous.'

Jim, who has his own special code, and who is a total professional, has to shoot from outside doors and around corners. He can't get on the plane except for one short hop from L.A. to San Diego. Ethan Russell, a tall, patrician-looking gentleman with a New England face to match his given name, and Annie Leibovitz, *Rolling Stone's* photography editor, and even the guy from *Time* magazine are getting all kinds of access simply because they fit in better and are more S.T.P.-acceptable. Backstage now, you can feel the tension, the subtle jockeying for position by the newly arrived group of people with cameras around their necks. Jagger, who is a bit scared to be working San Francisco anyway, is shuffling and running in place, trying to get warm. Awaiting outside is an audience of his peers, Neil Young and Jerry Garcia, most of the Airplane and the Dead, and five thousand expectant kids.

Once they go out, it's whomp! The band slashes into 'Brown Sugar' and 'Bitch' with the bass and drums coming together like a sledgehammer and the volume so loud that the music plays the crowds' bodies, the bass making their breastbones vibrate sympathetically, so that they *feel* it as much as hear it and have to dance. Sparkles rain down off Jagger's face and hair and the bells on his shoes tinkle as he leaps up and down. The set accelerates like a runaway freight train as soon as the Stones go into 'Midnight Rambler,' with Jagger the actor portraying Jagger the singer, and the band providing background music for the psychodrama. Jagger stalks from one side of the stage to the other until the music slows in back of him, with only the bass pulsing to keep time and the lights all blue and eerie in his face. Then it's Jagger on his knees like the James Brown of old. He undoes the studded belt around his waist and rises slowly to sneer, slashing the belt to the floor as the band crashes everything in sight in back of him and Chip Monck slaps his leg involuntarily and barks a command and pow!... it goes all red. Keith picks up the song's driving riff and begins bouncing as though his Les Paul was discharging electricity right into his body. In front of him, Jagger criss-crosses back and forth, waggling a finger, crooking his body, and pointing like an old arthritis-crippled gospel preacher. Mick Taylor is whistling leads over the rhythm and Charlie's there in back of everybody kicking shit out of the drums.

By the end of the set, Jagger is clinging to the tops of the amps and screaming, as Keith rocks and stumbles through 'Bye-Bye

Johnny,' cutting it into rhythms and playing through the breaks like the illegitimate son of Chuck Berry, ripping away at his guitar with his arm fully extended, a move that Pete Townsend of The Who first saw him make at the Richmond Station Hotel in 1964. Townsend took it and made it into the windmill that is his trademark.

The Stones leave the stage after 'Street Fighting Man.' The crowd kicks and howls and wails and stomps on the floor, demanding an encore, but the band is already out of the building, and in the mobile home on their way back to the hotel. The door at the top of the concrete passageway swings back and forth crazily in the breezy sunshine, as the crowd continues to scream.

As Bill Graham puts it, 'Say you got a blind date with a girl and over the phone she says, "Oh, am I going to give you head. Oh, am I going to fuck you." And then you go to pick her up and she's a two foot transvestite with one eye in the middle of her forehead and the other under her nose. And there you are, standing like a schmuck, with your good suit on...' In other words, all the hype in the world cannot replace one good show. When the Stones follow with another killer that night, word gets out on the street and scalpers' prices rise. The Stones have come back to San Francisco as champions. After it's all over, back on the hotel TV, the puddlefaced newsman has been replaced by the tanned, beaming face of Senator George McGovern. While the Stones played to ten thousand crazies, George has swept the California, Oregon, and Massachusetts primaries. Nothing can stop him now. He's on his way to the Democratic presidential nomination and his date with destiny. George is smiling a Liberace smile with all his gleaming white choppers showing. He's waving has arms in a victory salute and laughing, but now the sound on the TV has gone and all that comes through the static is George making like an Alka-Seltzer commercial and telling his delirious followers, 'I can't believe it... we won *the whole thing.*'

At this point in the tour, the individual members of the S.T.P. caravan are still getting to know each other and discovering how the tour works. In order to kill two birds with one stone and get into some basic journalism, I quiz Stan Moore about the large black guards who are on constant duty at the entrance to the Stones' hotel building.

'Stan, how come those black dudes at the door never smile?'

'Well, Bob, that's 'cause they *serious* fellows.'

'*Why* are they there?'

'To stop people from entering... you know, unauthorized people.'

'Like what *kind* of unauthorized people?'

'Well, mostly it's been chickies.'

'Uh... dangerous chickies?'

'I'll tell you, Bob, like the other day, this little chick comes round asking for Mickey. You know, Mick Taylor? So I call up to his room and say, "Mick, there's some girl down here to talk to you." And he say, "I don't know any girls in San Francisco." "Dig it," I say to him, "You ain't *got* to know her. Like she just here to push some leg on you." '

'To do what?'

'You know... the thang. To do the thang.'

'Oh yeah. What happened?'

'Well, he came down all right, but nothin go down.'

'Why not?'

'Aw, man. Like he too shy or somethin. Can you dig that?'

If the Stones stay in a city more than one night, word as to their whereabouts invariably gets out and the lobby of the hotel they're in begins to look like Christine Jorgenson's doctor's waiting room. In addition, in so-hip San Francisco, a lot of 'friends of the band' have managed to penetrate. A friend of the band can be anyone from a musician like Mike Bloomfield, who went to high school with Marshall Chess back in Winnetka, Illinois, and talks as fast as anyone in the world, to a person we'll call Flex, whose speciality is returning from Morocco and points east with stuff that you can smoke and snort.

What with the crush of freaks in the lobby and the clutch of groovies in the hotel rooms, the entire operation has gone up a notch or two in tempo. The Stones have a night off and the plans are to catch the Isley Brothers in some funky black club across the Bay. Better move quick if you're going to go through, since Mick and Keith, surrounded by a school of people, hop into the first limo and all the rest of the groovies clamber in where they can. 'Hey, man, try the next car down, we're full up. Yeah, I'm sure there's room back there.' A fine mist is falling in the parking lot and a chill wind blows through those not hip enough to win immediate acceptance into a car. High-paranoia time, with lots of eye games and people so intent on maintaining their own position close to the action that they're afraid to look an untouchable in the face for fear of contagion. The doctor's safely tucked in a car, he belongs, so's Marshall Chess, so is... when a loud voice cuts through the night, saying, 'if you knew as much about mouthpieces as you think you do...'

Lookee here. A guy talking loudly, even defiantly to Bobby Keys, who is a principal and a full-fledged inner circle member. 'Ah,' Keys tells the guy, 'take some of that wind and shove it back into your horn,' a remark which would kill someone without a definite position on the tour but doesn't seem to faze this guy at all. He just climbs into a car in back of Keys and keeps on talking.

Doors slam shut and engines rev. Robert Frank comes out of the hotel wrestling with his gear, but Jagger rolls down a window to tell him, 'Ah'm sorry, Robert, but wi the sound an all, it's just too much,' and the cordon pulls out, leaving those not nimble enough to catch a ride on the curb, literally holding their tools in hand. Frank at least has his camera to hang on to.

Bill Graham, however, is throwing a party at his favourite French restaurant, an affair which most of the Tac Squad is going to attend. It will be quieter without the Stones, but certainly acceptable, a peaceful meal in a gilded restaurant, with gathered silks that rise to form a pyramid near the ceiling and mirrors on the walls. It will be a nice sociable no-pressure night... as the door swings open and in come the boys, with Keith in the lead. 'The Isleys weren't on,' he explains, looking tired and slumping in a chair. 'So 'ere we are.'

And suddenly the evening is transformed into a party of the weirdest order. At one table Mick Jagger is being questioned by Tommy Thompson. Tommy is a tall, prosperous-looking, well-groomed man in fashionable sports clothes and highly polished brogans with chains on them.

'You know,' he tells Mick, 'I talked to every kid that came out of that place yesterday, and what impressed me was the way they said they were all able to see without any hassles. I mean, that's what it's all about, isn't it?'

Mick nods and reaches for a roll. Ho-hum. His eyes are like slits and he's yawning every now and then.

'Are you living in the South of France?' Tommy asks, looking for an opening. 'I bet the chancellor of the exchequer is glad to hear that.'

'DEMI-TAAAAAAAAASE,' moans this guy about three chairs down from Tommy. The guy from the parking lot has made it to the restaurant. In the brighter light, he is revealed to be Jack Nitzsche, master arranger and piano player, who has been rocking since the days of Phil Spector and the Teddy Bears. Jack has known the Stones forever. He played tambourine on 'Satisfaction' and is considered by Charlie Watts to be at least the funniest man in the world. Just that afternoon, Jack's gone to the trouble of telling Mick Jagger, 'You're supposed to be the leaders of the rock generation with that shit you're playin? Who you kiddin?' And although Jack is only half-joking, Jagger gets more or less upset by it because there aren't many people he respects who can get close to him and have the nerve to say something like that. Jack is a man who will not be daunted.

'DEMI-TAAAAAAASE,' he moans again, badly distracting Tommy Thompson from his line of questioning. Tommy seems a sincere, well-intentioned fellow, a hell of a good writer it's well known, who is definitely in over his head on this one. Who'd expect someone like Jagger to be able to converse about art, ballet, literature, and the theater and then lean over to Bobby Keys and, in the same breath, say, 'Yeah. I remember ballin her in the sink in your bathroom.'

'Do you own any ties?' Tommy asks Mick.

'Yeah.'

'Do you wear them?'

'Oh, yeah.'

'When?'

'When everyone else doesn't....'

The escargots have given way to the salmon, which has been served with the white wine and now the red. The waiters are all really Italians from Brooklyn, but no one cares because they're under the influence of various substances. Down at the end of Keith's table, a guy who hasn't touched any of the wine is, whoops, there he goes, on the nod, into the *framboise* and fresh cream. Nope, he pulls out at the last second, like a Stuka in flames leveling out. He holds on for a good minute, then snap! he falls right back asleep.

At Mick's table, Tommy's still trying to get a little give-and-take going, but the only guy interested in communicating is Jack. 'Bill,' he pleads with Bill Graham, 'don't go on any more of those talk shows, huh? I've seen ya. And don't let the Fillmore film out. Please? Huh? I'm beggin with ya... Bill? Promise me you'll say you won't release it... because I've seen *it...*'

'Jack,' Bill says solemnly, 'when you think of this moment in the future... be very careful.' Jack gets up to leave, with dignity, as the circus continues to rage around him at both tables, sentences left as unfinished as the plates of chocolate mousse.

'Who is that man?' Tommy Thompson asks Bill Graham.

'His name,' Bill says simply, 'is Nitzsche.'

'We've used his sewing machines for years,' a friend of Tommy's sniffs.

And from just outside the door comes Nitzsche's final comment on the evening. 'Waiter?' he says, with a note of clarity in his voice. 'Waiter? I should like a stinger, please. A double.'

It's all been so calm and friendly for three days that by the last gig, even Bill Graham wonders when the other shoe is going to drop. But aside from Graham shouting 'Who do you think you are, Johnny Superstar?' at some people trying to get in by the stage door, even he manages to hold on to his newfound Ian.

After the second show ends, the Stones are rushed to the airport for the flight back to Burbank and a weekend of concerts in Los Angeles. A smiling, cheery lady in hot pants, who looks like one of those breathtaking waitresses you meet once in a lifetime in an all-night coffee shop, is waiting for the Stones to board. 'Gee,' she says sweetly to Alan Dunn, 'could I ask them for an autograph? For my daughter? She loves them so.' And she is just so nice, with sunshine sweetness shining through her eyes that he lets her up to the plane.

She goes right over to Mick and coos, 'Are you Mick Jagger?' and when he nods yes, she pulls a sheaf of papers out of her bag and says, 'I am hereby serving you, Michael Philip Jagger, with the following...' and reads off a list of subpoenas all having to do with Altamont.

The next thing anyone knows, the sweet lady comes rocketing

unsteadily down the airplane stairway screaming, 'He hit me, he hit me.' She is followed through the door by Keith Richard who stands at the top of the stairway for a full second, silhouetted by the light from within, then swings an armful of papers up to the sky. The papers fly up, and then scatter out, down along the runway.

'The sonofabitch *hit* me,' the sweet lady shouts, to no avail. The plane taxis down the runway and heads for L.A. with five Rolling Stones tucked inside, safe as kids wrapped in their mother's quilt. And while all of it is a far cry from the fabled days of yesteryear, the world, in general, and the wages of time, in particular, still have a way to go before the Stones become completely respectable.

Chapter Three

Actually a person such as Jagger should be locked up. He would have been, had he tried to perform in the twenties or earlier, when we wouldn't have tolerated his mad offering.

RUDY VALLEE, IN A LETTER TO 'LIFE'

He tried. And he was wonderful. He spilled more blood on that floor than a five-thousand-man army but he didn't make it. He'd been tricked into acceptance... He was tired. He was too much money in. He was too famous. He sucked at the crowd. He tried to remember how it was when he first worked it. How it was when he was really and purely real...

CHARLES BUKOWSKI, ON JAGGER, L. A. FREE PRESS

Back into Los Angeles. Old whore Hollywood and her respectable madam of an older sister Beverly Hills. A city of stars. You could see them on the pavement when you walked down Hollywood Boulevard and catch them figuring out prices in their heads between the racks of beer and taco chips at the Safeway.

Like used cars, illusion was an L.A. industry. New York writers might traditionally leave the place snickering about its random blahness, the spiritless smoggy vacuum that was the city of L.A., but Hollywood always held on for the last laugh. America's fantasy life was generated on its back lots and sound stages, and pressed into records in its recording studios. L.A. made fantasy food for the country, and the world, and created the stars who were the physical embodiments of the fantasy.

But since proximity always breeds nonchalance, if not out-and-out contempt, those closest to the Hollywood fantasy-making process had few illusions about it all. They always knew which great 'star' who caused hearts to throb in Dubuque and Fall River and Brooklyn was in real life a dyke, a whore, a fag, a dope addict, or all of the aforementioned. And that knowledge was power. It freed them from the fantasy of the star as one who leads a higher, richer life and allowed them to go on with their business whether that be lighting the set, rigging props, or working in Schwab's.

So that in its own vacuous way, Los Angeles had this very hip thing going. A personality who might turn heads in Paris or New York could walk down a Beverly Hills street without attracting so much as a glance, save for the drug store cashier noting that today was the day they handed out unemployment checks so every actor's credit was good.

But with the golden days of Hollywood long gone, and the movies having given way to pop music and pro sports as America's prime fantasy obsessions, a new kind of star had come along. The rock star. Since musicians had always been considered outside or beneath the law and acted accordingly, lawlessness became part of the aura. The rock star was greater and more far out for his fans than any idol of the silver screen because he lived everyone's fantasy life right out in the open, where it could be picked at and discussed. Rock stars, as one groupie once said, are groovy because they smoke more cigarettes, take more dope, drink more whiskey, stay up later, and fuck more frequently and in odder positions than most people. In other words, in post-everything bizarro America, they do the things everybody wants to do.

With rock as the backing track, it was a brand new day in Hollywood. The sons and daughters of the illusion-makers were stoned out of their heads and trying to worm their way into the Stones' dressing room. Guys with English accents and velvet jackets were getting blown between floors in the elevator of that hotel on the Strip.

And right at the top of the whole pyramid was Michael Philip Jagger, the number one rock star in the world.

By his mere presence, Jagger changes any event that he is involved in. Any party that he gets dragged to becomes the party Mick was at. Any filmmaker who can persuade him to star in his movie no longer has a mere property, he has a Mick Jagger movie, with his name over the title and guaranteed box-office receipts, regardless of the film's merits.

The most famous one-shot concert of all time was the benefit for Bangladesh refugees in Madison Square Garden during the summer of 1971. George Harrison, Leon Russell, Eric Clapton, and famous others played together and Bob Dylan came out of semi-retirement to sing. Twenty thousand screaming people

packed the place, applauding everything deliriously, going wild
at just being in the presence of the greatest pantheon of rock stars
ever assembled on one stage.

At one time in preparations for the show, it was planned to
have Leon Russell begin singing 'Jumping Jack Flash' at the piano,
run through it once, then have Mick Jagger leap out to finish
it up. Jagger's sudden unannounced presence on stage during a
song that is heart attack material anyway would have escalated
the whole thing into another galaxy. The scream level would have
risen by three or four decibels and at least two people in the loges
would have died from excitement. Such is Jagger's power.

The more things change, the saying goes, the more they stay
the same. Truer words were never spoken especially in regard to
the new stars. For, despite all the changes in life style, the new
stars, like the old, are still defined by their fans.

Like Ronnie. 'So good, man, so good,' Ronnie is rattling, they
were just so good. They looked like refugees from *A Clockwork
Orange.*' A fairly mediocre show at the Hollywood Palladium
has just ended and despite all of Peter Rudge's fears (or perhaps
because of them), it has been a distinct nonevent. The streets
around the hall resembled nothing so much as a flood-struck
town under martial law, bereft of any life save for the blue-uni-
formed policemen walking in pairs. A few Bible freaks marched
up and down in front of the building chanting 'More Bible, less
Rolling Stones,' and a small, strange-looking man came to the
stage door claiming to be Brian Jones. He presented a card identifying himself to be a member of the Church of Satan then
handed over the 'microphone that Mick asked me to bring.' The
microphone was put into the first bucket of water that could be
found.

Aside from that, the gig was nothing special. Ronnie, though,
is solid gone. He is standing in the lobby of the Stones' hotel
in Beverly Hills. It is nearly midnight and in various rooms various Stones are climbing out of their stage clothes. Ronnie, too,
is shoeless and shirtless. Also walletless, keyless, and mindless,
having lost them all in the rush and crush of the four thousand
people on the packed Palladium floor.

'I'm knocked out. I *am*, man,' Ronnie jitters. 'Did I tell you?
That makeup, man... they looked like a fag show.'

Ronnie is not your ordinary L.A. kid. Oh, he lives in the requisite white house with the white-brick fireplace and the white wall-to-wall carpeting, with the pool out back, and his parents divorced, but Ronnie is hip.

Like when his father offered him a choice of presents for his high-school graduation, either a trip to Europe or a pair of JBL speakers and a Hitachi tape recorder. Ronnie figured, shee, Europe you can go to any time but JBLs are bitchin. For someone who has worn out five copies of 'Sticky Fingers,' that is, played the record so many times that the highs have become indistinct, it was an easy choice. No Europe. Speakers.

Ronnie is so hip that he has even managed to speak to Mick Jagger. Once. Backstage at a T. Rex concert at the Palladium. Jagger was there to catch Marc Bolan's act and Ronnie was there, well, just to be there and somehow got backstage and there was Mick, kind of leaning against this doorjamb, waiting for the action. It was almost mystical, the way Ronnie came to be standing next to M.J. Like a devoted pilgrim finally finding his master, and getting to ask *the* question. Ronnie, who is seventeen and a high-school senior, and Mick, who is *the* man. Ronnie approached him tentatively and said, 'Hey, Mick? Hey... how do you keep your head together?'

And Mick said, 'I don't.'

Too much. Too goddamn much. The guy who is on top of it all tells Ronnie that and he is blown away, like a little child again. Because if Mick says he doesn't keep it together and yet is able to maintain that kind of front, it's a lesson. It's a way to live. So that when Ronnie pulls off this remarkable coup of wheedling and trading tickets to every one of the Stones' four L.A. concerts, and is walking around school in his everyday incarnation as a normal teen-aged high-school person, he gets a chance to put Mick's advice into action.

The foxiest girl in the school, the one he's been after for a year and a half; sidles up to him one day in the library and just lets it slip that she knows he has Stones' tickets and if he wants to ask her to one of the concerts she'd be glad to go with him, and there's no telling what might develop from there. This, after eighteen months of Ronnie asking her out and getting the cold no. Ronnie plays his hand perfectly. 'Get down, you bitch,' he says, and walks away, having stepped on her, and with style, when he had the power. It makes no sense to take a girl anyway. She might go back to school the day after the concert with reports on how you had freaked out and started dancing by yourself in the aisles.

The best part of it all is that nine will get you ten, that sooner or later Miss Foxy starts thinking about the way she's acted toward Ronnie and wondering if she's been a bitch, ignoring him all that time, 'cause he is kinda *groovy*-looking, with his bushy hair and glasses, so that maybe he winds up with her anyway. Perfect! Mick! LA.! Rockbiz!

'Are they doin a lot of coke, man?' Ronnie sputters. 'I saw Richards crash into the amps once. I heard Sunset was gonna be closed shut, and that the National Guard was out. I heard Jagger is stuffin socks in his underwear to make himself look sexually big. I ditched school, man. I been standin in line since noon. Yeah. That's what I heard. About Jagger. Is it true, man?'

You've got to remember that I was brought up in a very protected environment. It was a middle-class home... I didn't go into the street and sell heroin... I mean, that's not where I come from.
                    MICK JAGGER, AS QUOTED IN THE 'N.Y. TIMES'

If you reflect at length on Ronnie's breathless backstage question, 'Mick, how do you keep your head?' it grows and grows into a showbiz koan. How do you hold it together if you are right at the top of the mountain with the final say on everything and everyone and the mountain is made up of money and people's lives?

Mick Jagger does it by having a go at playing everyone's game, and often doing it as well, if not better, than they do. Raised middle class, he got so good at a working-class art form that the upper classes ran to accept him as a snarling, sneering primitive, only to find that he had better manners than they did.

Jagger is the great poseur and role-player, and he knows it. One of the conservative businessmen who was in the running to take out the Stones' tour likes to tell of the time he spent two hours with Mick discussing facts, figures, and guarantees. Through it all, Mick conducted himself like a London School of Economics-trained financial whiz, then leaned back and sighed, 'But of course none a this'll mean a thing to me on tour. I won't care about it at all. I'll be completely out of me head.' And the businessman went away astounded at how aware and on top of it all M. J. was, how much he knew about the various masks he carries around.

Robert Frank likes to tell about the very long, very weird business meeting between Mick and former Stones' manager Allen Klein. Klein, a businessman of the first order, and a small battery of lawyers from both sides spent twelve hours haggling and fighting bitterly for the rights to various Jagger songs and the money they bring in. At the end of it all, out-talked and out-bargained, with hundreds of thousands of dollars sliding down the drain, Jagger, the one who would have to work to make it up, became a small child, and began scrawling a Buckminster Fuller quote upon a wall.

'I don't know,' Jagger says. 'It's just the way I was brought up. I was always... in England... people are brought up to always get on with everyone, in every circumstance, I've always found it easier to get on with people, regardless of class or group...

'I find the society thing, that scene very easy... I've been involved with it since I started, ten years ago, although I've had my times of reaction to it. There were times when I thought it was nice to dress up in sort of flashy clothes and be fashionable, which I did in fact for years in London. After coming from a drab background, it was chic.'

'But I was on the road for years and I never saw anyone or did anything but work. You know, it's like... I've never spent a lot of time with any one group of people at all. I never do. What I really like is to be with other musicians, but I find that... rather limiting too.'

There are few people in any walk of life who have Jagger's gift for being able to talk with anyone, from taxi drivers who shout his name in Chelsea to Princess Margaret. No matter who they are, he is able to perform for them. Even during the Rolling Stones' one and only year of obscurity, the winter of 1963, Jagger was different.

Keith had dropped out of art school and Brian Jones had been fired from his job in a London department store for stealing. They were bums, who had been told to fuck off by every organization they had ever come into contact with, until the feeling became mutual. In their Edith Grove flat, on the edge of Chelsea near World's End, all of the furniture is broken. There's no place to sit and hardly any to stand because the floor is covered with rubbish. Various forms of mold are growing in the forty empty milk bottles in the kitchen. The ceilings are covered with black candle smoke that Keith and Brian use to scrawl indecipherable messages.

Neither one of them has any money and whenever Bill Wyman or Stew visit, they make it a point to stop by the fish and chip shop first and casually leave a half-eaten meat pie around when they leave. The only thing anyone ever sees Keith and Brian eat regularly are apple tarts which sell for seven pence each and potatoes and eggs, which they buy with money collected by exchanging empty beer bottles they find in hallways and alleys.

Mick, though, is still attending the London School of Economics and receiving the government grant that, in Britain, finances a lot of students' first ventures into the madness of the real world. He is living at home, trying to make his parents happy, hovering between the two worlds. For the next ten years he continues to hover, while increasing the number of worlds he moves in beyond the scope of any other rock performer.

Which is not to say that it passes him all by, flowing like a gentle country river. Somewhere inside Jagger there is the hero kernel, the champion figure, that must reside at the centre of any person who rises up out of the circumstances they were born in to make a production of their own lives.

On the first Wednesday in July 1969, Brian Jones is found dead in the swimming pool of his home in Sussex. His death comes a month after he leaves the band and, while it is not expected, it is not illogical. For two years he has been slipping away, missing sessions, falling asleep on the floors of recording studios, getting so stoned and fragile that he first loses his lady, Anita Pallenberg, to Keith and then his band, to Jagger.

The night he dies, the Stones are rehearsing with Mick Taylor, who is to be his replacement. They have not worked live for nearly two years because of a series of life and business changes, and drug busts. On Saturday they have scheduled a massive free concert for Hyde Park. When they learn of Brian's death, they assemble early next morning in their office on Maddox Street. 'It's loik... how can I get upset,' Jagger says softly. 'It's Brian, man... he can't be dead. He can't be. He has to have gone on to another life...' That afternoon, they tape a 'Top of the Pops' TV show.

Jagger comes down with laryngitis the next day. On Sunday, he is supposed to fly to Australia to begin work on Tony Richardson's million-pound epic film, *Ned Kelly*. 'I can't go,' Mick is telling the movie people who are replying with detailed figures on shooting costs and production schedules and insisting that if he's not well enough to go on Sunday, then he's not well enough to sing on Saturday.

There's no explaining that if Mick doesn't sing, there will be 150 thousand angry people uprooting the trees in Hyde Park and draining the Serpentine. Anyway, now, the concert is for Brian.

A Granada television crew begins shadowing Jagger early on Saturday morning as he prepares for the concert. They're doing a documentary about it all. Kids from all over London and the rest of England filter into the park until the crowd is the size of a small city. Clad in a white medieval minstrel's shirt, Jagger reads two stanzas from 'Adonais,' Shelley's ode on the death of Keats. All these doves are let loose. They flutter into the sky in Brian's memory and then the band works.

The next day Jagger boards a one o'clock plane for Australia. He's greeted by a protest march at the airport. What's a convicted English longhair doin playin Ned Kelly? Give it to Chips Rafferty! No sense, in having one outlaw play another.

Two days later Jagger's lady, actress and singer Marianne Faithfull, who has come along for the trip, tries to kill herself by taking an overdose of sleeping pills. Three days later, some enterprising journalist sneaks into the intensive care unit of the hospital and takes her picture, and when Jagger returns from filming on location, he finds her, semiconscious, on the front page of a newspaper. Back in England, they're laying Brian Jones to his final rest.

Throughout the week, Jagger is on the set, working, fulfilling his commitments... and Mick, how do you keep your head?

Things are fairly dispersed in L.A. Four shows in three days with a full S.T.P. crew in attendance. Chris O'Dell is up at Michael Butler's house acting as hostess, Mrs. Jagger slash Richards she calls herself. Marshall Chess is chafing and unhappy because he's not been permitted to fly back from San Francisco with his lady on the tour plane, and Peter Rudge is recovering from the traumatic shock of opening the door to his hotel room and finding four turkeys and twenty-four chickens shitting, molting, clucking, and cackling on the bed and carpet. Being in L.A. is like not being on the road at all, it's an S.T.P. hometown, and a lot of people stay in their own homes. As the weekend unravels, the concerts become no more than rude interruptions of a long continuing party in the bars and big houses of Hollywood and Beverly Hills.

Party party party. The world is coming to an end and all that matters is where the next drink's coming from. The bar in the S.T.P. hotel is super red-plush and black leather, with lights so subtle you can't see your hand in front of your face, the kind of place where they keep shoving mixed drinks with cherries in them at you until you pass out in the men's room and wake up in Juarez with all the labels cut out of your clothes and a feeling you've seen this movie before.

The clientele is pretty well restricted to Sydney Greenstreet type businessmen and high-priced hookers who've got stage names and younger sisters who'd just love to see the Stones and do I have to fuck you *now* for these tickets or later?

Having to pay for sex is one thing rockers on the road are not accustomed to. After a strictly d class gig at the Arena in Long Beach where hundreds of kids show up with well-made counterfeit tickets, one S.T.P. dude sits down at the hotel bar for a quick beer. An attractive ginghamy Julie Andrews type is drinking coffee and they begin talking, with Miss Julie telling him how she's from New York and is just out here visiting her folks, who she's given all her money to so they can set themselves up in business. Now she's working again to get back East.

'Oh, yeah? Far out,' the S.T.P. dude says. 'What kinda work do you do?'

'I'm a *goddamned good hooker,*' she informs him indignantly.

'Oh, yeah, far out,' the dude says, falling into hippie talk. 'Really, man, that's... outta sight.' Then he goes upstairs and doesn't set foot in the bar again.

Also in the bar is an amazing-looking woman, in the Mae West tradition, with lots of makeup and false eyelashes, who insists her name is Joy Bang, but is decidedly not the actress of the same name. Her favorite Stones' song is (natch) 'Honky Tonk Women,' but she says she likes classical stuff too, like the 'Symphony of the Springs.' No one knows what to make of her, so they take her along to the party of the night, a Hollywood bash, for two hundred strangers up at Flip Wilson's house. She makes an entrance there that has people cracking vertebrae in their necks to get a good look.

The next day Alan Dunn is telling Pete Rudge all about her. 'Send for her,' Rudge says, and the next thing anyone knows she arrives by limo backstage at the Forum in pink hot pants. They put her on stage, to hand Jagger the bowl of rose petals at the end of 'Street Fighting Man.' Jagger is dancing and sweating and straining and the first time he sees her he doesn't believe it either and keeps on dancing.

But M.J. decides to play along, and he takes the flowers from her and the crowd loves it; she's as surreal as hell and part of the circus they paid to see. After the show ends, and the band sits cooling off, Jagger turns to Keith and says, 'Didya see Alan's girl-friend on stage? Quite noice I thought.' Then there's a long pause and he collapses with laughter.

On Sunday in Los Angeles, the Stones play two shows at the Forum, one of the few halls in the country to have a first name. In advertisements and radio broadcasts, it is unfailingly referred to as the 'Fabulous Forum,' a noxious bit of newspeak that has you doing promotion for the place in the course of ordinary conversation.

The Forum itself is a phony looking, white cakebox in the middle of an asphalt desert that is a security man's dream. For some reason, the Stones invariably play their asses off there and the second show is an absolute bitch. Unlike 1969, when the shows began late and ended in the predawn hours and traffic was so inextricably tangled you had to be a Stones' fanatic shooting methedrine to stick it out, this time around it is all very orderly and professional.

After the first show, Bill Graham, who is again promoting, goes back to the dressing room. 'Great show,' says Bill. 'May I tell you there are twenty thousand people here who will be very disappointed if you don't do an encore? They will leave easier and quicker if you give them a quick "Honky Tonk" or something.'

Well, this is real timebomb advice. Even as carefully as Graham chooses his words, he knows he is right on the brink, because people like the Stones, who have been in the business for years, don't like to be told go back and give 'em one more, sweetheart.

Not when they're sweat-soaked and exhausted with still another show to do.

But these are the new Stones. The new Bill Graham. So they go back on for an encore and in eight minutes the house is clean. 'It was like,' Graham says, 'they were balling and they had one drop left and... UNNAHAHAHAHAHAHAHHUHUH HHAHA.'

For security reasons, the Stones remain inside the Forum between shows. A special dinner has been arranged for them and Mick Jagger walks into the room where it is being served and makes straight for the table where Jo Bergman sits talking to Graham. Automatically that becomes the number one table, a fact reinforced when Chip Monck enters and sits down there.

Bill Graham has told Chip Monck that it is very necessary that he come and see Mick because Mick has something to ask him. It is a condition of Chip's life that if Mick Jagger needs a block of ice on Christmas morning and the precise block is located somewhere north of Anchorage, he will do everything in his power to get it. Which means... he *will* get it. There is no task too trivial for Mr. Monck if it concerns Michael Philip. What Chip would really like to be doing is to work for M. J. year round, helping him restore his historic house in the English countryside, caring for his automobiles, and generally overseeing the way he spends his money.

Chip is a big, rawboned, mustachioed, elegant-looking man who has such a beautifully constructed showbiz persona that there are people all over the world who have worked for him who use Chipmonck expressions like, 'But... how dear,' and 'Ah... how gratifying,' and 'What the principal requires...' He is a strong, talented man with a flaming redheaded temper, who is very, very good at lighting shows, but his relationship to Jagger is much like that of a child anxious for the affection of a busy parent.

So, because he has been summoned, he sits down next to Mick and has a drink, waiting to be consulted. But Jagger is talking to Graham about the prospects of hooking up a network of closed-circuit TV screens so that towns the Stones will never play live can get to see the band. It is an old plan, one that has been kicking around for a couple of years and although Chip has heard it all before, he sits and waits. Then someone hands Mick a note. It says:

Can you move your prick,
As well as you kick
When you dance, Mick?

I know that you can
That's why I'm a fan
You beautiful nasty young man

The way that you dance
Makes me just want a chance
To get at what's under your pants

I'm a honky-tonk chick
But I do know one trick
They call it the butterfly flick

I'd lick and I'd suck
If you wanted, we'd fuck
But, alas, I haven't such luck

Do you think this is crude?
Well, I'm really a prude
I'm just in a Jaggeresque mood...

The note is signed by a girl, who has also taken the time and trouble to include, her full address and phone number, both of which are scratched in pen at the bottom of the page. Jagger has seen such notes before, more or less, and he just smiles and lays it aside. Ah, Los Angeles.

By this time, Monck is slightly furious and about to fume, not being one who likes to be summoned by the principal when he has nothing to say to him. He stamps on back to the stage where he finds that while he was sitting upstairs, Bill Graham has supplied the entire stage crew with t-shirts with Chip Monck's face photo-screened on the front. Monck peering back at Monck from all over the stage. Chip is delighted. How dear. How gratifying. How Hollywood. He almost forgets to act embarrassed. All the anger generated by Michael Philip's silence passes, and is forgotten.

Monck, like Alan Dunn, Jo Bergman, Peter Rudge, Chris

O'Dell, and Marshall Chess, is a Pisces, rotating insecurely
around Jagger, the Sun, a double Leo.

Although the tour is but one week old at this point, Gary Stromberg comes into relieve Bob Gibson, on whom the strain is beginning to tell.

Gibson is no newcomer to rock and roll. He owned the Chee-
tah in L.A. and did concert advertising for years before getting
into full-time rock PR and many's the night he's flown to some
god-forsaken city like Cleveland with a writer under his arm for
a wild night on the road with some band.

But that's as far as it goes. One night. Bob has never before had
to be a policeman, a roadie, and a walking directory of information. When Rudge shouts wildly in the middle of a set, 'Who's
that?... Who's that photographer?' Gibson has to try and find out
instead of saying, 'How the fuck do I know?' and go on sipping
at his brandy and soda. It's reached the point where Gibson is
even carrying guitars into the hall. Gibson! The king! Carrying
guitars... carrying them into the hall... like a roadie.

It's not so much the pressure as it is the way the tour is boring.
It's both exciting and boring at the very same time, which is right
on the edge of minor psychosis, where you don't know if just you
are crazy or if everyone else is. Also, Bob cannot talk to M. J..
Cannot. In tense situations, Gibson is known to get a little hyper,
but around Mick he freezes. Mick has so many responsibilities, so
many problems. When Bob needs to ask him something he feels
guilty. He doesn't want to hassle him, and the only time he feels
comfortable with him is when everyone's wrecked after a good
show.

'So, no thank you,' Bob decides. He will retire back to the
home office on the Strip, High Paranoia Central, where reputa-
tions are made and lost in that spine-and-kidney-chilling moment
just after you call and are told by the receptionist to hold on
while she shouts your name to Bob, who'll say 'Sure, let me talk
to him,' or 'I'm not in... that is, not into talking to that schmuck,'
and that will be it, an early return, a first vote of no confidence
to confirm that you've become a cheap hustler no one wants to
deal with.

Gibson is out, and Stromberg, a small, thin, dark man whose
face is covered by a thick black beard and floppy framing hair,

whose eyes swim like goldfish behind aquarium-thick glasses, is in. Stromberg is recovering from a fair-sized case of hepatitis and has been warned by his doctor not to drink, not to take drugs, get plenty of sleep, and should he fail on any of the first three, to supplement them with regular vitamin B^{12} shots. During the tour, he gets lots of B^{12} shots. After the Forum concerts, he throws a party for the Stones that every transvestite on the Strip crashes. Stromberg has to call security guards from the Whiskey to bounce them and since he doesn't really know all the people on the tour yet, he instructs them to throw out most of Stevie's band. Pencil Stromberg in. He fits.

With the weekend over and the L.A. concerts in back of them, the Stones stay on in the City of the Angels, and begin commuting to concerts in San Diego and Tucson and then Albuquerque, after which they will be authentically on their ways toward New York.

On June 13, the Stones play the sports arena in San Diego, where the Republicans, more or less the party in power, were to hold their presidential nominating convention. A lot of private memos made public revealed that the GOP and ITT, last of the really great combines, had some kind of telephone exchange of their own going and the resulting furor got the whole thing moved to Miami Beach.

Which is a downright shame. Because San Diego is a tough town, for conventions as well as rock concerts, not to mention an authentically weird place in its own right, the very last bastion of the Orange County Creed, a haven for surfers, dopers, bikers, and retired military men. Everyone is very far to their side of the fulcrum down there, very extreme, which is the way of things in southern Southern California.

'Where is it?' Jagger would ask after the tour was over, meaning the radical political spirit that was rampant in America in 1969. 'It's nowhere. It's just a lot of people dopin up now. All the dopin's got to stop before anything else. All that smack and everything. If that's their thing, if they wanna take smack and downers and two gallons of some chemical wine, okay; you're never gonna do what I thought people were gonna do.

'I don't blame people for wantin to get fucked up. Everyone likes to get fucked up once in a while, but you can't go through life like that. You can't blot it out. It keeps coming back, man, and in the end you just kill yourself trying to blot it out.

'People say all the dope on the street has stopped people from bein active... and I wonder... which is the best thing to do? Whether it's better... aw, fuckit, I just wanna be naïve about it. I think you just have to make your country a better place to live and bring kids up in and think in, and sitting at home taking smack and listening to records just ain't gonna do it. That's old-fashioned, maybe, but you got to take the bull by the horns and it's a huge fuckin bull, America... and the horns are very nasty.'

Let's call them to order then, the street-fighting men of San Diego, as they assemble outside the arena to the left of the main ramp, in a crude semicircle twenty degrees around with half-gallons of wine dangling off their crooked fingers and joints going around. Let's inspect them, as they slouch by cars in the parking lot getting wasted.

'Hey,' one blond longhair yells to a visored-helmeted cop who looks like a robot, 'you're a fuckin pig, man. Jeesus, you are... you want some wine, pig?'

'How come you got longhair, man?' one kid sneers in the face of one of the hall security men. 'You're a worse pig bastard than them.'

Pig/ prick/ motherfucker/ cocksucker/ bastard/ coward. That's how the two sides still talk to each other in parking lots. The cops form up and stand their ground. Bill Graham, who is again the promoter, is screaming at the officer in charge to have his men move the kids out before it gets too heavy. 'This is not just another concert,' he shouts. 'Shu-muck, this is the Rolling Stones....'

By six o'clock, the number of kids and wine bottles has increased appreciably and a few rocks come spinning out of the back fringes of the crowd. Lowlife motherfucker coward sonofabitch/you're the lowest piece of scum on earth/you don't have the balls to come in front/rock-slinging bastard. The litany goes on.

When the Stones get driven through the pack and inside the arena, the crowd realize that if they don't make their move soon, it'll be too late. Someone piles ten or twelve wooden police barriers together, shoves some cardboard underneath them and lights it. The thing blazes into life, and when someone tries to put it out, he's met by a hail of rocks and the first Molotov cocktail of the evening. The people's army has armed itself and skirmishes begin in earnest. Three windows get broken, nine cops and six kids are injured, and sixty arrests are made for everything from assault on a police officer to possession.

Quite a charade. There are no issues and the kids are too stoned to have any politics. They can all probably afford the price of a ticket, and because they're mostly white and middle class, the cops can't shoot them. Shooting white kids in post-Kent State America is definitely out. The press doesn't like it. So the cops have to wait and wait until they can go for their ultimate weapon, tear gas. Tear gas gets everyone off. The cops love to throw it because it vents all their frustrations and anger. 'Gimme a tommy gun,' one cop mutters when he sees a kid break a window. In a parking lot war, a broken window is an affair of honour that can be rectified only by lobbing a smoking, throbbing, tear gas canister. Which the kids will lob back. Sometimes one lands in the wrong spot, causing the cops to retreat, coughing and choking, from their own smoky onslaught. Both sides are clearly insane and enjoying themselves thoroughly. One patrolman heaves a baseball-sized rock through a windshield and fractures the nose of a seventeen-year-old girl. Two days later the girl graduates from high school and the patrolman goes from cop to criminal, as he gets suspended from the force and charged with assault with a deadly weapon.

And all of it is in accordance with the Orange County Creed, which says in essence, 'We're gonna make this American Dream work. Yessir, we are. By God, yes. Even if we have to kill everyone to do it.'

The next night in Tucson the cops let the kids collect too close to the building and by the time Stevie Wonder comes on, the kids charge the place. A few windows go and then a door and the cops pull out Mace and let fly with it and soon enough the tear gas is floating down over the community center and three thousand dollars' worth of damage has been done.

Coming right on the heels of the San Diego set-to, the incident makes a good follow-up story and it gets a fair bit of play in the papers, to Bob Gibson's manifest dismay back in L.A.. None of it has touched the Stones or really had anything to do with them. Some nights there's trouble and some nights there isn't, so it can't be the Stones' fault. That's tour thinking. The boys in blue outside the hall—they're the ones who make it different each night. Them and the kids.

By the time the Stones' plane leaves Los Angeles two days later, for the very last time, en route to Albuquerque, a rather fabulous police intelligence report awaits them there. Obviously filed by some student working his way through the University of New Mexico as a police informer, the report states that everyone who is 'straight' is afraid because the Stones' concert will be the start of a riot in the city. 'We didn't get our riot in May so we'll have it in June,' some radical is quoted as saying. The local Spanish population will also be involved.

What with the Albuquerque police jumpy ever since May when someone got shot during a blockade of a highway to protest Nixon's escalation of the Vietnam War into Cambodia, there's enough in the report to implicate half the city. No less than three police forces—campus, city, and state—are present on a windy, gusty night as the Stones play.

All that happens is that one kid gets thrown out a back door, then crashes back in looking for a fight. Uniformed cops are joined by plainclothesmen, and they form a semicircle around him and beat the kid to the floor until he's bloody and unconscious. Then they arrest him for resisting arrest.

Things like that are becoming commonplace on tour and the only way you get to see them is if you go to the trouble of looking for them. Everyone's pleased that the criminal intelligence report has proved to be hooey and that the tour's in no danger of beginning criminal insurrection in the Southwest; so there's no need even to discuss it.

When the plane leaves after the concert that night, it turns north for the first time, toward Denver and the open road, full throttle, six weeks of trucking to New York ahead. And there's no way of saying what's out there. No saying it at all. California's been good, but as even Jagger will tell you if you ask him, 'California... well, I mean... it doesn't have anything to do with the rest of America, does it?' And it's a question so obvious, no answer is required.

THE POP STAR

The pop star sat in a car in the parking lot outside of the hotel in Denver. He sat on the passenger side, in the front seat, and he was all hunched over and whispering. 'There's a cat... in this hotel... who's gonna get himself a blade,' he rasped, in a voice made hoarse by coke and sets that went on for much too long. 'And that cat's name is... Keith Richard... here I am, on my own turf, and he comes in... and I'm gonna fucking call him out.'

The pop star began as one of the better singer-songwriters of his time, and even now there were few people who could play their instrument as well as he. But too long a time, behind coke and in the studio, on the road, and wallowing in the wake of rock and roll madness, had led him deeper and deeper into his own special hole.

So that now the brilliant musician, the writer of fine songs, and the singer of beautiful harmonies, carried an expensive hunting knife around with him, one that had been pulled so often and flashed so many times that the blade came out flick! with a snap of his wrist, like a cheap switchblade. He owned a sword that he liked to swing back and forth across hotel rooms in samurai fashion, getting it nearer and nearer to someone's head, watching for their reaction as they silently prayed he wasn't too wasted and wouldn't slip, and clean them out once and for all.

Most of the musicians who had started out with him and made it too had given up on him. They'd written songs about him or just come to accept the strange role he had chosen to live out. The people who bought his records and came to his concerts got younger each year. They had only heard about the legendary bands he'd played with in his early days. The process was complete. The musician had become a pop star.

And people in the rockbiz kept asking each other how long he'd be able to keep it up. They'd greet each other with reports on his condition, no one being immune to a good piece of gossip about one of the rock aristocrats, and always it would be the same... 'Not much longer, man....' 'Really gone this time....' 'I hear... he's strung.'

The pop star was a tightrope walker, balanced on a fine wire, with the crowd below watching breathless, waiting for the fall.

'I come to the party and there's no blow,' the pop star rasped, 'so I get everybody high. Now I ask that cat for a blow and he tells me to fuck off... that cat... he's gonna get a blade.'

Blow, also known as dust, rocks, powder, nose, and girl. Along with grass, also known as muggles, boo, shit, doobie, and weed, it was one of the traditional allies of the musician. Swing bands in the forties threw so many grass seeds out behind the stage doors of midwestern ballrooms that in the early sixties it grew wild. Ten years later, rock musicians would go out in back of the clubs, pick it, hang it in a closet to dry, then walk down Main Street smoking a pipeful. No one but blacks and other musicians knew what it was. Dope came with the territory. Any place you found music being made, you'd find people getting high.

The pop star had been asked to leave Keith Richard's room, a feat of no small consequence. Despite the security arrangements, Keith's room was party headquarters. Occasionally, people no one had ever seen before could be found sitting on his bed trying on his boots. Once or twice, they'd walked away in them.

But the pop star had offended. He'd walked in with his hat over his eyes and his nostrils flaring, expecting them to be filled, and after some harsh words, was told to get out.

Which is how he comes to be sitting in the parking lot, hunched over and mumbling.

Rock and roll is an easy business to lose your mind in, to lose your life in. If you had a lot of talent at the start, and you wanted to make it real bad, there would be people who'd see that you got whatever you needed to keep working. Sometimes much of it is like a bad old movie, except that the dialogue is better. The rush to fame is always very fast, very confusing, and right there just before the end, very lonely.

And as they liked to say in the schoolyard, the first taste was always free.

Chapter Four

Flaming torches, wicki-wicki luau tables; floating, flat-stomached ladies. Lucky Strike flat fifties', green-metal cigarette cases filled with joints. Bottles row on row, tequila and mescal. Bathrooms clogged with coke snorters, crab and oysters, abalone with snow peas and mushrooms, plates of hen and pig and duck, hollowed out water-melons stuffed with bananas and strawberries, a severed pineapple head. Iced plastic wading pools crammed with Coors and Diet Pepsi; Robert Johnson and Bessie Smith moaning over the speakers in the backyard.

'It's a bar mitzvah,' Robert Frank says solemnly, gnawing on a chicken bone, 'and they've put us at the dais.'

It's a party, a suburban, Saturday-night party in a big ranch-style house outside Denver in honor of the visiting dignitaries, the R. Stones and their S.T.P. helpers.

Downtown on Larimer Street, people are leaning on store windows and crumpling on the corners, waiting for the economy to fold and the crops to blow like sand. Out in the suburbs the more prosperous natives are engaged in some kind of weird tribal rite.

'Anybody seen Jagga?' one very stoned guest asks. 'I gotta talk with him.'

'He just left,' someone says. Standing right next to the kid who asked the question, Jagger nods in agreement. He is wearing a feathery blue boa top and there is no one else in the world he could be tonight with the exception of Carmen Miranda, who is deceased. 'He's gone, man,' Mick says sympathetically.

The Tac Squad is gathered around the dining-room table, getting loose, when Keith Richard stumbles into the room, gasps, 'Jo... Jo... I've got to...' takes two more steps and crashes head-first into the middle of the table. There's this sharp intake of breath all round as though someone's been stabbed in the heart then Keith springs back upright, smiles and continues talking. 'I've got to ask you about the hotel rooms....'

A small circle of people surrounds Peter Rudge in the living room. He is bouncing up and down from the waist. 'Question

one,' he says, 'a limousine is...' He searches the faces around
him. It is Rudge's theory that he is conveying a group of largely
unconscious people around the country. He bounces again from
the waist. 'Keith plays?... Two promoters we've worked for are?...
Too tough, are they? All right, then, how about.... The equipment travels by (a) truck (bounce), (b) choo-choo (bounce), (c)
sheer good fortune (bounce, bounce, bounce)...'

'He's really gone, huh?' the kid says sincerely, pointing to
Rudge. 'I wouldn't even bother him by asking him where Jagga
is.'

In the kitchen, Marshall Chess struggles to get some ice cream
on a plate. Denver is old home grounds for him. He went to the
university here for a while before dropping out to work for his
father. Chess has a fierce sweet tooth and the ice cream is really
frozen, so he very carefully and precisely works at it, ten ardu-
ous minutes, to get the ice cream on the plate, then five more
to spoon the caramel topping on it and smooth it into the perfect end to the orgy of eating, drinking, and smoking that's been
going on for the past three hours. It's all ready, ready to be eaten,
when Robert Frank walks into the room and bumps into Marshall so that the plate falls neatly into the kitchen sink, the vanilla
ice cream floating off in the dishwater like an errant iceberg. It's
such a stoned perfect thing to do that Chess falls against the
refrigerator, laughing helplessly, able to gasp only, 'Robert... oh,
man, Robert...' and keep laughing.

'When the English flip,' Rudge says quietly to no one in particular, 'they go badly, boy. Oh yes. But I've stopped answerin
questions now. And we're leavin people behind too. It's grand.'
Around him the locals are trying not to stare at the Stones. The
S.T.P. honchos are hustling for women like defrocked priests. All
of it feels like a high school party in some girl's house on the
weekend when her parents are away. 'Yes, indeed,' Rudge repeats.
'Grand.'

In the backyard, not far from the shadow of a basket-ball hoop,
across from the spotted plaster toadstool that burbles forth soapy
bubbles, Mick Taylor sits alone at one of the low, red banquet
tables. By torchlight, with his frizzy blond hair and pale skin,
with the party swirling furiously around him, he looks like some
visiting British anthropologist observing native rites in the Solo-
mons. When he speaks, it is with the civilized tone of a man just

offered the King's 280-pound baby daughter for the night who is doing his best to maintain, ah, uh, retain a modicum of dignity in the face of it all.

'It is healthier here,' he says. 'Definitely. You don't see that L.A. pallor. But this party does have a certain Satyricon touch, doesn't it? Without the decadence and perversity. You'll be seeing that soon, I reckon. But not here. In L.A. Soon, I reckon.'

Taylor is twenty-four years old. Of all the Stones, he is the one closest in age and outlook to the people who jam the halls to watch them play. He is a member of the generation of people who entered their twenties when acid was considered the way to find out what was true and what was not. In terms of sensibility, he is as removed as any of those in the band from the freak in the street.

Born in Hatfield, an industrial new town outside of London, he is the son of a factory worker, and was brought up solid working class. His wife, Rose, describes him as 'Being like a mutant in Hatfield... no one knew where he came from, it was as though he'd been dropped in. Fortunately, he had parents who trusted him and let him become what he wanted.'

At the age of ten, Taylor's uncle bought him a guitar. By the time he was thirteen, he was already playing with a local band, the Gods, having never thought of himself as anything *but* a professional musician.

By the time he was sixteen, he was good enough to come down to London and be invited to join John Mayall's Blues Breakers. Mayall, a genial eccentric, now in his forties and still working, has fronted a series of bands that have served as the training ground for half the working musicians in England. At that time, Mayall had just lost a pretty fair lead guitarist named Eric Clapton.

Mick Taylor's London debut took place at the Manor House, an old blues club in North London where all the greats like Sonny Boy Williamson and Freddy King played when they came to town. For those already into the music scene, the night was an event... let's go down and see this sixteen-year-old kid try to replace Eric.

A smoky club jammed with good English faces, fingers clamped around pints of bitter and brown ale, the funny damp smell of Players and Woodbines burning down in ashtrays, as the band takes its place on the stand, with this kid up there with a fine soft face and blond hair, who has listened to every old blues record he could get his hands on and has practiced every run until he is technically brilliant. And he's quite good! Awfully nervous, but quite good. And schoolgirls who have sneaked in are saying, 'OOO, 'ee's lovely, inn't he? Let's go back and say hello.'

For the next four years, Taylor tours with Mayall, learning, working seven nights a week, sometimes two shows a night, crossing America on tours four times. In 1967, when he is but seventeen, he plays the old Fillmore in San Francisco just after Clapton and Cream have blown the place apart with a historic set that paves the way for English bands in post-Beatle psychedelic America.

He decides to leave Mayall, and is thinking of starting his own band or joining up with Paul Butterfield when Mick Jagger comes to him to ask if he'll replace Brian Jones. Taylor takes a week to decide, then says yes.

In his years on the road with Mayall and then increasingly with the Stones, he begins to read, avariciously. He embarks on the kind of self-education process usually associated with immigrants to America in the thirties who wind up becoming judges or mayors. Never one to talk much anyway, it gets so that the easiest subject to draw him out on is James or Conrad. If someone mentions something that he has not read, he makes a mental checkmark to put it on his list. He begins to write, poetry and prose, and learns how to read music in order to begin playing piano, an instrument better suited for writing music on than the guitar. He starts collaborating with Jagger on songs. 'You just watch,' his wife says. 'He started out a musician, but he's going to wind up some kind of writer and composer yet, I know it.'

As the party dribbles itself to death around him and people stumble into their cars to go back to the hotel, Mick Taylor sits alone, then leaves quietly, very much a tourist in the midst of it all, being honored by people who do not know him at all, but who still offer tribute, because he is a Rolling Stone.

Maybe this is it. Maybe it starts here. Two full weeks into the tour and everyone is waiting for America to begin, the real America, the one they saw in *Easy Rider*, where everyone isn't stoned, with long hair, faded jeans, and suntans. It's got to be out there somewhere.

Maybe old beat Denver, the Denver of Jack and Neal, of Dean Moriarty and Cody Pomeray. Bob Frank knew both Cassady and Kerouac and he'll tell you that Jagger's got that Cassady facility for giving you total attention so that when it's gone, you miss it, and that nonstop energy that burns up people around him who try to keep up. There are guys on the corners on Larimer Street who look like they've been through it all and can tell you half a thousand stories about the way things useta be. They're the people Frank would be filming if he was in town for any reason other than a rock and roll tour. They're his faces, his Americans, but there's no contact at all between them and the S.T.P. caravan.

Instead, Frank shoots a little scene staged to suggest what a rock tour is supposed to be like. After it's over, Bobby Keys, Jim Price, Keith, and Mick Taylor pile into the rear of an acre-long, red Lincoln Continental limousine with a bar and a TV set in the back and one of those bubble patches in the roof that Ike and John Glenn used to wave through to the cheering thousands outside. There've been some plush four-wheel jobs around, but this is the all-time cherry ride of the tour except that the bubble patch refuses to close and halfway to the airport the sky goes pastel pink and gray, and soft Colorado rain begins filtering into the back seat.

A never-ending empty Sunday, the eighteenth day of June, Father's Day, in another town in the provinces, with nothing to break the monotony. So just before the limo leaves, Keith and Bobby rip a TV set off its hinges and send it ten floors out the hotel window to its explodo death. Robert Frank films it, and it becomes another chapter in the saga of Keith and Keys on the road. Born within minutes of each other on the same day in 1943, the two have a kinship based on getting crazy and seeing what happens. In Sweden once this guy kept bugging Keys at lunch, so Keith hit him across the head with a bottle, then persuaded the police to arrest the guy while he was still semiconscious. Keys repaid the favour in a city a few stops farther along by asking a hotel manager if he could stop the drilling noise on the street outside so that Keith's young son could get to sleep. When the manager informed Keys that street noise was out of his province, Bobby repaired directly to the hotel kitchen where

he began dropping valuable pieces of crockery on the stone floor,
one by one, until the noise outside abated.

'They got you now,' Jim Price says, in his quiet clipped way.
'They got you on film this time.'

'Wasn't us,' Keys drawls.

'Actors,' Keith explains. 'The things they can do with makeup
these days is amazin.'

'Oh yeah?' Price says, his attention shifting to the problem at
hand. 'Where we goin? Where we stayin? Who we playin for,
what time, where?'

'Minneapolis,' someone says.

'Almost died last time I was in Minneapolis,' Price notes.
'That's how cold it was. Nearly froze on my way to the hall.
Hey, Bobby?' he says to Keys, 'you know what I was thinkin
about? That time on the European tour...' He turns to Keith,
'Bobby had this habit of talking to chicks on the planes in English knowin they couldn't understand him? One time we're on
the plane and this good-lookin blond is sittin there and he tells
her, "Ah'd shore lahk to eat yore pussy, baby... Ah'd shore lahk to
fuck you." Went on for about ten minutes, then I leaned over
and asked her where she was from "Rotterdam," she said, real
clear. Dutch she was. Spoke English perfectly.'

Keith begins laughing in the corner. You can tell he's laughing
because his shades ride up and down on his face.

'Goddahm chick understood English all the tahm,' Keys complains, looking up at the rain as though it might explain his
unending hard luck. 'Where do you live, baby?' he repeats. 'Philadelphia!'

The limo cruises through the outskirts of the city with the soft
rhythm of an old Four Tops song coming from the radio. Outside
the window in front of their comfortable frame houses, guys are
working on their lawns, raking the earth into furrows and tamp-
ing down new grass seed. Their cars stand newly washed behind
them in the driveways, and they're thinking that if the Denver
Bears had themselves a quarterback to go with Floyd Little in the
backfield, there's no telling which way the whole thing could go
next year.

'One of the guys in Stevie's band,' Keith says, launching a story,
'told me about the time he was playin with Butterfield. They
were in some town and these seventeen-year-old chicks came up

to the hotel to interview Butterfield... the livin blues legend an all, right? One of his roadies walks in and sees them and says, "Hey, you girls wanna see a psychedelic light show?" '
' "OOOOOOh yeah," they say, all giggly an all. So he takes down his pants and pisses all over the back of the TV set and sparks come shootin out of the picture tube.'

'The other thang that's good,' Keys says in between laughs, 'is pushin the room service tray into the screen. Also flushin fire-crackers down the toilet. You get yourself one with them water-proof fuses and light it, and boom, you can blow up the crapper in some salesman's room three floors down.'

'Hey, Jim,' Keith asks, 'how come you didn't come to the party in my room last night?'

'Well,' Price says, 'about six or seven this morning I did hear someone playing Bobby's album real loud.'

'Yeah, yeah,' Keith says. 'That was us. Should have walked in. You were on the eleventh floor too, right?'

'Ninth,' Price says succinctly.

'Ninth?... Oh, yeah,' Keith says. 'I guess we were a bit loud at that.' He settles back to consider that and doesn't speak again until the flight is well on its way to Minneapolis.

It takes the Stones' plane three hours to fly from Denver to Minneapolis. Three hours of Kahlua and cream, tequila and grenadine, shrimps and yoghurt and fresh fruit, with sun stream-ing in from a blue and cloudless sky.

It takes Cynthia Sagittarius twenty-six hours to make the same trip, leaving Denver right after the last concert on Friday night, hitching with a rolled sleeping bag and all her clothes in a bulging knapsack. Sleeping in cars that pick her up, she gets to Minne-apolis on the day of the gig just in time to begin waiting outside the hall for someone to let her in.

Cynthia. She knows how to wait perfectly. She waits like a pil-grim outside the temple gate. If she waits long enough, someone will always let her in, someone will give her an extra ticket or a guard will turn his head and let her walk by. For Cynthia lives in the gaps that exist in the network of things, outside of the money rules that concerts are based on. Cynthia doesn't want to pay to see the Stones. She doesn't want to meet them. She just wants to go from city to city and hear them play because it makes her feel good.

Cynthia is a freckled, moon-faced girl who is twenty-one. People who know her well kid her by saying that she's going to wind up like one of those old lady bums you see in Grand Central Station with Middle European relief maps for faces and all their belongings in a shopping cart they wheel in front of them. There is already something old about Cynthia, the loose, floppy dresses she wears, the arthritic sound her slippers make when she walks.

Cynthia began the tour by hitching from New York to Vancouver for the first concert, with stopovers in Ohio and California. When she reached the Canadian border, she had two dollars in her pocket and had to wait until a friendly lady came to her aid and assured the immigration people she would be responsible for Cynthia's welfare. From Vancouver she hitched to Seattle and then on down the coast. One ride was in a milk truck full of freaks, with haunted faces and dead-end eyes. Every time the truck passed a hitchhiker, it stopped and another body clambered in. One guy kept asking, 'We near that Oregon highway yet?' only to be told it was two hundred miles away. Five minutes later, he'd ask again. Then he began poring intently over maps of the East Coast. No one spoke for three hundred miles, then the truck stopped to let a dog out to piss.

In L.A., Cynthia slept in the lounge of a college dorm and used the bathroom to get clean. Outside one of the concerts, she saw Bill Graham, whom she knew from four years of standing in front of the Fillmore East in New York. Bill introduced her to Gary Stromberg and soon enough a little note about her appeared in the newsletter Jo Bergman is mimeographing and slipping under people's doors every day.

As Cynthia moves from city to city, following the tour, she meets up with two guys named Charlie and Robert and a girl named Michelle and they all start travelling together, as much as possible. In Denver, Jo-Anne comes to join them. Jo-Anne is from Brooklyn, and that's not her real name but it's what everyone calls her. Jo-Anne is twenty-six but acts like a kid. She's got lots of blond hair and torn, funky clothes.

But Cynthia is the one who has the Faith, the implicit pure trust in the goodness of people that gets her from Denver to Minneapolis every time, that allows her to say, 'oh, you know how it is... if you don't worry about money, it's not a hassle... Krishna provides.'

Krishna hasn't provided the Metropolitan Sports Center in Minneapolis. Not likely. It's a smoky hockey arena, with signs for Grain Belt Beer plastered on the walls and fat-armed Hennepin County sheriffs at every entrance. Concrete walls and concrete floors, and ballpark concessions; none of it has anything to do with music. Only a kid who was crazy for rock and roll or crazy for something to break the boredom, for something to get off on, would come to a place like this, stoned, and be able to concentrate on a stage miles away while ignoring the spilled beer and stepped-on popcorn, the locked iron gratings and barricaded blue doors.

Minneapolis, as everyone knows, is a twin city, in the heartland, with lots of wheat and Scandinavian faces. They fish through the ice in the winter and right down front by the stage there's a fifteen-year-old boy with bright spots of rouge on his face and a silk kerchief wrapped around his head. In full drag on Sunday afternoon with the green plains stretching away outside the parking lot... what does he do after the concert? Ride the bus back home, then walk down the street he grew up on and go to his room in his parents' house?

At a quick-shot gig like this one, in and out on the same day, the S.T.P. crew sticks together closely. No use hustling women because you'll be sleeping in a different city tonight. No use trying to see anything outside of the dressing room; it's just another gig. In such a situation, every S.T.P. badge-wearer is a brother, another mote in the showbiz whirl, a trooper. Allegiance to the tour supersedes all human and ethnic ties. Stan Moore is making his rounds outside the building when a band of very together young brothers stop him, and say, 'Hey! You with the show, ain't you, broth? How 'bout us? Dig. We are like the co-mune-i-tee, man, you know? Like we wanna see Stevie, and later for the rest.'

And Stan says, 'All right. How many of you are there?' He counts them very carefully, and there are eight of them, so he tells them to wait right there.

'Hey, man,' one says, 'you wouldn't hang us, would you?'

'Hey,' Stan says, really sincere and more than a little hurt, 'I counted, right?'

As soon as he gets around a corner of the building from them, he pulls a handkerchief out of his pocket and wipes away the beads of sweat off his face and sighs, 'Whew!... How'd I do?... I hate to do that to those brothers...' He shrugs and starts walking again. 'But what am I gonna do with eight of 'em? If I don't find me some cops to clear all these kids away, there's gonna be trouble out here yet.'

No trouble of any kind is evident inside the dressing room. It is a peaceful, orderly world, the buffet table stretching down the middle of the room, groaning under the weight of the fruit, nuts, shrimp, fried chicken, English cheese, English cigarettes, Blue Nun white wine, Charrington Bass ale, Courvoisier, Kahlua, Cokes, Seven-Ups, and a large square cake in the middle of it all with a great red-sequinned tongue into which someone has inserted a cigar. Stew is addressing the girl who arranged it all on the subject of whether or not English ale ought ever to be chilled. The makeup man is doing a few card tricks for Bill Wyman, who is both delighted and bewildered at the way he can make cards reappear at will.

'Ace of clubs, right Bill?' the makeup man says.

'Amazin,' Wyman laughs. 'Didn't take it out of your pocket, didya?'

'Haven't got any pockets.'

'Amazin,' Wyman laughs.

Wyman is somewhere in his midthirties. He is the oldest Stone and Wyman is not his real name, Andrew Oldham having changed that one too. In many ways, he is the most respectable member of the band, and certainly the straightest. Like Charlie Watts, he has never taken acid. He feels hesitant about talking about drugs and will tell you, 'I don't need a half-a-dozen joints to get a session together. I don't really drink, and I don't take pills. I'm perfectly content and happy with my girlfriend, my home, my kids, and my music.'

Along with Wyman's one-fifth share in the profits from Stones' albums and tours (like Watts and Taylor, he gets no writer's royalties; those are divided between Jagger and Keith), he has had to share their publicity. 'Everyone tried to get us,' he says of the Stones' early days. 'The papers in every country abused us when we'd get there for bein dirty and long-haired. We needed teachin a lesson, they said... and if Mick or Keith or Brian got arrested for somethin, it was always STONES ON DRUG CHARGES and you're punched in right with it.'

With the Stones on top this time around, there aren't many who can even recall their first American tour in June 1964. The Stones were then the first English band to come to the States without a number one record. They were more or less unknown and, although Tom Wolfe and Baby Jane Holzer were hip enough to pick up on them in New York, they played to half-empty halls in the Midwest. Two days after they arrived, they taped their first American television show, 'Hollywood Palace,' hosted by Dean Martin.

'It was the only TV show we did that time through,' Wyman recalls, 'and Dean Martin was so insultin, sayin... "Don't leave me backstage with those morons... The smell back there is awful... I can see the fleas jumpin off them, ha-ha-ha." We did three songs for 'em and when the thing was shown, there was about two and a half minutes of us.

'We were like a joke act for them. We watched it on tour and got sick. It was our only way of gettin across, and after we saw it, we said, "That's it. Let's go home then. Let's just pack it in and forget it."

'But then we got lucky and had a couple good shows in a row and after we'd had some big records in the States, they reran that Hollywood Palace show six times, with new emcees saying, "And now the fabulous Rolling Stones," with screams and cheers added in the background...'

A solemn, stone-faced man, Wyman moves on stage as though he were mounted on a track that runs from the amps to the front of the deck, but then only occasionally. In his spare time he looks after the Stones' finances in Europe. He was born in South London, the son of a bricklayer who was one of ten children and a mother who was one of seven. Rationing went on in postwar England until 1951, with sweets impossible to come by and things so tough that Wyman was pulled out of school at the age of fifteen and a half to go to work for a local bookmaker. The house he grew up in had no hot water, no inside toilet, and gas lighting.

He began playing guitar at the age of twenty, fairly late for a professional musician. Since the only guitar he could afford had a wide neck and his fingers were too small to form chords, he began picking.

When it became apparent to him that he wasn't going to become a lead guitarist, he took up the bass. By tuning the bottom strings of a regular guitar seven frets down he could play Chuck Berry riffs on them. Wyman saw Berry in *Rock, Rock, Rock* at the local cinema and, while the audience laughed at his funny pigeon-toed duckwalk, Wyman sat awestruck watching his hands. Back then, a Chuck Berry record was a prized commodity in England. Record stores took months to get them (possibly because the kid in the Chess mailroom in Chicago was Marshall).

Wyman began picking up a fiver a night playing in town halls and clubs in the provinces. Then a drummer friend of his told him that the Stones—Brian, Keith, Mick, and Ian Stewart—were rehearsing in the back room of a pub and were in need of a bass player. Wyman auditioned.

'I brought all me stuff with me, includin a spare amp... they all knew who I was but no one spoke to me. Stew I'd met once before and I kind of said hello to him, but Brian and Keith were sittin at the bar drinkin and they totally ignored me for an hour and a half. Which is how they are, and it still freaks people out even now... Mick came over and said somethin... then this amp appeared and it was a bit more interestin. We began playin "I'm a King Bee," the Jimmy Reed thing, and I found it easy to get into, a simple twelve-bar riff...

'The amp had some sway with gettin me into the band in the beginnin I'm sure. "Well, he's not too bad, an we need the amp... But we don't like the drummer." So he went, and since he's my friend, he says, "Comin, Bill?" And I said no. I don't know why. It just felt right. I had gotten quite into the music and besides, they were talkin to me by that time as well...'

Charlie Watts became the drummer, and a month later the six Rolling Stones (Stew included) cut five tracks in a small studio off Oxford Street. They auditioned for the BBC and were told, 'Sorry the band's okay and we might be able to use them to back up various artists, but the singer sounds too colored.'

Not long after that the Stones started to work at the Marquee and the Richmond Station Hotel and from then on it got bigger. Wyman can still remember that Edith Grove flat. 'I could never have lived like that,' he says with a shudder. 'I drive past that place even now and it still looks the same on the outside. Pillars outside, six steps down, and on one of the pillars we stuck up a poster that said, "Rolling Stones at Ealing Jazz Club." Eight years later, there's still a little piece of it there, four by three, yellow, it says, R... St..." or something. I look for it every time I go past. It's like... it's a bit silly... but I think that as long as that's still there, well, we're gonna be all right. It's like the touchstone.'

'Got your makeup on yet?' Charlie asks Wyman.

Bill smiles and points to Jagger. ' 'E says Minneapolis doesn't deserve any.' Jagger wears a purple rhinestone jumpsuit with a pink and purple cummerbund wrapped around his middle. He's got white shoes with red and blue tassels and little bells that ring-tinkle-jangle when he jumps. The temperature outside is in the nineties and the kids down front are drooling and pushing, gasping for breath and fighting for room. The band walks out and Keith hits a solo in 'Bitch' that wasn't there before and everyone looks at him for a half second then follows him through, Charlie whaling away with his sticks. Right from the start, the band is cooking, with Keith cutting it right on time every time, playing fills and breaks that he's never rehearsed. The energy he generates when he's absolutely on is scary. On 'Happy' a song that he wrote, he gets so carried away ripping notes out of his guitar back by the amps, he forgets to make his little run up to the mike and Jagger has to sing the chorus alone.

Some nights it was as though they brought Keith to the hall in a cage and his hour and a half on stage was the only freedom he was going to get. There was no way of telling when he'd crash into an amp or fall the last three steps off the back of the stage. He was dangerous and unpredictable, which made him exciting to watch.

Unlike Jagger, who had a never-ending bag of stage tricks and brilliant spur-of-the-moment mad acts that could get a crowd on its feet, Keith was right *there*, all the time, playing for his life. He possessed none of Jagger's aesthetic distance. It was never a performance for him. Keith was always putting out all he was worth, doing the best he knew how at the moment.

'Watch out!' Jagger shouts into the mike. Charlie has his eyes closed in back, building the song. The beat is brutal. A girl passes out down in front and they hand her out over the stage. When the fresh air outside the stage door hits her, she faints again and urinates all over the guy who's carrying her.

In the middle of 'Midnight Rambler,' Jagger lets fly with a falsetto scream that no one has ever heard before, 'OHHHHHHH-HHHHH BAY-BEE... ooo, ooo... don't do it to me...oooooooh, ooooooh, AHHHHHHHHHHHHHHHHHHHH.' Two girls down front twitch in fear. 'Oh, oh, oh,' he moans, softly, as Keith picks up the riff and dips his shoulder and they boogie, with the lights gone all white. The silver chain around Jagger's neck splits and the sweat soaks through his jumpsuit, into 'Bye-Bye Johnny,' and the kids are laughing at the utter outrageousness of it and waving their hands in the air. Jagger's like some rag doll being jerked and bounced by the unseen hand of a gargantuan child.

Backstage, Peter Rudge is furious. Through half-cracked doors, the choking, acrid smell of tear gas is floating into the hall. The cops are doing it to the kids again in the parking lot. Rudge wants to leap on stage, grab the mike and shout, 'You cunts! We're goin. We've come here and no one's given us a chance. No one. There's no air-conditioning, the police are beatin heads, the kids are throwin bricks through the windows... we're goin.'

The cops, with their clubs and green froggy masks, are outside. Inside, Jagger is howling. As the light bridge comes down and goes up again, and the band wheels into 'Street Fighting Man,' the kids inside are dancing, the ones outside are running. Backstage, the limos rev, ready to roll, guys holding the arena doors shut until the very last second. The cops are scared or indifferent; all they want is for the circus to be gone, out of their town. So move it, move it, get that first car out. 'Buttons down,' they shout, 'buttons down.' Keep the buttons down or the kids will rip open the doors and take over the limos. Will they? Really? How much of the security madness is a hype? It's impossible to find out.

With one last Charlie Watts drum roll, the Stones leave the stage. They're into the mobile home and off and rolling out the back door as the feed-back cacophony of 'Street Fighting Man' still hangs over the screaming, thundering audience.

It's quiet at the airport. You can't hear the cheers, the kids crying for an encore. You can't see them finally give up and struggle out into the still midwestern June night with the streetlamps casting patterns on the asphalt through freshly bloomed leaves.

The hot, close smell of the tear gas is still a faint tickler in the nostrils, the kids are sweat soaked, trying to get it set in their heads how they'll talk about it, what they'll tell their friends who weren't there about the night the Stones worked Minneapolis and the cops threw gas.

' "Jumpin Gas Flash," it was tonight,' Jagger sniffs philosophically on the plane. 'I could feel me voice goin about halfway through. Reminds me of a night in Sco'land when it was so hot there was steam risin from the audience and we thought the place was on fire. They built a metal cage around the stage to protect us and young girls persisted in climbin it, like insects goin to their deaths.' He yawns and tilts a bottle of beer to his mouth and slides into a seat. Keith is stretched across the back of the plane laughing as Bobby Keys looks over the doctor's shoulder, into his bag, smacks his lips with relish and says, 'Mah, mah. Tahm for mah midnight snack.'

By the time the kids at the hall get into their cars to drive home, the Stones are halfway to Chicago, and the concert's already been forgotten.

Chapter Five

Sensation is the soul of essence.

JOHN KEATS

I've never seen people be so stoned and talk so straight.
MICK TAYLOR

One realizes, after a while, that indiscriminate association with the opposite sex has its drawbacks.

KEITH RICHARD

Much like a rock band whose music is preceded by the flowering legend of its publicity, a city tends to come prehyped by the poets and writers who have loved and lost her, and then written all about it.

So it is with a sense of joy in their hearts that the S.T.P. crew wake up to find themselves in Chicago on Monday, a hot, windy, smoggy, shit-stinking bristly hog of a day, with the aroma of the stockyards filling the International Amphitheater where the Stones will play three shows.

Four summers ago, good Mayor Daley told Abe Ribicoff to fuck off from the very same stage, on national television, and the cops bent limbs in Grant Park and lobbed tear gas into the cocktail lounge of the classier downtown hotels.

Chicago! Hog butcher, oh, baby. It was where the blood ran out when they hung the meat upside down. It was where they ground it all into pieces and patted it into burgers, and burgers fed the nation. The machoburger city of America.

The day after the Stones arrive, the *Chicago Tribune* reports that the FBI is hard at work on the identities of five Chicago uniformed cops who operated as assassins and are responsible for the six dead black men found decomposing in the Chicago River. All are reported to have been part of a police-criminal narcotics ring, which also had plans to rob a bank in broad daylight. This would have put the FBI in the indelicate position of having to fire on uniformed cops in police squad cars. Legitimate police then arriving on the scene would have been, in the words of the *Tribune*, 'thoroughly confused.'

No doubt. The upheaval in the violence quotient of a major city like Chicago is like a whiff of strong smelling salts or good cocaine. It clears the head, starts the blood to racing and generates all kinds of razor-sharp thinking, such as the plan the Tac Squad has worked out to protect the Stones.

With all the downtown hotels filled to bursting by conventions of furniture dealers from Grand Rapids and hardware retailers from Fargo and Omaha, the Tac Squad has to find a place for the band that is both secure and geographically convenient. The answer... the Playboy Mansion, the house that Hef built, located on a leafy, parked-up, downtown street. And although Hugh Hefner, the man responsible for it all, is not in the habit of inviting stoned-out rock bands to his home, when the Tac Squad calls and explains the bind they're in, Hef mulls it over and says sure, come on in. He's seen Mick in *Performance* and has even met Jagger once at a party out in L.A. Since one of the mansion's purposes is to give Hef a chance to get to know people whose work he admires, he graciously agrees to allow the circus into his living room.

The rest of the S.T.P. family is put into a hotel thirty miles outside the city, on a green strip of parking lot between freeways and airports, just a convenient twenty-seven-dollar cab ride from all the action. The hotel looks like a cross between the hanging gardens of Babylon and a Kinney parking lot in midtown Manhattan, all concrete, built around an inside mall, like some Moorish palace. Sparkling crystal, Art Deco elevators rise up on pillars to a translucent roof, measureless to man. The elevators are cluttered with bleached-out blondes clutching champagne bottles and looking like the honeymoon just ended. The lobby, coffee shop, bars, swimming pool, and steam rooms are congested by eight hundred McDonald's executives, come together in Chicago to 'Make the Big Mac Safe for America,' and sell another ten billion of those ground chuck delights every kid loves to munch. In that curious mixture of evangelical religiosity and personal self-expansion that always seems to accompany big-business conventions in America, each and every one of them wears a lapel sticker that says, 'Be All You Can Be.'

Right on! Eight hundred of 'em, being all they can be. On convention. Ten billion of 'em sold under the Golden Arches of McDonald's. It is enough to make you run out, buy a bagful, and take 'em home to the kids. Machoburger.

Chicago is one hell of a convention city. The International Amphitheater alone has hosted three national political conventions in the last twenty years. The amphitheater calls itself the world's largest building, in terms of total area, and if it isn't, it's certainly the world's ugliest. A great barn of a place, it's played host to the horse show just before the Stones, and the thick, rich smell of manure is still redolent.

The unions at the hall are so powerful that Chip Monck, who on his last time through the place duked out a stagehand who aided in breaking his light truss, is present under the name of Harry Pine of Newark, New Jersey; Monck-Pine can only sit watching from the stands as they set up his stage.

Outside the back door, the cops begin forming in the early afternoon and by the time Stevie Wonder goes on, every other car moving around the outside of the arena is a police car. The cops stand on corners in fours, their bare arms jutting out from under short sleeves, their stomachs bulging against regulation summer shirts. They take no shit from anyone, forcing kids to take off their boots and stand in the middle of the street while they search them for dope, then leaning right into their faces to shout, 'NOW! Put that boot on. SHUT UP! GOWAN HOME. YOU DON'T BELONG HERE.'

Chicago's cops had the city locked up tight. They were an occupying army and the kids who came through the doors were like prisoners who could only mumble to themselves impotently about what they'd do to them one day if they had a chance. You had to wonder about the cops; they were getting paid, sure, but it couldn't be much of a joy for them to have to work a rock concert by the Rolling Stones, with every long-haired freak in Chicago assembled in a four-block area.

One of the cops, in his late twenties and Irish, with one of those simpy mustaches that ends precisely at the corner of the mouth stood by the back door. 'Where I live,' he said, 'over by Hyde Park, I got the shortest hair on the block, so it don't bother me none. We might have a lot of the force down but there ain't no way we'd go for the tear gas like they did in some of those other cities. We got us some bad publicity here a few years ago, maybe you read about, which we are still tryin to lose.

'Couple weeks ago right here, I'm workin an Elton John concert. No, it was Humble Pie, yeah, that's right, the Humble Pie, full house, kids drinkin Ripple and Bali Hai like it was goin outta style. Swear to God. Cheapest shit you can buy, yet when we frisk 'em at the door, we get piles of it. Mountains of it.

'But what's worse is they're blowin pot. You can smell it the minute you walk inna hall. You stand there more'n five minutes and your skin tingles, and your heart starts pumpin. As I stand here talkin to ya, that's how bad it was. We gotta do somethin about that, right? We can't ignore it.

'Ah,' he shrugged tiredly. 'Fuckit. Couple weeks ago I worked one that was a beaut. Elvis. You know him? That's a performer. They had me right next to him on stage by the piano. Some broad got so excited she took off her shoe and threw it at him. Hit me right in the head. Yeah, that's what I call... a *beaut*.'

Cynthia Sagittarius walks into the hall. Not only has she managed to hitch successfully from Minneapolis, but in quick succession she refuses offers of food (she doesn't eat meat) and money (she doesn't accept it from people she knows, it's a rule). Inside the dressing room, things are less pure. A guy in a porkpie hat hits Peter Rudge with a writ attaching all the instruments and the sequins on Jagger's face for nonpayment of something or other. The just-before-the-show writ is a time-honored showbiz way of extracting money and Rudge and the Tac Squad have prepared for it. They have lawyers in every city, hired to defend the Stones in the event of such an occurrence. Rudge nonchalantly gives the process server the name of their local attorney.

Jagger is prowling around the room, with an Eclair just like Bob Frank's stuck to his eye. He's filming Frank as Frank films him. Robert's wife, June, is along for the show and she takes a Polaroid of Jagger filming. When she pulls it out of the camera and shows it to Mick, he films it. 'Is that all of you?' he leers, staring at her breasts encased in a tight-fitting 'Exile on Main Street' t-shirt.

'Uh,' she says, 'it blew up....'

Jagger is just about to pursue that one when Charlie Watts

brushes past, on his way to the door. 'Where *you* goin?' Jagger asks.

'Uh... goin on,' Charlie says, as though he's just remembered.

Charlie Watts is a sad-eyed, wistful, funny, dapper little man with an impassive jack-o'-lantern face and a Cary Grant way of exploding the word 'Fan-tast-ic' so that it sounds like a cymbal crash at the end of an eight-bar riff.

Watts began playing the drums at the age of thirteen in Wembbley, the same North London neighborhood where Nicky Hopkins grew up, and the two have known each other since they were teenagers playing in pick-up bands. The son of a truck driver for British Rail, Watts' fantasy was always to be a jazz drummer. Hollywood held no glamor for him, it was New York where he wanted to be, 'walk-in' about in an Ivy League suit in front of the Half-Note. 'Now, I'm not from New York, I'm not black, I'm thirteen years old and all I want is to look like Miles Davis. For me, he is the sharpest man in the world.'

Watts graduated from Harrow Art School, put together a book of sketches about another of his idols, Charlie 'Yardbird' Parker, and went to work for Hobson and Gray, a respectable advertising firm, while continuing to play with bands in pubs and clubs. He caught on as Alexis Korner's drummer, working with the band while Cyril Davies, a legendary harmonica-playing panel beater from North London, was still alive. From Korner, he joined the Stones and although he was not overly familiar with all the Jerry Lee Lewis and Chuck Berry stuff they were into, Keith and Brian played the songs so often and so intensely that it soon became part of his subconscious.

The band started making it then, with TV appearances and girls fainting in ballrooms, and Watts says, 'Beatle-a-Rama days I call 'em. Ridiculous. But very necessary, I guess. It was like being a puppet. Girls screamin for good-lookin guys... those were the most hateful times for me. I couldn't even go shoppin if I wanted to. Girls used to come knockin on my door lookin for me and I was almost married, and then I was. I used to sit there and think, "Well, I'm goin to work now" 'cause that's the only way I got through all that shit. I never believed it then and I don't believe it now.'

After the jelly-baby-throwing-scream-fab-gear-crunchy days ended, Mick and Keith and Brian started getting high, stopped working for two years and recorded 'Satanic Majesties,' an album which was a departure from the kind of music they had been making up to that point. 'Regretfully,' Charlie says, 'I never took acid. I say regretfully because I've been terrified of the fuckin stuff and I wish I'd taken it to know about it. I think I was the only rock star never to wear a pair of beads. I wished I could have done, but it never looked right on me. But I thought it was great. It fucked a lot of people up, the psychedelic thing, but it made people really talk to each other too...

'People say I've always been Charlie. I dunno. Maybe I'd been a better person if I had gone through all that. Like junk. I don't like it. I've never had it. I don't want it. I can hear better behind a smoke but I can cope with that. But I drink, too, and I can't cope with that sometimes.

'Part of it is that I never was a teenager, man. I'd be off in the corner talkin about Kierkegaard. I always took meself seriously and thought Buddy Holly was a great joke....'

Of all the Stones, Watts is still very much the person he was before it all began, and yet very changed by the years of touring, recording, and notoriety. He is an extremely charming man, in a way that only musicians who have been totally cared for and looked after for much of their lives can be. Protected for a decade in order to concentrate on playing the drums he possesses a child-like innocence that is beautiful. 'I get bored anywhere,' he says. 'The only time I'm not bored is when I'm drawin, playin the drums, or talkin. I talk a lot, about nothin usually, and all contradictory. Shirley [his wife] always accuses me of havin no beliefs. Maybe that's why I can talk to anyone.'

As the tour progresses, Watts keeps adding to a book of drawings he is making, carefully recording all the beds he sleeps in, the Magic Finger massage units, the 'THIS DOOR IS ALWAYS LOCKED FROM THE OUTSIDE' plates on the doors, the room keys, the way he looks staring at himself in a hotel mirror. In Chicago he writes, 'At this point in the proceedings I cannot fault the luxury (but I also cannot stand it).' 'I don't sleep when we're on the road,' he says, ' 'cause I got no one to sleep with. So I'll draw.' By the time the tour ends, there are a hundred and one drawings in the book.

'I'm a bit pedestrian,' he says. 'My drummin's a bit pedestrian,

I've been told that on several occasions. My personality's a bit
pedestrian.

'All the people who latched on to the tour don't give a shit
about me. Mick is the star, and he remembers their names.
I'm a sweaty bugger sittin' in the corner who plays the drums.
'Cause drummers are always black Africans who sweat a lot. And
they swear all the time. Which is true of me in a way. They do
silly things and never say a word. And mumble. All drummers
mumble and are offensively black or something... so they don't
remember me. I don't want people like that to remember me. I'd
sooner have some kid come up in the fuckin street and say he
likes the band.'

Jagger follows Watts out onto an amphitheater stage adrift in a
boiling steamroom of clenched fists and gritted teeth, four thousand kids leaping up on their chairs from the first drumbeat,
prisoners no more, released by the whipping cross-rhythms of
'Brown Sugar' and 'Bitch.'

People start fainting down in front, the crush is so bad that the
only way out of it is up, over the stage... first a girl... then three
guys, then six, and seven. A Coke can bounces off an amplifier...
someone grabs for the Jack Daniels... a long-haired kid in a cut-
off t-shirt leaps up on stage with clenched fists and a wild look
on his face and crashes into Jagger. Chip tears off his earphones
and tackles the kid high as Leroy rushes up like an express train
and unnnh! chops a punch to the kid's kidneys. The kid keeps
on flailing and thrashing and the three of them are caught in
the spotlight, joined together like a human pinwheel, then they
fall to the stage and begin rolling around. Jagger pirouettes away
from it all with a dancer's grace, his lips pursed in an 'O,' as
though he cannot believe it's really happening.

Strange hands reach for the monitors, people claw and cry and
kick. Brawny bare-chested kids with sweat streaming off them
vault on stage and stand there proudly, gleaming, showing their
friends they've made it, one short moment of glory before they're
grabbed and thrown off. To gain the stage is a triumph, to throw
up your fists and laugh and say fuck you to the world. One kid
leaps on playing an imaginary guitar. He skids past Bill Wyman
and is lowered off the back of the stage still playing.

'Cool 'em off,' Keith shouts to Jagger, who baptizes the circle
of upturned faces in front with a spray of water. Keith is impa-

tient, angry, shouting at security guards to leave the kids alone. He cuts short Jagger's introduction by slashing into songs, stamping out the beat on stage. The hall is lurching around on its foundations, as kids with their shirts off, their heads thrown back and their eyes closed suck on metal hash pipes and guzzle cheap wine and shout and dance. The joint was rocking.

Get this man a drink. Waiter? What the hell? Are they waiters or butlers? Butler? A tequila sunrise for this gentleman. Put it on the table, right by his boots.

Snakeskin boots on a polished wooden table. Keith Richard on his ass on a sofa on the left side of the football field-sized main room of the house that *Playboy* built. At play in the first temple of the American Dream, Keith the human scarecrow, whose arms are a series of black and blue marks from crashing into amps and falling down steps, who one day in Chicago shreds four nickel-wrapped steel guitar strings with his bare hands while playing. Keith Richard, the son of working class folk from the tough Dartford area of London, who three years ago would have been stopped by the black-suited, walkie-talkied, presidential-caliber security operatives outside the mansion's front door and told to get a haircut, a job, and a new attitude and *then* try coming around, is sprawled on the couch, digging it all. 'It's the funkiest this house has ever been,' he muses over the rim of a tequila sunrise, 'and it's still formal.' He laughs and rumples his thatched hair. 'Look at 'im,' he says, indicating with a nod of his head, Hugh Hefner, who founded the magazine that made the money that makes this particular show possible. Hef sits talking to Peter Rudge. 'Doin well, ain't he?' Keith laughs. 'Makin conversation, bridgin the generation gap. 'E's my father's dream, 'e is... yeah, ai been thinkin about doin a Black and Decker job on my room. Paintin' the walls black vinyl or something. Just to remember us by.'

Talk about your cultures running together in post-Woodstock America. Polished boots on a snakeskin table. Here's Hef sitting on a couch beneath the huge Picasso of a reclining female nude, about a hundred yards down from the two suits of armor that flank the stairs into the main room, with a pipe in one hand and a Pepsi-Cola in the other, being asked by Peter Rudge, 'Who runs your record company then?'

It's a goddamned great moment, this, the first contact between the rock and roll dynamo Rudge and Hef, a self-made man of the first order, who plugged his adolescent fantasies into the mainline American wet dream and came out a multimillionaire. Here they are, both still young men, representing the best money can buy in two distinctly alternate life styles and they're about to get right down and communicate.

'Uh,' Hef says. 'Uh... John. John uh... no, that's not right. Sal... uh, geez, I'm hell on names.'

'Sal Iannucci?' Rudge suggests helpfully.

'Uh...' Hef reloads his pipe and runs an absent-minded hand through the blond hair of the girl by his knee. She smiles automatically like one of those cats in a car's back window whose eyes light every time you brake.

'Damned if I know,' Hef concedes. 'I've been in a meeting that dragged on until one thirty this morning and this is the first chance I've had to relax all day. I guess I'm still a little punchy from it all.' He smiles and puffs away at his pipe.

Geez. Hef is a pleasant son-of-a-gun. He's the kind of guy you'd like to have as a fraternity brother, the one who'd lend you his car for big dates and lay money on you when you ran short at the end of the month. There's an authentic midwestern campus feel to him, like when the Glenn Miller orchestra plays 'Moonlight Serenade' and couples stroll through the quad as the bells ring softly from the tower.

But despite all that, the vibes the night the Stones arrive are terrible. They come direct from tear-gas Minneapolis, exhausted, to find the couches adrift with long-stemmed ladies and some dull X-rated movie being screened. It's all very quiet and uptight and Charlie Watts has trouble getting past the guards at the front door.

When Charlies does get inside, he takes one look at the hungry-eyed ladies and thinks, 'Uh-oh. This is a star situation, let me out... I don't care if I'm a star or not... let Mick handle it,' and he turns right around and goes down the street to stay with Marshall Chess. And for the next three days, Charlie drifts through the mansion, because wherever Mick and Keith are is okay with him and you've got to be somewhere at five in the morning when you can't sleep and don't want to go to bed, but still he'd like to blow the place up. There's something about it that just offends him, it's like hospitality without a host or something, even though Hef's for sure a reasonable guy.

When the Stones awake the next day, they are ready to shine it on, trek out and look for other accommodations. Despite the fact that the rooms are color coded and stocked with hair dryers, razors, cabinets full of cosmetics, soaps, and after-shave lotions, despite the fact that there's a stereo, a tape recorder, and enough books in each one to keep you occupied for two years, there's still that main room and those vibes, and the Stones don't want it.

Until Leroy says to Keith, 'Hey, man, have you taken a good look around this place?' by which he means have you walked down the staircase that leads to the oval-shaped swimming pool, the gym, the steam and sun rooms, the underwater bar, the child's fantasy of a gameroom with flashing pinball machines, a full-sized pool table with cubes of purple chalk on the rails, the Red Baron game, the table football set, the Test-Your-Skill driver game, the computer game. The Stones' bodyguard gets them to open their noses and dig... the house is a no-time island where your every wish comes true. It's Disneyland for sense freaks. If you're hungry, you just stop one of the butler-waiters and ask him what's for supper.

'For supper, sir? Why, whatever you like.'

If you hesitate and mumble, 'Fish? Got any fish?' he'll just smile pleasantly and say, 'of course, sir. Shrimp, lobster, sole? Boiled, baked, broiled, fried? With string beans, or potatoes, or salad? Whatever you desire, sir.' Because Hef keeps a chef on duty twenty-four hours a day and the kitchen is so well stocked, they've got it no matter what it is.

And after the so-so dull hotels the Stones have been seques-tered in, the mansion is a place to let go. After they tumble back in after tearing up the Amphitheater with the wildass kind of show that made them ban Alan Freed in Boston, the first thing that goes is the sound system. Like guerrillas come out of the mountains to seize the local radio station, the Stones get Marshall Chess to get hold of Hef who gets hold of his personal electrician who links up Keith's cassette player with the house stereo. And it's no longer great hits of the forties and fifties coming out of the speakers, but Clifton Chenier honking and moaning black bayou blues. Most of Stevie's band has taken Keith up on his generous invitation to dig on the house and S.T.P. people are arriving in droves and giving their name at the door and coming up the wide flight of stairs to the door that says 'If you don't swing, don't ring' in Latin. It's turning into a rock and roll party, a hop at the gym. Aretha and Jerry Lee and the Coasters come spilling out of the speakers and down in the gameroom Jim Price is sucking on a cigar and squinting down a pool cue. The baggage man and the Stones' bodyguard are dancing with one another and the chaos is starting to spread.

The couches pulse with women. In the nights to come, the Stones will have their own man on the door, selecting talent, but tonight the gathering is official... mostly bunnies, ex-Playmates, future Playmates, glossy four-color ladies with polished faces and made-up eyes. None of your New York city darkness here, no clean puritan New England faces or spaced-out California smiles; these ladies are the real thing, products of the heartland, from Rockport, Illinois, and Gary, Indiana. One of them has the nerve to ask the reporter: 'Excuse me, but are you from this planet?'

'How do you mean?'

'Well, the way you're sitting there... it's like this party has nothing to do with you. Aren't you having fun?' She breaks the last word into two syllables, like a suburban mother asking her drooling child, 'Aren't you going to eat your car-rots?'

A clutch of bunnies sit chattering away on the sofa and the floor.

'I'm a libra,' one says.

'I licked a couple half-trips of acid and after the Stones finished I leaned back and the whole row of chairs fell on the floor. The whole row,' another smiles.

'Got any beans?' a third asks.

Beans? 'Oh, you know,' she giggles, 'Quaaludes. Sopors. Even Seconals. They're my second-favourite drug.'

And the first?

She smiles and holds up a tiny silver coke spoon that hangs from a chain around her neck.

The bunnies are girls who like to get high, in every way imaginable, but mostly through the use of methaqualone, a drug respectable America is just swinging into in the summer of '72. Quaaludes, or quacks, as they are known on the street because of the way they tend to make you rap, are hypnotics. They insert a warm and fuzzy feeling into that portion of the brain that usually inhibits action. So they are great for falling down, fucking people you might not otherwise speak to, and forgetting your name. Without stretching a point, or overlooking a drug, one could even say that Quaalude is the drug of the year for 1972, much as 1967 was a good year for acid, and 1969 an excellent one for developing a discreet coke habit.

Anyway, in the next few days, these girls are going to be given their shot of Nirvana. Hundreds of Quaaludes are available, spoons of cocaine, pills, drink, and grass. All the best to smoke, drop, and sniff. But no matter how much medicine they pound into their systems, these ladies will still look like your sister's best friends at her Sweet Sixteen. It's the makeup, the teased hair, the stockings and charm bracelets, the sweet perfume dabbed in the warm throbbing spots, the good color job to keep the roots from showing and the Touch and Glow. These girls are all prisoners of Revlon and if you squeeze too hard, it comes off on your hands.

'Did you meet the doctor yet?' Libra Bunny says. 'He's cute...'

'Marshall? I thought he runs the record company,' Bunny Two sparkles.

'I met Bobby Keys. He plays trumpet,' Bunny Three says. 'By the way, I love your dress. Where did you get it?'

It costs the bunnies fifty bucks a month to live in the mansion and they have to pay for all the food they eat. No such stricture applies to the S.T.P. crowd and they're going at it like a Mongol horde, ingesting lobsters and downing the booze like they were born to such situations. A good way to look at the bunnies is as soldiers in the Playboy army. They're even subject to memos.

June 20
Dear Bunnies,
When was the last time you took a really good look at yourselves and your job? Have you considered how important you are to us? ...YOU, each and every one—make Playboy different and exciting. The bunny concept has been responsible for the founding of an empire....

The memo then rambles on for seven paragraphs about the rules for bunny punctuality. It concludes:

...Get your acts together, ladies! We are running a business here. You

realize, I hope, that there are no Bunny Mothers in other organiza-
tions who would go through the changes we do to get you to work.
Keep in mind that no one else would take the time or make the effort
we do—you'd be out the door.

Get your shit together, girls, or go back from whence you
came. It's no great life being a Bunny. Most bunnies are girls who
take the job to get away from home or out of a lousy marriage,
there being no real experience required other than a tight body
and fairly good skin. And although Playboy itself runs a tight
ship where the clubs are concerned, on their own time the girls
do what they like. As Hef says, 'What America is doing now in
terms of drug use is hypocrisy. What we do is reality, and sur-
vival, and a recognition of how things really are, which is not
how I think they should be... of course, what people do on their
own time is always their own business.'

So it comes as no shock to Hef that the bunnies like to get
loaded and fuck. Everyone likes to get loaded these days. The
counter-culture's greatest contribution to America was to point
the way to unbridled drug use. As the party gets more intense,
it's obvious that ladies are being passed hand to hand like good
joints, going off first with one person, then another. Some of the
braver dears are walking right up to S.T.P. honchos and saying,
'Joy tells me you're a bitch. Dominate me?' and there's nothing
you can do with a macho challenge like that but respond, and
quickly. One S.T.P. dude finds out about that 'sheik thing,' which
he describes as being able to fuck six or eight women in one
night, do it and then forget it, and start all over again because it's
a brand new trip.

Chauvinism of the first order, male and female. Everything out
front. Legs getting wobbly as that last Quaalude hits the pleasure
centre and the warm feeling whirls centrifugally down the spine
into your groin. And a little something extra special is being
planned to cap off the evening. Some of the girls have giggled
and leaned over to Hef... and asked if it's okay if they could...
and he said yes... so they've gone about inviting the inner circle
of grooviest people... to do a little number in Hef's private bath.

Now Hef is a very aware fellow. He knows that the two
most popular fantasies extant about him and Playboy are (1) He
invented sex and is getting it so often as to challenge the laws of

God, Nature, Gravity, and Science, and (2) the whole Playboy Dream is nothing more than a popcorn and Pepsi-Cola sham, and that Hef himself is queer. The second fantasy, Hef knows, is the one the man in the street uses to get through, to persevere and go on living his own quiet little life. Because, as Hef will gladly tell you, the truth is closer to the former than the latter.

For what Hef never realized when he began publishing *Playboy* is that all his fantasies would become real and that he would begin living a life filled with some of the most physically beautiful ladies on two legs. And that there would be A LOT OF SEX. In fact, it downright makes Hef's hackles rise when he talks about journalists who have come to public Playboy functions and then gone away snickering behind their hands at the impotence of it all, at the *sterility* behind the image. What did they expect? As Hef puts it, 'Fucking on the floor at a reception for the ACLU?' No way. But in private, Hef wants the world to know, a lot of real action goes on.

But even for worldly-wise Hef, the Stones are taking it apart and putting it back together a new way. It's a little more intense and out in the open than it's ever been before. Although there have been groovy scenes before, and groovy scenes are a practice out at the L.A. Playboy Mansion where the gang is, well, uh, just groovier... it's never been quite like this; there have never before been so many knockdown-loaded people openly getting it on and inviting their friends to come along for a ride.

So by the time the Roman bath comes up, no one knows what to expect. Hef and all these superstars and shiny ladies... the mansion roof might come off. Everyone that's been invited goes down through Hef's bedroom to this great pool of a bathtub that can hold as many as twenty-five people. The water's all fragrant with special oils and a little of the special stash is going around and everyone's waiting for Hef to slip out of his robe and get into the swim.

But it's so late in the evening and everyone is already so multi-satiated that nothing happens. Nothing more than a friendly dip, with some pleasant conversation and lots of eyes, watching eyes.

Hef clambers out when he's had enough and goes back to his round bed with his two ladies for the evening. He flicks on the videotape recorder to watch a film and orders something to eat, and when the bathers troop back on their way upstairs, there is Hef, the gentle ringmaster, sitting between two pneumatic ladies, smoking his pipe and watching late-night TV, like the most charming parody of what life must be like in the suburbs. Kind of like 'Leave It To Beaver' on DMT.

When the invading S.T.P. forces gather themselves together and stagger into the street to go home, with the party dead behind them, the first gray light of dawn is coming up over the city roofs. Everyone reeks from dried sweat, stale cigarette smoke, and whiskey. The bloodshot sun has the nerve to announce another day. Passers-by on the street are freshly showered, talcum-powdered, and cologned, on their way to their offices, hurrying to catch an early bus. It seems incredible. Outside the mansion, people still have to get up to go to work. Life actually goes on, day to day. Imagine.

Back at the hotel, those not fortunate enough to gain entrance to the mansion are forced to entertain themselves. At a little party thrown by a very conservative, hard-working, New York business-type, Gary Stromberg and Chip Monck and a small marble chip of girl named Janice find themselves sitting on the bathroom floor discussing the way things are, and the way they should be. The very next night, Janice will distinguish herself by getting zonked beyond belief at the concert and then more wasted at the mansion, finally to burst into the hotel at 4:00A.M. where she will be seized by security guards only to shout hysterically, 'It's okay, it's okay, I'm with a chipmunk.' 'Sure you are, lady,' the guards will say, 'come with us...', but right now Janice is still an unknown factor. The three have left the main body of the party because in some circles it is still considered in poor taste to whip out joints and start smoking them in mixed company. Anyway, the discussion is just getting interesting when Chip reaches casually under the bathroom sink and comes out with the drain pipe in his hand.

Stromberg stares goggle-eyed for an instant then begins this high piercing laugh where he tugs at his beard in order to hold on to his head as it rolls around on its moorings. He reaches up and pulls the shower curtain off the bar. Touch . Chip yanks all the toilet paper out of the wall and wraps Gary and Janice in it. Then he removes all the remaining pipes from under the sink so that when you turn the faucet on, the water runs on the floor. In rapid succession then, the toilet is taken apart, the flush cabinet, the shower rods, the handles, the shower head, the towel rack... everything that is removable is... Stromberg getting more hysterical with each volley. Here and here! Take that! Top this! It's a psychedelic destructo tennis match and when the business-type throwing the party walks in to take a leak, the place looks like a retail plumbing-supply outfit. The three are asked to leave.

Outside, the concrete, open-air corridors are filled with McDonald's men who feel no pain, and who for the moment have forgotten about the Holy Grail of stuffing the American duodenum with ten billion more burgers, and are shouting balcony to balcony, 'YEAHYEAHINNNABAR HALFANHOUR WHYNOT?'

Chip decides the only reasonable thing to do is break into the swimming pool. Instead he gets into the kitchen, opens a wallbox filled with circuits and disconnects all the downstairs lights. Along the edge of each of the hotel's floors runs a long planter box filled with flowering ivy. How does the ivy get watered, Chip wonders. Not by God, nor by little children with blue-and-white sprinkling cans. No, the ivy is tended by a network of hoses that run the length of the box, having a little nozzle for each plant. All day long Monck has been pondering... with the ceiling so high and the hotel so obviously intent on creating an artificial environment (which, after all, is exactly what the Monck specialises in), why not go all out and have weather inside the building, as well as out? Why not? So Monck instructs Stromberg and the two take out every little nozzle they can find and hang it over the edge of the balcony so that the next time the hotel people water their flowers, it will rain, real live drops, on to the cranium of every last God-fearing McDonald's man standing in the lobby. And having completed a fair night's work, Monck and Stromberg repair to their respective rooms.

Nighttime is the right time for rock and roll, as well as other things. Daylight kills its magic, the dusty beams of light that slide into the Amphitheater during the afternoon show the next day are too real, too much a reminder that it will still be the same day out there when it's all over.

Playing in t-shirts in the smoky afternoon, the Stones do a laidback but satisfying show, with Jagger working himself into

the by-now traditional horse-race lather at the finish. After a
night in the mansion, it's remarkable they don't have to wheel
him on stage.

'You don't always feel like the show,' Jagger will say. 'You don't.
But that's all right. You can do it. Once you get up there, you
don't have to fake it anymore. Because though you felt 'orrible
when you woke up, by the time you're on stage, you're all right.
Because if you can't get up by that, you can't get up by anything
and you might as well forget it.' And hang up your rock and roll
shoes.

So despite all the activity in Hef's pleasure palace, Mick is still
able to run and jump all over the place, during the second of
the shows the Stones will do in Chicago. He winds up the set
with one leg stuck straight out behind him, like Nureyev, with
the silver bowl that holds the flowers balanced on his head like a
polished steel helmet.

It's after this show that things authentically begin to blur. The
Stones go back to the mansion and then return for yet another
show at the Amphitheater that night, but with everything going
full tilt inside the mansion twenty-four hours a day, and, in fact,
intensifying after midnight when Hef is up and about, and with
all those pills around to relax with, a little coke to get your head
up for the show, a little grass to take the edge off the coke, and a
little tequila to give the whole buzz some depth, it's easy to start
feeling definitely... a... little... spaced... out.

Which means that things are happening in more or less
a dreamlike manner. They're going on and you know you're
involved in them, but it's all so much shadow play. Someone is
holding a flashlight behind all these characters, and the weirder
and more surrealistic it gets, the better sense it makes because it's
Punch and Judy time inside your brain. A fine example of this is
the long and involved story one S.T.P. dude tells of fucking some
lady in the steamroom when Hef walked in. The dude asked
Hef's permission to get someone to photograph him watching
them as they balled, so that he could send the picture to a mutual
friend of theirs in L.A. Just to dig on the incongruity, you understand. And Hef said 'Sure,' but they couldn't find a camera. 'Fantasy,' Hef says later. 'Nothing remotely like it even happened. But
it's not unusual. I'm supposed to be a lot of places I'm not'.

Spaced... out... it hardly matters if it didn't happen. In fact, one of the great dangers of being on the road, of all the constant moving, partying, and getting loaded is getting so out of your head you can't go out there and do the show anymore. Yet you have to get high, some way or the boredom will kill you. Both Bobby Keys and Keith survive it the way musicians have traditionally coped... get as high as possible and blow, and anything that comes down around you, you accept. Because your focus is the music, and as long as that's where your real action is, you're safe. It's the way bands have always careened around the country... get loaded and carry your horn with you at all times.

Which is one reason rock and rollers have come to be considered junkie outlaws, scum who don't even deserve the courtesy you'd extend to a jazz musician, who is, in his way, infinitely more respectable. Rock musicians play music for *kids* to dance to.

Keith Richard, of all the Stones, has best accepted that particular role. Okay, man, if we're outlaws, then I guess that's what we are. So that a great deal of his personality is generated by that non-acceptance, by not even wanting to become respectable or to be accepted by those who don't respect his music. But on this tour, in the Playboy Mansion, it is no longer possible to deny that if rock itself had not become completely respectable, then the Rolling Stones themselves were being accepted in social situations that no other band could ever expect to gain entry to.

And despite all the changes Keith had gone through in his time with the band, he still had to fight for his role as the highwayman. Forced to leave England for tax purposes, then exiled from the country of his exile, France, because of legal difficulties, he had become some kind of international gypsy, whose family had to break into contingents and file through different immigration aisles when they entered countries. His son was English, his lady Anita maintained Italian nationality. His daughter had been born in Switzerland and would have her choice of passports.

The Stones' financial affairs were shepherded by a White Russian prince; they were incorporated in several countries; they supported a financial structure as complex as any small nation, and they had influence. Despite all the money and power, Keith still clung to the role of rebel and misfit, the kid who no one talks to until the night he comes out of the corner at some party playing his guitar like a-ringin a bell. So that while the rest of the

Stones are outraged and amused and bored and titillated by Hef's
wonder house, only Keith will say, 'It's not always like this here,
man. Oh, I'm sure a few weird things have come down, but
nothin' like this... it's *us*, man. Ten different chicks have told me.
I bet they haven't seen a hard cock here in years...' He'll grudg-
ingly admit, 'Aw, Hef's okay. He'll talk to anyone, pass an occasional joint around... he's as liberal a gentleman as you'll find in
Chicago, I guess, but I don't know if I can put him all together.
He borrows a bit from everywhere. It's a very ambiguous respect-
ability.'

And Hef, who *is* a very liberal gentleman and well-schooled in
the psychological insight, accepts it all easily, saying, 'Keith is so
obviously turned on by it all, he feels the need to explain... "It's
not the house, it's us." What could be more of a compliment? I
think Keith is more aware of people being aware of Keith than
the others. I think you could say... he *is* a little farther out than
the rest.'

More ladies from the mansion than one would have thought feasible are in attendance at the Stones' final Chicago show. The
most obvious of them is Lisa, snub-nosed, with wide eyes, cas-
cades of platinum-blond hair, and upstanding rose-tipped breasts
that are to grace the centerfold of *Playboy*, and what is usually
described in toothpaste ads as a 'winning smile.' 'My goodness,'
Lisa says, as the Stones dress around her. 'You know how I am,
usually the straightest of them all, but last night, oh it was just so
different! Lawd, I've got bumps and bruises and bites all over my
ass. And tomorrow's my birthday. I feel just like Cinderella. They
were *all* so nice.'

After the show, there's a distinctly different scene at the mansion than the night before. Every freeloader in the city seems to
have gotten wind of the goings on and infiltrated. They crowd
the bar, ordering exotic drinks... 'Uh, introduce the Galliano into
the vodka with a syringe, and then pass the brandy over it...'
They fall into the pool and create a definite gap between the
public party and the private one.

Down in the gameroom, Chris O'Dell is locked into the Red
Baron game, shooting down Spads and Fokkers over the skies of
France in World War I, only she thinks the name of the game is
the Green Baron. Whewww, Chris. All the flying she's done has

got her a little jet-lagged and then this hand comes from nowhere and something cracks and whooooooooooooo the Red Baron is like whooooooooooooo sliding off the machine wow whooooooo. That characteristic burnt odor—amyl nitrate goes rushing up the nasal cavities like a flash fire in a wheat silo, setting the heart to pound and the brain to rush as everyone in the room gets off at once and begins laughing hysterically.

Half an hour later this waiter-butler who's been telling everyone how much he likes to get high walks into Keith's room with a tray full of tequila sunrises, Kahlua and creams, and bloody marys. They hit him with an amy and the guy smiles to show he's hip and has been through it all before and then the rush hits him in the front brain and he goes wheeling and staggering like a moth in flames spiraling to its death. The tray whirls once, twice, then goes bomp-crash ka-chunk! and slides and spills all over the floor in stoned super-slow motion.

Later in the night Keith and Bobby are just sitting around, getting more relaxed, when Keith says, 'Hey, man, you smell something burning?' Keys shrugs and they both look around for a glowing cigarette butt on the carpet. There's no cigarette to be found and they go back to relaxing when someone starts pounding on the door, shouting, 'HEY... HEY, ANYONE IN THERE? THE PLACE IS ON FIRE.'

'What's he talkin' about?' Keys asks laconically, wiping the tears from his eyes. The smoke is so thick he can't see Keith. 'Ain nothin goin on here at all. Be cool.'

'Yeah,' Keith mumbles, 'just be cool.'

Down in the gameroom, a bumper pool bunny is hanging out of her low-cut red dress, with everyone watching and wondering which breast will strike the cushion first, and whether it will be a mass shot or... ah the hell with it. She looks familiar, and if she took off all her clothes maybe you could place the month she appeared stapled at the navel in the middle of the magazine. With all these centerfold ladies gliding about, ladies whose graven images have graced the walls of army urinals and hung over dismantled Fords in body and fender shops across the land, you have to wonder if it's proper to go up and say... 'Uh, ma'm, just wanted to... to tell you that everyone in my platoon has, uh...your picture... it's given my friends, well, reams of pleasure.'

'Here's Charlie,' someone says to Miss Riting Pectorals. 'Play with him.'

Charlie looks bleary-eyed. 'Charlie?' the bumper pool lady says. 'Charlie? What's he do?'

'Charlie?' someone says, incredulously. 'Charlie's a *STONE*.'

'Uh, oh-oh,' says Charlie, grabbing for the door. 'That lets me out. Thank you and goodnight.' The door closes behind him and the bumper pool lady hitches her assets back into place a little drunkenly, lays her pool cue on the table and surveys the crowd. 'Next?' she says.

Barricaded behind closed doors at the most private of the several little parties that swirl around the mansion this night is Mick Jagger, sitting on a large double bed reading a review of 'Exile on Main Street,' with Lisa sitting near him. The door swings open and Marshall Chess enters with a blond in tow.

'I need this room *now!*' Chess says, a little wildly. 'For private reasons.'

'Uh, well, we're all kind of *in here,*' Mick says vaguely, gesturing around at the other people 'Use mine. Upstairs.'

'It's locked,' Chess says, jittering badly. 'Gimme those keys *now*, motherfucker.' The lady-behind him is in third, itching to shift into high for the long swooping run down the straightaway. Mick hands over his keys, notices her motor idling, and kindly says, 'Don't worry, dear, I'll fuck you later.'

'Will you?' she says, very brittle. 'You better. You wouldn't lie, would you?'

Mick sinks back onto the bed. He looks a bit weary and worn as he gets up, pads around the room barefooted, then sits back again. 'Ai mean,' he says, gesturing toward the record review. 'What do they want from us? We put together a side you can listen to late at night or early in the mornin and they say it's the only one without a barrelhouse rocker...' He sighs and shakes his head, very much the exile on Main Street in a world where no one understands.

'God, look at all these marks,' Lisa says quietly, examining herself on the bed.

'Not awl mine, are they, luv?' Mick says without looking. 'I'll have to be more gentle next time.'

'Oh' Mick,' she sighs 'You looked so sexy tonight on stage. Much prettier than in your pictures.'

'Well,' Mick says softly, 'one hopes so. Ai mean, it would be a drag if it was the other way round, wouldn't it? Ai mean, 'orrible ugly in person.'

'Mick?'

'Luv?'

'Did you know I'm a designer? I do things for bands.'

'Yeah? What you think of me outfit? Designed it meself. Shrinks a bit, but otherwise it's quite awrite, inn't it?'

'Oh... it is. Tonight, at the concert, Mick, I was standing next to this bald-headed guy who was all clean shaven and when he saw you cut your lip on the mike, he bit down on his lip until it bled in the very same place. The very same.'

'Yeah... the things I see down front. The guy beggin me to whip him with the belt durin "Midnight Rambler." Another holdin up a burnin cigarette for me to look at 'im then crushin it in his palm and, holdin it up all fucked up and black with ash. It's weird, inn't it?'

'Mick?' Lisa says, plaintively. 'You're going to sing "Happy Birthday" for me tomorrow, aren't you?'

'Sure, luv...'

Her eyes widen and she looks at her watch. 'God, it's after twelve right now,' she says. 'It's my birthday. I've been queen for a day here, for a month...' she giggles. 'But I guess it's all over now. Gee, it really is my birthday,' she repeats to herself, awestruck and more than a little out of it. 'I'm not twenty-one anymore.'

By the third night, the mansion strain is beginning to tell. The body *is* only flesh and blood, after all, and the only thing keeping people going is the hot gossip that all the phones are tapped and that Hef has videotaped all the pairs and doubles competitions and free-style events for his own consumption. It fits so well. Mick, the world's number one sex-fantasy object, and Hef, the ultimate voyeur.

And when confronted with the rumor Hef almost gets indignant. 'It's true, then...' he sighs. 'It's really true that the Stones are as guilty of accepting the fantasies that exist about *Playboy* as John Q. Public. Bullshit. Complete bullshit.'

For although Hef does have a complete range of videotape equipment and does use it, he is only too glad to tell you, 'I enjoy visual sex if I'm groovin' with a lady but not as a replacement for

it. I take great pleasure in my own life and my fantasy isn't to be
Mick... I'm my own fantasy, and I don't need to watch anyone
else.' Then there's that funny broken Hef laugh as he sucks dry
on his pipe and scrapes the match against the matchbook.

It's been a good three days for Hef. Although he hasn't managed to get out of the house to see the Stones, and won't, on
account of Manson fear, which is a peculiar 1970s paranoia that
affects the very rich and hip who maintain at least one big house
in L.A.. Ever since Manson's Family slaughtered Sharon Tate and
others, Hef tends to avoid big crowds and public gatherings. But
to have had the boys in his house, and to make contact with
Mick on kind of a star-to-star basis, has been a joy. Jagger is so
aware of the star trip, and so on top of it all that he's been a gas.

As Hef sits playing backgammon at a long table under a spotlight, with Bill Wyman, the butler-waiters line the sideboards
with trays of sweet, creamy chocolate eclairs. They fill chafing
dishes to the brim with steaming lobster tails and place bowls
of drawn butter where they'll be easy to reach. The Stones and
S.T.P. people sit down to their last free meal at Hef's.

A tired-looking man with a thick mustache, wearing a black
cap and holding black driving gloves, trudges tiredly up the back-
stairs into the kitchen. He looks like the chauffeur in the home
of some industrial prince or investment banker in the Chicago
of the 1890s when the robber barons ran the land and wheat
fortunes changed hands every day in the 'Pit.'

Not so much is different. All the things you'd ever want were
all available in Hef's house, but they still needed black-uniformed
servants to put it on the plate for you. And as the guests, invited
and otherwise, press closer to the banquet table for another helping of lobster, the tired-looking man with the mustache trudges
back down the stairs with his lunch in his hand. You had to figure
he had at least another three hours to go before the end of his
shift, when he could finally drive home to where all was not so
glossy and where it didn't all wash off and start again the next
night. Some people still did have to get up every day and go to
work. Imagine.

Tales from Rock and Roll Heaven

B MOVIES

PRINCESS LEE RADZIWILL: 'Who is responsible for organizing everything?'
MICK JAGGER: 'Peter Rudge is....'
PRINCESS LEE RADZIWILL: 'He's so funny. He'd be a good actor in a movie.'
MICK JAGGER: 'He's a riot.'
FROM AN INTERVIEW IN 'INTERVIEW'

Camera dollies in on a ringing phone. A woman's hand picks it up. A voice on the line speaks.
VOICE: It would be in everyone's interest if Mick gets in touch with us.
FEMALE VOICE (*worried*): Yes, but who are you?
VOICE: The New Yawk chaptah of the... Hell's Angels.

The hand drops the phone. It clatters to the desk. Cut to an extreme close-up of Peter Rudge's face, an extralong Dunhill cigarette nesting in the crook of his mouth.
RUDGE: We'll wait. (*Blows smoke directly into camera.*) Let's see if they keep calling.

A montage of stock shots of San Francisco, cable cars, Coit Tower, then an exterior of Winterland. Concert footage. Cut to ringing phone.
VOICE: It would be in everyone's interest....

Montage of Los Angeles, Santa Monica beach, Capitol Tower, exterior of the Forum. Concert footage. Cut to the phone.
VOICE: It would be in everyone's interest....

Cut to a medium shot of Peter Rudge under a sign reading, 'Minneapolis Sports Stadium'. Cigarette smoke curls about his head; he stares into space for an instant, then reaches out for a phone and begins dialling.

RUDGE (*in a low voice*): Awright boys, this is Pete Rudge. Whatcha want?

VOICE: We wanna talk. We wanna clear up some misunderstandings,

RUDGE: Talk.

VOICE: Not on the phone. We wanna meet.

RUDGE: Well, I'll be comin to New York. We can do it there.

VOICE: Where you stayin?

RUDGE: Don't know yet (*a worried look in his face*). I'll call you when I get in.

Rudge hangs up the phone, drags on the cigarette, looks up at the sign and smiles.

RUDGE: At least Minneapolis is safe.

Cut to Rudge slumped in the seat of a crowded commercial jetliner filled with business types. Rudge looks tired, as though he's been at an all-night party.

STEWARDESS: And in just five minutes, we'll be making our descent into the New York metropolitan area.

Cut to exterior of Madison Square Garden. Camera picks up Rudge riding an elevator up to a plush, carpeted suite of offices, where he is greeted warmly by three businessmen in suits. Cut to Rudge on the phone.

RUDGE: Right. Here I am. Let's talk.

VOICE: Not on the phone. You wanna meet, come down to our place.

RUDGE: No, no... not there.

VOICE: Where?

RUDGE: Where?

VOICE: Awright. You know the Broadway Pub? On Forty-sixth?

RUDGE: What time?

VOICE: Six.

RUDGE: How will I know you?

VOICE: You kiddin'? Haw! You'll know us awright. (*Click*).

Cut to Rudge in the middle of a top-level business meeting. Three businessmen sit around table, facing him.

RUDGE: (*casually*): I've got to be going, gentlemen.

BUSINESSMAN ONE: Why?

RUDGE (*casually*): Got a date with the Angels. Gotta meet 'em by seven (*sing-song... then serious*). By six actually.

Pan the table for reaction shots. Jaws drop; cigarettes fall.

BUSINESSMAN ONE: Peter, you're joking.

BUSINESSMAN TWO: You need protection.

BUSINESSMAN THREE: They're animals.

Hands reach for phones. Three men on three different lines.

BUSINESSMAN ONE: Captain? Yes, he's one of our men and he needs protection. How many can you spare?... Four men, in plain clothes? Good.

BUSINESSMAN TWO: We'll need a car, we're going down ourselves... incognito, of course.

Dolly shot down Forty-sixth Street. Pick up shadows on the side-walk as people rush toward the subway entrances. Camera picks up Rudge in the crowd, follows him past a sign that says 'Broadway Pub' into a dark, empty bar. Camera, from Rudge's point of view, picks up two nervous businessmen trying to look casual, looking like nervous businessmen; four cops at the bar looking like obvious cops, and farther back, four Angels in full colors, leathers and death's head emblems, faded denims, and grease-caked jackets. Rudge shakes hands with them and sits down.

FIRST ANGEL: There's a few misunderstandins we want cleared up. We paid the tab at Altamont. Sixty grand it cost us in legal fees, and it was the Stones what did the hirin.

SECOND ANGEL (*excitedly*): We been shit on.

FIRST ANGEL (*sternly*): Be quiet.

THIRD ANGEL: A lotta Angels had to go through shit to get that money up.

SECOND ANGEL (*excitedly*): We been shit on.

FIRST ANGEL (*obviously the leader*): Be quiet. We want you to do another concert for us. We'll promote it.

RUDGE (*hard-voiced*): No way.

FIRST ANGEL: Maybe you don't understand us....

RUDGE: There's no way the Stones are going to play a concert for the Hell's Angels. It's bad for you and it's bad for us. Forget it.

FIRST ANGEL: Look Pete (*grins*), we can see you're a nice guy. If youdda been at Altamont, maybe this wouldna happened. But you owe us....

THIRD ANGEL: 'Cause we doan wanna hurt the Stones. We dig 'em. We wanna party with 'em.

FIRST ANGEL: We got lawyers. We wanna piece of paper between your lawyers and ours for that money.

RUDGE: All right, then. But I'll have to go back to Kansas City and talk to the boys.

FIRST ANGEL: I hope it's awright. 'Cause we wouldna want to cook an Englishman alive. (*Angels trade glances, all guffaw at once.*)

SECOND ANGEL: 'Cause if we don't get paid, Pete, it's you.

THIRD ANGEL: You're our man now.

FIRST ANGEL: And we can get on a plane to anywhere in the world and get you.

RUDGE (*very English*): Yes. I believe I understand. Let me get the check.

Camera follows them as they walk out in between the cops and businessmen. To the left of the door is what is obviously another Angel, acting as a lookout. Camera follows them around the corner, Rudge looking very small and clean in the middle of the pack. Camera focuses in on four gleaming choppers, then cuts to Rudge's face. Without a word the Angels leap on their bikes and roar down the street. Extreme close-up of Rudge's face as he sighs. Cut to Rudge talking to two uniformed cops in a precinct backroom.

COP: Think you can identify 'em?

RUDGE: I think so.

Rudge, poring over mug shots. Face lights up, he points to a picture.

RUDGE: This one, him, and him.

Cop leans over Rudge's shoulder, shakes his head slowly from side to side, makes clucking noises deep in his throat.

COP: Nasty. You really met with the bad boys.

RUDGE: What now?

COP: You got three choices. Pay the money. Don't pay it... (*grins*) and take your chances. Set up another meeting with 'em and go in carrying a bug. We'll entrap 'em... it's extortion.

RUDGE: No good (*shakes his head*). They half-searched me when I sat down this time.... it'll have to be lawyers.

Cut to Rudge on the phone, surrounded by cigarette smoke.

RUDGE: There's to be no concert... no... arrange a meeting with their lawyers... and stall.... The Stones'll be out of the country in five weeks. With any luck we can drag it out past then.

Cut to Rudge walking through an airport departure gate marked 'Kansas City.' Rudge on the plane, drawing deep on a Dunhill. The plane takes off into the dusk with the lights of the city behind it. Cut to Rudge switching on his overhead light. Bring up the theme music in the background (check on feasibility of getting Shirley Bassey for this):

Cut to Rudge's face, a small smile flickering on his lips. Cut to the paperback on his knee. Zoom in on the title, Raymond Chandler's *The Big Sleep*.

Roll the credits.

Chapter Six

And a year before they would never come. There was no certainty then... They never wasted their time nor their charm on something that was not sure. Why should they?

ERNEST HEMINGWAY, 'A MOVEABLE FEAST'

Some airplane rides are a downright lie, implying that there is a connection between places that have nothing more in common than airport facilities. The Stones leave Chicago on June 22, a windy cloud-driven Thursday, stop over in Kansas City for a quick gig, then board the plane again to head for Texas.

Maybe the partying in Hef's house has robbed them of more than energy. Because now, it starts to fall apart. The group mind that Peter Rudge has so carefully constructed during the tour's first three weeks, the we're-all-at-camp-for-the-summer *esprit de corps* that has kept the thing humming, disappears.

Separate power centers that have been slowly developing burst into statehood along these lines: The Tac Squad, composed of Peter, Jo, and Alan, with its soldier Stan Moore out front and Leroy, the Stones' bodyguard, as its commando behind the lines; the Film Crew, headed by Marshall Chess (who Rudge has started referring to as 'von Chess'), Robert Frank, and Danny Seymour; and the Inner Circle, Mick and Keith, Bobby Keys, Chris O'Dell, Marshall, the doctor, and Keith's friend Flex. There are other power cliques, the Girls, a fluctuating number of musicians' ladies, and the Musicians, Bill Wyman, Charlie Watts, Mick Taylor, and Jim Price. The first three dominate because each has direct access to a power source, the Tac Squad (Peter), the Film Crew (Chess, who in turn has access to Jagger), and the Inner Circle (M. J. himself).

Four shows are scheduled in Texas, two in Dallas-Fort Worth and two in Houston, and they are both to be filmed by a full-sized Hollywood crew, and recorded, for a live album, by a six-teen-track mobile studio. This intensifies the pressure on the Musicians, the inner Circle, and the Film Crew, as well as on

Rudge and Jagger, the two individuals already under more pressure than anyone else.

In addition, during this leg of the journey the tour attracts the presence of a small host of people who have no firsthand knowledge of the world of rock or the music that is its lifeblood. They are around for various reasons, some valid, some not so valid, but their presence is a distraction, for they are, in the main, self-centered, important people who are not used to deferring to others, who demand recognition and 'equal' treatment. On a showbiz tour the only available equality is the brand Orwell spoke of in *Animal Farm*, namely, that the guys who go out on stage every night are more equal than anyone else.

And so by the time the tour gets into Houston, several cracks have appeared in the shiny black S.T.P. wet suit that has kept everyone dry. Small arguments become major incidents, and feuds mushroom in the wet Texas heat like orchids bursting into bloom in a tropical rain forest. Much of the joyous madness and innocence of trucking around with crazies evaporates and the sticky residue that remains is nothing to write home about.

It begins with the Stones in flight from Chicago to Kansas City, where in the red-plush bar of the Muehlenback Hotel, Truman Capote awaits, sipping a gin and tonic. Some months before, the idea to have Capote write about the tour for *Rolling Stone* magazine came up. Obviously a brilliant idea, it would apparently profit everyone involved. Now in his forty-eighth year, Capote is a writer on his way to becoming a national institution by dint of his frequent late-night television appearances. All of his projects are well publicized; he has a genius for self-promotion, and the thought of his razor wit at work on the raw funk of the rockin Stones is irresistible. It has been seven years since *In Cold Blood*, but no one has forgotten that one yet so there are only two small problems in arranging it all... would Capote do it? Would Jagger let him?

The two had already met in New York and neither came away impressed, Capote describing Jagger as a 'scared little boy, very much off his turf' and Jagger recalling Capote as 'tryin to make everyone laugh. Everyone laughs at a cocktail party anyway, but no one laughed wi him because he wasn't funny. He tole me he was goin to do the tour for the money and when he tole me how much they offered, I said, "I'm sure that's not' enough"; and "Besides," I said, "we don't want you...." '

But the idea is a hot one and both Marshall Chess and *Rolling Stone*'s editor like it so much that cables and telephone calls begin whizzing back and forth across the country. *Rolling Stone*'s publisher in New York gets in touch with an old school friend, a Montauk-based photographer named Peter Beard, who is close to Capote. Beard gets on Truman's case about it, saying, 'Look, this is terrific! You ought to do it!' over and over until Truman agrees and flies to Kansas City, accompanied by Beard and a dark-haired lady with the high cheekbones and finely pursed, aristocratic Bouvier face that is instantly recognizable throughout the world.

Even at thirty thousand feet in the Stones' plane, the word is out and going up and down the aisle. 'Jackie Kennedy is waiting for us in Kansas City.'

'Onassis,' Chris O'Dell giggles, trying to explain some etiquette to Mick and Keith. 'You're all English and you keep calling her Kennedy. That's like calling the Queen... Lizzie or something.'

After four spaced days in Hef's house, it seems entirely possible to one and all that the former First Lady of the United States and the current wife of one of the richest men in the world has nothing better to do with her time than rendezvous with the Rolling Stones on the banks of the old Mississip. The Tac Squad has gone to the trouble of calling ahead to arrange a small banquet dinner for Ms. Onassis after the concert so that everyone can get acquainted. As the S.T.P folks file out of the plane, Danny Seymour tells Keith, 'See if you can lay a joint on her,' meaning Jackie. 'Put it right in the middle of her palm so I can zoom in on it.' Keith nods, mumbles assent, and keeps walking. 'Oh and yeah,' Danny says, as an afterthought, 'and if you can dick her, outta site.'

The dark lady in the bar, however, is not Jackie, but her sister, Lee, the Princess Radziwill, who has come along for the ride with her good friend Truman, in order to have something to do. The Capote entourage is filled in on things by the Stones' advance man, who holds down the fort until Peter Rudge, fresh from his sit-down confrontation with the Angels in New York, arrives. Then the advance man slips away and quietly cancels the dinner.

In the space of a day Rudge has gone from bikers to Beautiful People, but as always he is a fountainhead of propriety. In longhand, he scrawls out a pass instructing whoever is at the stage door to allow these people, Capote, the princess, and Peter Beard access to the hall.

The hall itself is a mellow movie house of a place that smells of melted butter and has inlaid lights in the ceiling and fake marble floors. Huck Finn longhairs try to *sneak* rather than break in and the entire feeling is of an earlier, more innocent time.

Backstage, a loud argument suddenly flares between Marshall Chess and Stan Moore. Marshall's asked the guy who's going to head the film crew in Texas along to watch the concert and they're both in a limo reserved for musicians so Stan tries to clear them out. Marshall won't stand for it; it's a combination of that showbiz arrogance that everyone in the Inner Circle is capable of flashing when they feel their rights are impinged upon and that primal therapy doctrine, if you feel it, say it, and within no time it's fuck-yous and go talk to Peter and I don't give a shit who you are—tempers and yelling—an ugly taste of what's to come.

Chess goes out into the hall after it's ended and comes back with Capote and the princess. In a wide-brimmed hat and a summer seer-sucker jacket, Capote looks like a very small, very dignified United States senator. 'Truman's here,' someone says excitedly to Jagger. 'Let me introduce you.'

'Oh, yeah, well,' Mick says laconically. 'Loik I already know him.'

And when the introduction is finally made, Jagger grins his impudent little boy grin and says, 'What you doin in a dump like this?'

And Capote, who has spent quite a bit of time in Kansas City and been to the University of Kansas in Lawrence many times, immediately thinks, Well, this *isn't* a dump. It's a swingy city. He feels this attitude the Stones have, their lack of respect for a country they really know nothing about.

It is immediately apparent that there is no way Jagger and Capote are going to get on. Mick is too aware of Capote's reputation. Capote is going to be looking for Mick's slightest flaws, and because he's in the midst of a grueling tour, he is very vulnerable.

The mask can slip at any time in a high-pressure situation like this, and society's games are hard to play on the road, so the best they can hope for is an uneasy detente where they don't speak much to one another.

After the nonstop partying in Chicago, the Kansas City show is, to put it kindly, subdued. Capote stands beneath the amps, watching, as the band manages to stay on its feet throughout the whole set. When they come off, Keith says grimly, 'Tomorrow we rehearse. For sure.'

At 2:30 in the morning, they straggle out of the plane into the eighty-degree heat of Dallas' Love Field. The hot air smacks you in the face like an asbestos glove. The businessman in the hotel elevator sizes you up and drawls, 'Ah wish ah could grow mah air like you. Ah shorely do.' A circle of plain-faced stewardesses keeps a vigil in the lobby, waiting for the party to begin. A girl in a white plaster body cast that makes her look like a deformed mummy keeps asking people for their room numbers.

The party is in Keith's room. Mick has asked Chris O'Dell to come and sew sequins on his costume and the never-ending party that began in Chicago continues, people snorting, smoking, popping amys on these straight but solidly crazed stewardesses who want to welcome the Stones to Big D.

Jagger sits in the middle of the party on a bed looking into a mirror, like in a scene from *Juliet of the Spirits*. He just sits there, at the center of things, totally relaxed, ignoring this chick who is in the bed too, under the covers, with all her clothes on. Everyone is just sort of waiting... for something to happen... for it to begin, whatever it may be.

Annie Leibovitz, who is twenty-three years old and one of the premier rock photo-journalists, is at the party. She has joined the tour in Kansas City and this is her first on-the-road social encounter with the Stones. She's gone through all kinds of nervous changes before going on about whether it's cool or not to take along her camera. She decides to leave it behind and go as a person and the first thing she notices is that Jagger has this thing he does with his eyes; he focuses in on you, zooms in, looks through the back of your head and then moves on. Annie, who is nothing if not a strong lady, the Margaret Bourke-White of the amps and roadies set, finds herself looking at Jagger more than she wants to and taking far too many pictures, searching for the

Jagger picture, the one that will capture him totally, define him as completely as those zoomar looks of his do when they pin you to the wall.

The next afternoon, when the Capote entourage arrives in Dallas, with both Truman and the princess in the city for the first time, they take that cab ride, the one which must keep Dallas taxi drivers in eating money these days, through Dealey Plaza, and go slowly, driver; so that we can look. Peter Beard points out the window where the shots came from and Lee turns away, not wanting to look, having been as Truman puts it, 'Very close to her brother-in-law. The entire city is a very depressing place for her.'

There's no way anyone's going to feel good in Dallas. Sure, sure, everybody knows that the city existed for a long time before November 22, 1963, and that there are lots of fine, upstanding people that live there even now, but for a whole generation of people who grew up by the light of their television sets, Dallas means only one thing—assassination, as the TV newsmen drew those carefully marked diagrams of the motorcade route and Lee Harvey Oswald went down again and again grimacing from a bullet in the side, as they reran the tape.

If you draw back the two sets of dusty drapes at the hotel the Stones are staying in and peer over the pink and yellow lights that shine against the white stucco of the building, across a couple of freeways and in back of a row of buildings, you can make out the large square structure with the words 'Texas Schoolbook Depository' on top.

The hotel itself is worn and lame, and tired, like some drunked-out hooker who never got more than fifteen a night in her prime and now can't give it away. As Jagger says, 'Someone suggested we stay in places cheaper than Holiday Inns and I said, "Great" to save the money. It doesn't bother me 'cause I don't need luxury. Nonetheless, this is one cheap, fuckin, horrible, shitty place....' In the morning, the local paper carries an item out of Greenville, Texas, about the Dallas man who stabbed another to death and was sentenced to 999 years in jail. The district attorney had asked for a thousand years.

Outside the lobby, the sun's heating the air to blast-furnace temperatures. The air itself is wet and heavy and the combination of the sun and the humidity makes it impossible to keep your eyes open and breathe at the same time. If you try to go anywhere, your shirt gets sodden with sweat and you can't tell where you've been, or if the trip was worth it.

Willie the baggage man has done a yeoman job of getting everyone's stuff into the hotel, but the Film Crew find they're missing an important box. Robert Frank calls him. 'Where's that box, Willie?'

'What do I know where it is?' Willie snorts. He's trying to shave; he's sweating, Dallas sucks.

'Go get it.'

'Hey, Robert... who you orderin around? Fuck you.' And he hangs up. It's not more than a minute later then that there's a banging at his door and Robert Frank, in a reasonable state of agitation, charges in, demanding, 'Who you hangin up on?'

'Hey, Bob,' Willie says, in his best Wallace Beery tones, 'I'm shavin now. Lemme alone, willya... Hey, Bob... get outta my room, huh?... You want somethin, go tell Peter, he's in charge... Hey, Bob, what are you, crayzee? Stay outta here...'

And the very next thing, Robert is lying on the floor, having either been punched or shoved. ('A shove,' Willie says later. 'I punch him, I woulda laid him out') 'Willllllieeeee,' Keith Richard shouts from down the hall, 'what's goin on in that damn room?'

'Okay, Keith baby, okay,' Willie says, and a few minutes later he goes to find the box.

That evening the Stones rehearse. The show in Kansas City was fairly rotten and with the recording truck around, there's a need to get things back together. Called for 4:00 P.M., the rehearsal begins at eight, and consists of a lot of musicians sitting in, standing up, switching off on instruments, dozing, humming breaks, going for beer, and playing maybe one song all the way through. It goes on until 2:00 A.M., and when it's over everyone feels good at having worked hard to get the show in shape.

While the Stones work, the Dallas social whirl begins. There's a small soir e in a downtown French restaurant so that the Tac Squad and the Capote entourage can become better acquainted. And the Tac Squad approves... Truman has such a watchful manner. Why, he's the kind of person who finds out all about you merely by looking at you, and it's all you can do from spewing out your life history to him before they put the soup down. Jo Bergman's impressed with the way the princess says, 'Thank you so very much,' every time a waiter puts down a plate or takes one away, as though someone had just given her the most amazing present. Peter Beard is the wild card. No one knew Truman would be bringing his own photographer along, and no one knows for sure who Beard is shooting rolls and rolls of film for. He is *very* concerned about fitting in and being nice to everyone and somehow his anxiety makes him fit in a lot less than Truman and the princess who don't seem to be worried about much at all.

While some people are dining graciously, Jagger and Charlie Watts are in search of soul food. With Annie Leibovitz tagging along, they decide to check out the South Side of Dallas, make a lightning raid on the ghetto, where the heat has the people standing in the street, drinking and knocking each other down, looking for something to burn. Mick and Charlie want to eat barbecue. They've got Leroy with them, of course, and his main concern is keeping the white chauffeur from turning the limo around. He's never been in this part of town after dark, much less on a Friday night at 3:00 A.M.

Annie tells Jagger that she's just come from photographing Huey Newton. 'He's not at all the way I thought he'd be,' she says. 'Actually he's very priestly, almost saintly.... a nonviolent man. He told me he'd done a *Playboy* interview... for the money.'

'Ai'd never do one a those,' Jagger snorts. 'They offered.'

Annie looks at him incredulously. 'You'd never do one of those?' she laughs. 'You just stayed in his house for four days.'

'Iss the principle,' Jagger says. 'Ai don't loik the principle... I've never agreed. Aw, Charlie loiks the magazine, but ai don't. I know they can afford good writers an awl, but even the best writers need the money so maybe Nabokov gets one outta the drawer for 'em....'

'But Heffner's a noice guy, inn't he?' Charlie says. 'Didn't like his house though. Went a bit crazy in 'ere...' (He points to his head.) 'The best fun I had there was talkin to the cook; he'd been there sixteen years, ever since the road was full up wit Chicago's biggest gangsters. He'd been a driver back in the bad days, or as 'e called 'em, the "fun" days....'

'The house,' Jagger sighs, '... yeah...' He laughs, 'I got a bit loaded meself. Got a memory blank about most of it.'

The limo rolls past a corner where a circle of young brothers

stand in the shadow of a building. As the car rolls by, they turn
to watch, wondering who's driving a hog that size at this hour,
what pimp is going where. Jagger sits staring out the window,
watching street-lights flow together in the humid heat. Out of
nowhere, he asks Annie, 'Wha's your sign?'

'Are you kidding?' she says. Jagger has to be putting her on.
The question is such a bad hippie clich , hey, maan, what's your
sign; that all she can do is laugh and say, 'Get serious.'

'Ah,' Jagger says, laughing, liking that she won't tell him. 'All
right,' he smiles and turns back to staring out the window until
they find a joint that has ribs, a jukebox, and a pool table. As
Mick and Charlie and Annie sit and eat, the Stones' bodyguard
keeps a watch on the brothers shooting pool, gauging the distance to the door, wondering if the five rounds in the snubnose
revolver he carries will be enough if he has to shoot it out to get
to the door.

Back in the hotel, those not out on the town or down in the
ghetto are getting loose in Bobby Keys' room, passing pills and
potions as the cassettes start spinning and the local stewardess
contingent slides off the side of the bed onto the carpet. Still
tingling from his night of destruction in Chicago, Gary Stromberg finds Keith and says, 'Where's Capote? Let's bring him to
the party. He's covering the tour, right?' And Keith says, 'Sure.'
If Stromberg has some mad plan, some fantasy of what he would
do if he were Keith, there's no reason not to try it out and see
what happens.

Into an empty elevator and down a deserted corridor, two midnight ramblers. Up to the door of the room where Truman, the
respected man of letters, sleeps. Quiet, as quiet as it can get only
in the small hours of the night in a strange hotel, with the creak-
ing elevator cables and the humming air conditioner singing a
lullaby to the guests in dreamland. Suddenly... BANGABANG-
ABANGBANG.

'Huh? Wha? You hear somethin, Herb?'

BANGBANGABANGBANG. 'Wake up in there,' Keith shouts
through the locked door. 'Wake up, you queen. Come to the
party.'

'Who is it?' comes the familiar Capote singsong from within.

BANG BANG BANG. 'C'mon, you bitch. Fuckin wake up!
Come to the party and find out what rock and roll's all about.'

'Go away,' Truman says. 'Go away. I'm sleeping. And besides, I already know.'

Down a few doors to where the princess sleeps. BANG BANG BANG. 'Princess Radish!' Keith howls. 'C'mon, you old tart. There's a party goin downstairs.'

By this time, Stromberg is laughing so hard his sides hurt. The utter outrageousness of it all, these high-society folk out on the road and Keith treating them the way they deserve... God... between laughs, he spies a bottle of ketchup lying on a room-service tray outside someone's door. He hands it to Keith and they spurt and smear it all over Capote's door, so that it looks really grotesque and blood-spattered... Keith and Gary as Terry and Smith, offing Truman Capote in Dallas, in the nonfiction novel entitled *In Cold Ketchup.*

Looking none the worse for wear the next afternoon, Truman, the princess, and Peter Beard sit assembled on a couch in the hotel lobby, waiting for the limousine fleet to leave for the Tarrant County Convention Center in Fort Worth. It is a twenty-seven mile ride to the hall and most people will go by bus. The entourage goes by limo.

'Are you sulking, Truman?' the princess asks, in her Lauren Bacall cigarette-smoke-and-whiskey voice.

'Just thinking,' he says wistfully.

'One and the same, aren't they?' she observes. 'Why, when I think I've given you the most *divine* present of your life and you've never even used it....'

Just a couch away, Gary Stromberg has his nose in Sheriff Jesse Curry's personal account of the assassination of JFK. Keith exits from the elevator, flanked by a mean-looking, possibly razor-toting girl a good head-and-a-half taller than he. 'See ya, deah,' he says. Turning to the couch full of people, he says, 'Ready for the mornin show?'

Even as he speaks, planes are landing at Love Field with visitors who are looking forward to a wild weekend in Big D with the Stones. Chris O'Dell's on her way back from L.A., having made an emergency flight for necessary supplies. Richard Elman is arriving from New York to write a piece for *Esquire* that will eventually appear in *Oui.* Ethan Russell returns to take photographs for *Saturday Review,* which has Terry Southern landing in place of William Burroughs. Mario Medious, known to disc jockeys and friends as the 'Big M,' a sharp-dressing, fast-talking parody of everyone's fantasy of what a super-fly record-promotion man should look like, will be on the scene, along with Ahmet Erteg n, the Turkish-born president of Atlantic Records, the firm that distributes Rolling Stones' Records.

A host of writers and photographers and recordbiz people. A contingent, descending on the narrow dressing room in Fort Worth, so that in between the afternoon and evening shows, it's like a swarm of locusts in a bell jar, a dressing room crowded with new faces, with strange bodies angling for drinks at the buffet table and making conversation.

'Look,' the princess says in her husky voice. 'We've found a good corner over here.' In a scoop-necked black top with her official Rolling Stones badge that says 'Access' pasted on her back, in a print skirt, with a chain link shoulder bag and sandals with chain link backs, the princess stands smiling as a puff of fragrant smoke billows in the air: 'Shhh, baby,' a clandestine voice says. 'For this they give you twenty-five years in Texas.'

Mr. Capote meet Mr. Southern; Mr. Elman meet Mr. Russell, Mario meet anybody you like.

'Helllllo there, uh, big bopper,' Terry Southern says to Keith. Southern is a bearded man whose clothes are wrinkled from his plane ride. He wears black-frame eye glasses Scotch-taped together in one corner. Southern has known Keith since the days of the Living Theater in Rome, when he was scripting and rescripting *Barbarella,* a film directed by Roger Vadim, featuring Keith's lady, Anita Pallenberg.

Southern tends to ramble when he speaks, drawing out his words in broken sentences, sliding into tangents that always intersect sooner or later. Often there are long silent gulfs, on the other side of which whole new subjects begin. He often seems on the verge of saying what it is he precisely means, but soon gets into another tale about the people he's known and the insanity he's seen.

There was that time in London when the great Stanley Kubrick was filming *Dr. Strangelove* and 'Sellers hurt his leg and couldn't play the bomber captain... and Stanley didn't want a mere actor, so he sent for Slim Pickens, the legendary Slim, who came straight out of the Texarkana-Okie rodeo circuit and flew to London, where they sent this Oxford fag in a blue blazer to greet him. The two looked at each other and neither could understand a word the other was saying....'

The crush is so heavy in the dressing room that the Stones are dressing down the hall, popping in only occasionally for a bird-like swoop toward the food and drink. They're guests at a literary gathering of some significance, catered in the spirit of a histrionic Long Island bar mitzvah.

The princess takes two steps out from her corner, gets lost in a fishpond of people talking and clutching greasy hors d'oeuvres, then quickens her step and manages to hook Jagger by one bare arm. He turns to look at her and she stage whispers, 'How's Tony?'

'Who's Tony?' Chris O'Dell says out loud. She's just stepped off a plane and the question jams in her jet-lagged brain and sticks there. Who's Tony? Tony who? So that the first chance she gets, she vows she'll corner Mick and find out who Tony is. And that doesn't happen for a while and then Chris forgets his answer and has to ask him again, but it's worth all the trouble because she finds out the princess is enquiring after the husband of another princess, Tony Armstrong-Jones.

'Like there is no privacy at all in this dressing room,' Mario the 'Big M' says from his end of the social spectrum. 'Like none. I saw all kinds of farmers in that place. They was pointin out the big-bread people to me. Everyone bowin down and kissin ass. I said hello to Capote and the Princess Roz, what's her name, man? But I don't rap to no one less they rap to me. I tells 'm I work for Ahmet 'cause I know they know him and I gotta be cool. But I ain't gonna say, "I admire your sister, she dress real well." Or, "I admire your book." The cat know somebody admire it, right? 'Cause it dun sold three million copies. What he care about me tellin him?'

'Stanley called me up,' Terry says, picking up the story for a small semicircle of enchanted listeners, 'and said, "You're from Texas. Go down there and translate." I did and there's Slim with his pants tucked into his boots and a big Stetson. "Hah're you Slayum," I says to him, "how 'bout a drank?" It's ten in the morning and slim says, "Whall, snort, snort, ah nevah says no to that." So I pour him a shot of Wild Turkey.'

'I'm looking for something to drink,' Truman Capote says very precisely from his end of the buffet table. 'But the apple juice does not agree with me.'

' "Thanks, padnuh," Slim says. "Slayum," I ask him, "you set-tlin in all right here?" The fag in the Oxford blazer cannot understand either of us by this time. Slim looks around at the hotel suite, takes a drink and says, "You know what an ole boy ah once knew used to say: All ah needs is some loose-fittin shoes, a taght pussy, and a warm place to shit and ah'm fahn." ' Terry waits for his laugh.

By special fiat, as a friend of Keith's, the Tac Squad permits Southern to watch the evening show from the stage, and halfway through the set he reaches into his pocket for something or other and this box falls out on to the deck and amyl nitrates come rolling out... it's enough to cause heart problems... for some reason even Mick and Keith look back and notice them... little corncob amys that flush the system and rush the brain... rolling... over... the stage, past the the shoes of the Chief of Police of Fort Worth who is *fascinated.* He doesn't know what those little thingies are, but they sure are cute. He's bending over to pick one up. Terry is bending over to pick them up. Gary Stromberg is down on the floor before anyone, because if Terry bends, he'll fall, and the police chief will be looking down at him, *fascinated.* So Stromberg crawls around for awhile on his hands and knees, gazing up at the well-polished police shoes of the chief and does his job, gathering amys and heading off a good deal of publicity.

After the concert, the Capote entourage hops into a limo, rides it around the corner, then hops out to go somewhere with a friend, leaving it half-empty for the ride back to the hotel. On the S.T.P. bus, the new crop of tourists and the Tac Squad sit like the Big Red Team plus cheerleaders on their way home after an away game. Outside the darkened windows, the freeway unrolls, the Six Flags Over Texas amusement park off to one side and Terry Southern up front spinning out stories and passing around a leather-covered hip flask. 'Okay, now,' he says, 'Pree-tend we're in the desert and we got only one canteen left. Jes' one swig now, boy, or we're both goners.'

Terry passes the flask to Janice, who has come down to Dallas on a bus ride that took two years. At least it seemed that long, that's how stoned she was from the action in Chicago. The guy in back of her on the bus had a regulation foaming-at-the-mouth fit so she had to fill out an accident report and maybe she'll get to collect some money, on account of being foamed on.

Janice, it develops, is nineteen years old and an original. She's skinny, pretty, and modeled for a while in New York, and now just drifts. She got into town a couple nights ago and a S.T.P. dude spied her in the lobby and took her upstairs, having scored for the night. Then the phone rang. 'She doesn't fuck,' a familiar-sounding voice said.

'What are you talking about? Christ, lower your voice, Chip. She's right here, in the bathroom. What do you mean, she doesn't fuck? Everyone fucks.'

'Not her.'

'Oh... shit... that's *you*. Of course she wouldn't fuck *you*, but...'

But she doesn't. What she's doing is sleeping her way toward Mick Jagger. Chastely, facing the wall, with the covers drawn tight for protection. Tonight she's sitting next to Terry. This nine-teen-year-old piece of bone and hank of hair, with big innocent eyes, who is rootless and just drifts, like a rolling tumbleweed out on the mesquite, sitting next to the man who co-wrote *Candy*. She *is* Candy, and she doesn't even know who he is. 'Take a swallow and pass it on,' Terry, as Gabby Hayes, says, 'and, little girl, take extra care you don't take... a double swig.'

Back at the hotel, the party is in the minisuite occupied by the princess on one of the hotel's top floors. All the social levels are going to run together tonight, one way or another. The cassette player's whirring 'Sister Morphine' with Jagger crying 'Tell me whyyyyy/ The doctor has no faaaaaace.' The doctor himself is present, along with Charlie Watts, Rudge, Terry Southern, Keith, two beds' worth of stoned locals, and Peter Beard. The princess comes through a door, surveys the gathering, pronounces, 'The party's over,' and leaves.

With the princess gone, Peter Beard plays host. A bluff, ath-letic-looking fellow, Peter has already been dubbed the 'Great White Hunter' by Keith, who doesn't understand why he talks the way he does. Beard is American, yet he has this clipped, almost English manner of speech, that 'Have a good show, old sport'-type thing he must have picked up at some school back East. There's a definite Francis Macomber feel to him, gin and tonics at the hunt club after a day stalking the beastly rhino, and he did, in fact, live in Kenya for a while. Keith takes action and slips three Quaaludes into Beard's tomato-colored drink. 'To get some truth out of him,' Keith says, 'to see him involved.' Why the hell else are these people out here on the road, crowding into sweaty dressing rooms and smiling all the time as though they were delighted at the unique anthropological opportunity to get a firsthand look at a dying herd of antelope, or a bunch of nearly extinct killer apes. Don't get too close to the animals now, folks, they're liable to get nasty and try to get you down on their level with three Quaaludes... and everyone in the room is waiting to see if Beard is going to start hallucinating and see God or just fall down on the carpet and moan.

The culprit, Keith Richard, sits on the floor with his back against the wall. Having done two shows in a day, he is well entitled to some relaxation. Between his knees is the black leather bag everyone knows so well from childhood days when the kindly family M.D. swung it on the sickbed and withdrew the stethoscope.

'Hey,' Stoned Local Number One inquires, 'whose bag *is* that?'

'His,' Keith says, pointing to the doctor. 'And mine.'

'Ahhhhhh,' Terry Southern says very slowly, easing himself down on the floor next to Keith. 'And what, ole buddy, have we here? Aha...' Terry sticks a hand down into the bag, sifts its contents and says, 'Uh... that is... may I presume it to be... the, uh, Big M?' meaning morphine.

'Desoxyn,' Keith says, with the authority of a man who has read the *PDR (Physician's Desk Reference,* the *Encyclopaedia Britannic*-Neiman-Marcus catalogue of dope) more than once.

'Ah-*ha*,' Terry says, enlightened.

'Hey,' Stoned Local Number One inquires, 'who's the doctor here?'

'Him,' someone next to him says.

'Richards?' the local says, horrified.

'This one in the middle.'

'The one in the middle's a bellhop,' someone else notes, passing a joint. 'Whyn't we go and dick the princess?'

'Lissen, man', Stoned Local Number One whines. 'I'm dyin. I got sinus congestion. You got any APC?'

'What's that?' Keith asks. 'A downer?'

'No... oh, maaaaan... my head's throbbin like hell.'

'This man's head is throbbin like hell,' Keith parrots. He plunges the bag and comes out with a Quaalude. 'Take one of these and come back tomorrow.'

Terry's removed his black-frame glasses and leaned them against the rim of a scarlet tequila sunrise that stands by the open black leather bag. They ought to use the picture as the cover for the tour album, because it tells the story as well as any one shot is going to. Across the room, Peter Beard seems to have lost all interest in his crimson-coloured drink. With the party still pulsing around him, he's yawning a good deal and turning back the covers on his bed. Keith and Terry sit holding bottles up to the light, discussing dosages. 'It's seconal, man... has that characteristic barbiturate odor when snorted...'

'How's this?' someone says, dipping into the bag and coming out with a bottle of rainbow capsules. 'How do these look with my eyes? These Valiums... they go with my shirt, you think?'

A lot of people seem to have left the party, but time has little or no meaning at this stage of the game. Terry is leaning over and pitching to Keith trying to sell him a movie. 'Fantastic thing is, Keith, it's you and Mick... musicians, see, from Kansas City... open on a great shot of the two of ya in a bar... long-distance call, cut to New York City and all these fucked-up changes you go through makin it.'

'Us from Kansas City?' Keith says. 'You jokin?'

For years people have been trying to lay movie deals on the Stones, drag them into films that they'll have to write the music for. Donald Cammel, who succeeded in getting Jagger and Anita Pallenberg for *Performance,* Southern, even William Burroughs and Brion Gysin, who are interested in having Jagger write the music for the film version of *Naked Lunch.* Somehow the Stones relate to it easily, as though it were only proper that they be consulted for the soundtrack for the best in anarchy their generation has produced.

'I've spoken to William about it,' Southern says now, 'and it all depends on you doin the music....'

'Ah, no, don't really know at this time, Terry,' Keith mumbles.

'Ah, well, a certain person there... we uh both know... would love you bein obstreperous about it.'

'Me bein physical, you mean?'

'No, actually, I've uh spoken to William about it and he assures me ah em aha (in low voice) you would not have to... or even, uh, unless of course you wanted to.'

'*Tell me whyyy/the doctor has no faaaaaace,*' the cassette cries, unwinding again. No one in the room has the strength to turn it off, or try and answer the question.

Sunday, June 25th, dawns hotter and more humid than the previous two days. In the steambath hotel coffee shop, waitresses in white crinkled-nylon uniforms slap tuna combos, fries, and chili with a burger onto long plates and push them down the counters. Sweat forms tiny beads and crystal mustaches on their upper lips and soaks dark moons under their armpits. The clatter of knives and forks, the chink of heavy china, and Terry Southern and Truman Capote sitting like two dons in an Oxford staff room, discussing the relative merits of the Dixieburger versus the Mexburger.

'Stay away from the french fries,' Truman cautions. Each one is like a potato.

In the lobby, Keith asks Beard, 'Did you sleep well, Peter?'

'Yes! Fine! Very well!' Peter says enthusiastically, as Keith says, under his breath, 'I put a Mickey Finn in your drink, you stupid bugger.'

Willie the baggage man is struggling with his arms full of suitcases. He has nowhere to put them because the Film Crew has hijacked his truck to go back to the hall. So there are more exchanges of get away from me before I knock you on your fucking ass, but it quiets before the Stones come down. Bianca Jagger has arrived sometime after the midnight hour the previous night, and her entrance into the lobby, like nearly everything she does, is a superb piece of theater. She wears a khaki walking suit, a straw hat, carries a walking stick, and looks like Charlie Chaplin dressed for a day's shooting on the veldt.

It's ninety-six degrees outside the lobby and the Capote entourage, minus the princess, who's gone back to New York of her own accord, hops into a limo while the regular S.T.P. crew jams into a sweaty little transit van. 'Oh, honey,' a broken-hearted Dallas belle sighs, as the transit starts to pull out. 'Ah wanna go down and see y'awl puhform in Houston *so* bad. Ah know a boy who maght drahv me...'

'Oh yeah?' the guy she's spent the night with says. 'Here,' he flips her the key to the hotel room he's just left. 'I slipped her a Placidon,' he tells the guy next to him. 'You feel that pill yet, honey?' Her answer is lost in a rush of hot asphalt and carbon monoxide as the transit lurches into gear and pulls away.

It's only three degrees shy of a hundred in Houston, and the Stones are scheduled for two shows, which they do without Stevie Wonder. Stevie's drummer has had an authentic nervous break-down—and split the band, and they haven't even gone to the trouble of traveling to Houston. They're still back in Dallas, and the first Rudge and the Stones learn of it is when they enter the antiseptic baseball locker room.

Keith freaks. People curse, and even Jagger, who rarely, if ever, blows it, is obviously pissed off. Lockers get banged and Peter Rudge sees red, and heads for the nearest phone. In their ten years on the road, the Stones have missed exactly one show, through a booking error, in the north of England eight years ago. The Stones' time-honored tradition is... if you can walk, you can make the gig. And here's Stevie with a big band in back of him, and he doesn't bother to show because of one missing musician.

A lot of fantasies about how a band on the road lives are hard facts for WonderLove, Stevie's band. They don't have it easy, and it's a wonder someone hasn't cracked before this. After some con-certs they have to be up to catch a flight that leaves at seven in the morning. They get into Atlanta or some other strange air-port, then have to wait for three hours in order to catch a thirty-minute flight that gets them to the gig city eight hours early. Their accommodations are always straight roadside motels, with Stevie, who is a star, staying right with the band. As one S.T.P. wit suggests, 'Maybe it's a good thing Stevie's blind. That way he can't see some of the places they've got him in.'

Stevie and his band have been on the road for the better part of a year, having done a cross-country Joe Cocker tour just before going out with the Stones. In the business since he was thirteen, unlike Frankie Lymon and his brother, Louie, two talented black performers who made it as kids and then both died of overdoses, Wonder has grown, his talents have expanded, and he is certain to be one of the big stars of the future.

'The man is blind,' Mario the 'Big M' explains. 'So he goes where you take him. He loves to play. So it's got to be the management. The road crew, or whoever, shoulda been on the case. If they gonna party all night, get high and wasted, then the damn road manager gotta go out there with a ball bat and beat the momma jommas 'cross the head and throw them into the bus 'cause it's a stone bringdown to miss a gig. Like you dig, right now the Stones don't need Stevie Wonder. He's big in his own right, but he ain't gonna draw no white people to a soul show. Ike and Tina, B.B. King, and Muddy, how you think they got big, Jack? The Rolling Stones. They opened a whole new market for 'em. That's why Jagger was so pissed, cursin, sayin, "Fire 'em. Fire the whole band." I can dig where he's from.'

Hot, weird Texas karma has gotten into everything, like dust from a desert windstorm and there's no joy in the Houston dressing room. Thirty-nine people crowd it, elbowing for the hot Mexican food and snapping pictures in the shower stalls. Photographers are tucked into every corner so that every time you turn someone's got you in their lens, and you begin to envision yourself as a role of contact sheets, each movement broken down into sections, frame by frame. Click click. The song of the Nikon. Click, click click.

Ahmet Erteg n, resplendent in a crisp white shirt, pressed blue blazer, and neatly trimmed goatee, has arrived. A tanned balding man with glasses and large round eyes, he heads one of the most successful rhythm and blues record companies in America and makes it a point to come out on the road to see his artists perform, especially ones like the Stones. 'M'sieu Keats,' he says, and Keith turns around and tries to smile. During the first show, the tempo on stage got a little tangled with Charlie hanging back a beat or two and Keith began shouting, 'Faster, Charlie, faster. Fuck you. COME ON,' stamping in time to show him what he meant. It's something that's happened before, and the two of them go offstage with their arms around each other, but it's undeniable that the strain is starting to get to Keith, who is the band's barometer, with emotions close to the surface. More easily read than anyone else, Keith is always what he appears to be. Now, he looks wasted, drawn, drained by the heat, and dislocated by all the people who have hopped on the tour to watch and take notes. He flashes Ahmet a weary smile and says that he's looking forward to driving to New Orleans.

'Gonna be a quiet change,' he says. 'Dig up some Cajuns or something.'

There's no swamps between here and there,' Ahmet says, like a merchant advising against buying a particular brand. 'You want swamps, you drive from Lake Ponchartrain and look at 'em. What do you expect? Cajun fiddlers by the side of the road?'

Keith shrugs. Bobby Keys comes up to greet Ahmet. 'Hey, Bobby,' Ahmet says warmly, 'what you think? You going to stay in tune this time out?'

'Yes,' Truman Capote says saucily to Mick Taylor. 'Try to play on key this time, will you?'

'We always do, Truman,' Taylor answers, unsmiling.

People aren't even making it out of the dressing rooms for the show any more. They've become a by-product, hardly worth discussing, unless you're trying to impress one of the musicians by telling him what you thought of his individual performance. Everyone around the tour is hanging on for dear life, as though being permitted to be near the Stones was like a membership in the League in Hesse's *Journey To The East.*

There's no task too trivial, no act too demeaning for those who want to be around. Flex, Keith's friend, says, 'I'm back and I'm gonna stay until I burn up.' Janice is outside in the shimmering heat, chewing on a massive corn dog, juggling a box of popcorn and a large Coke, looking like an advertisement for the county fairs of America, trying to get someone to take a note in to Mick Taylor, who is her next rung on the ladder that leads to Jagger.

It's really no surprise, then, that when the band comes off after the show with Keith sweat-soaked and in pain, that Terry Southern goes right up to him, loops an arm over his shoulder and picks up where he left off, hustling the movie. And Keith, who just doesn't know what people want from him anymore, explodes, shouting, 'Can't you see I'm sick? What the fuck do you want from me? Just fuck off and leave me alone.'

'Ohhh-kay,' Terry mumbles. 'If that's how you feel, Keith ole buddy oh, ohh-kay.'

And the milk train that has brought everyone so far seems in precarious shape, shunted off onto a siding in the heat, and looking as though it definitely might tumble off the rails at any moment.

Chapter Seven

'Southern stops here. 'Ee's out.' Peter Rudge sighs softly the next day, ignoring the blinking red button on his phone that informs him there's a message in his name waiting down at the desk. 'It was out of hand in Texas, yes, I grant you that.' Rudge picks a piece of tobacco off his teeth with a fingernail and leans back into the pillow on his bed. The red light keeps on blinking. 'Too many people hoppin into limos like they owned 'em. But... *c'est fini*. We got changes to make.'

It's a well-steamed, uneasy breeze that blows off the coffee-colored Mississippi River, down by the Jax Brewery in old New Orleans. Outside Rudge's hotel room, a line has commenced to form, writers and photographers with metaphorical hats in hand being asked to explain why they should not be sent back to from where they came. The Texas debacle has hit the S.T.P. organization from top to bottom, and action will be taken.

Terry Southern, an obvious Scapegoat, will be the first to catch it. For what Ethan Russell calls the 'unpardonable sin... getting too close to one of the principals,' he will be asked to leave the tour. Ethan will as well. As will this writer. And maybe even Capote and Beard. Up on the hotel's alabaster white rooftop, Stan Moore watches an orange sunset behind skyscrapers under construction and mutters darkly, 'I might be goin home Monday mahself. Yeah. Because I can really get down if I have to and I want Peter to have confidence in me... I can do my job, man.'

Chris O'Dell sleeps away the day. Every time she shows her face lately, someone asks her when she plans to leave, which is kind of awkward since she doesn't. Mick and Keith absolutely need someone around like her to take care of the small things, and all these people acting in the Stones' name make Chris really annoyed. It's not like it was when she worked for the Beatles at Apple. People ripped the Beatles off right and left, but at least when they walked into a room, they commanded respect. People treat the Stones like children. Like this New Orleans purge. The Stones don't even know about it. No one's even asked them what they think. This party is getting to be a drag. Chris sleeps on.

'Anyway,' Peter Rudge says, taking time out from a series of consultations with Jo, who hated Texas and is only now locked back into rushing in and out of rooms and talking away quickly in a series of extravagant accents, 'it's over.' The phone rings and Rudge lifts the receiver to his ear.

'Who? Yes, of course, Troube-y,' Rudge croons, smiling down the wire. 'Troube-y, we know you're giving us a dinner. What can we say? We're overwhelmed. You are too? Perfect. Troube-y bay-bee, constrain yourself... Mick Taylor is in 416. I'll send you a room list and you can make your invitations from that. Certainly yes, by-bye.'

Well now. Just because some people have stepped over the line and had their wrists slapped is no reason for everyone to enter a monastery. After all, one must have a minimum of social inter-course. And what could be more fun than a dinner party thrown by Truman Capote, the man who tossed *the party* of the sixties, the black and white ball at the Plaza Hotel that *The New York Times* published the guest list for the very next day. Pete Hamill, columnist for the *New York Post*, was so outraged by it all, he wrote an entire column, alternating paragraphs about the party with paragraphs about guys on a Vietnam battlefield getting shot at and chopped and chewed to ribbons by Vietcong mortar and small-arms fire. Everybody in New York without money loved that column. It was an angry blast at a country where people went to parties while its young men were being shipped home from war in aluminum caskets.

But the sixties are over now, and Capote is still going strong. Although he's been around the tour for only four days he's already decided which of the S.T.P. crew are professionals, and which are rank amateurs. For instance, he considers Gary Stromberg a 'rude New York person.' In the copious notes he takes for an article he later decides not to write, Capote describes his '...glassy eyes shifting behind aviator shades, his hair-framed lips so painfully producing the supplicant, boot-licking smile so indigenous to his image.' Also on Capote's list is Marshall Chess, the very man who conceived the idea of having him on tour. Chess had 'fat little legs' and can be seen 'pumping them nymphomaniacally' on stage as he edges 'as near to the stars sweating under the spotlighted blaze' as possible.

And those are just his notes. But, in the month between Capote's little fete in new Orleans and the climactic three concerts that end the tour in New York, this remarkable thing happens. He appears on both the Johnny Carson and Dick Cavett late-night talk shows. He discusses drug intake on the chartered plane, mentions Bobby Keys as a good ole boy from Texas, itemizes the ingredients of a tequila sunrise, and generally does the kind of advance publicity for the Stones that money cannot buy.

Although he does refer to the band as the 'Beatles' two or three times on the Carson show ('The Stones, right?' Johnny says helpfully. 'I thought that's what you meant.'), everything Capote has to say is more or less complimentary and he makes the whole shebang sound like a great adventure.

Asked about it some months after the tour ends, he says of the Stones, 'They're complete idiots. Mick Taylor is pretty, a little Jean Harlow blond-type, but dumb, and totally uninteresting. What I like is something beyond my imagination that (pop! snaps his fingers) sets me off. A vision. Nothing on the tour was remotely like that, and I had no insight into any of it that any other half-sensitive person who was along couldn't have had.'

As a matter of fact, Capote hardly has a good word for anyone associated with the thing. Nicky Hopkins he finds 'has the mark of death upon him. Not interesting but obviously a very sick boy.' Jim Price is 'that little blond boy from Texas, a nothing.' Bobby Keys is 'either better or worse than the Stones; I can't tell which, but certainly totally undisciplined and headed for disaster.

'Intuition tells me they'll never tour this country again and in fact will not exist in three years. They are evanescent people who are not important. There's no correlation at all between Jagger and a Sinatra ....Jagger can't sing, his voice is not in the least charming, he can't dance... he has no talent save for a kind of fly-eyed wonder. He will never be a star. That unisex thing is a no-sex thing. Believe me, he's about as sexy as a pissing toad.

'He could, I suppose, be a businessman. He has that facility of being able to focus in on the receipts in the middle of "Midnight Rambler," while he's beating away with that whip. Maybe it's his financial advisor, the Prince, that he's whipping...'

Despite the way he feels about it all once it's over, during the life of the tour Capote is so absolutely polite and well-mannered that no one can tell if he likes or hates them, and some people are very concerned about which it is. So the tremors that run through the S.T.P. hierarchy when it's learned that Capote is throwing a dinner party and has his own guest list are considerable. The Tac Squad is quite taken with Troube-y, as Rudge calls him; he's a breath of civilisation out here in the boon-docks, an authentic arbiter of American taste who is on the road with the Stones, so that must say something about everyone else who is fortunate enough to be along.

Here's how the party at Amaud's in the French Quarter looks. Capote down at one end of the table with his coat over his shoulders like an Italian film director. Jo Bergman to his left, then Charlie Watts. Bill Wyman next, with his lady Astrud next to him, Ahmet Erteg n, who's flown into town earlier in the day on his private jet, and Peter Beard. On the right, a visiting promoter who's a friend of Rudge and Jo Bergman, Mick Taylor, Annie Leibovitz, and Peter Rudge. Mick and Keith and Bianca are still in transit.

Just east of New Orleans, Cynthia Sagittarius stands waiting for a ride on a narrow, two-lane country road. She stands there for a long, long time until what looks like a guy and his wife pick her up. The guy has some kind of speech impediment and he talks really slowly and very spaced out, as though they've been feeding him institutional Thorazine for a long time. In halting sentences, he tells Cynthia that his wife, who's driving, has just come out of a mental institution where she'd been sent for cutting her parents into small cubes with a butcher knife. Only he knows all these details that only the person who did it could know. Then he starts wrestling with the lock on the glove compartment. He says there's a butcher knife in there that Cynthia should see. His wife tries to pull over to the side of the road, but he grabs the wheel out of her hand, jams his foot down on hers on the accelerator and keeps it there until they are careening out of control at a hundred miles an hour.

Someone tells a story about the Shah of Persia, and the waiter brings white wine. Down at their end of the table, Ahmet and Peter Beard are keeping the conversation going by disagreeing over everything. Ahmet's known Peter forever, from back East, and they seem to really get on with each other.

It's not very long afterward that Cynthia gets picked up by a guy driving alone who doesn't talk much and stares straight ahead, and right away she knows she's in trouble. When he turns off the main highway onto a side road, she's sure of it, and she asks the guy to let her out. He refuses, and keeps on driving, and Cynthia yanks on the handle and opens the door. In a car doing over forty, opening the door usually freaks the driver into slowing down. This guy goes to the door of the car and comes up with a snub-nosed revolver in his hand. He points it at her head and tells her she can jump out now if she wants. Cynthia leans out, about to do it, wondering how bad it will be hitting the asphalt at that speed, when something takes hold of the guy. He slams on his brakes and lets her out.

In Tuscaloosa, Jo-Anne gets arrested. Her clothes are in bad shape by now. She's got crabs and fleas and lice in her frizzy blond hair. She's been raped a couple of times while hitching and when the cops collar her outside the hall and put her into the paddy wagon for loitering, she just breaks down and starts to cry, like a little girl.

Yes, Mick Taylor tells Annie, the architecture in L.A. is weird, especially when you consider that they could have planned it. Annie's amazed at the way these little soirees work. For instance, the promoter sitting down the table from her has more than once instructed his security guards to get her to move her ass off the stage while she's trying to shoot some concert and now they're politely making small talk over the *escargots*. The promoter asks her to pass the water. She does.

After the dinner is over, everyone converges on a warehouse at 748 Camp Street where Ahmet is hosting his own little party. Everyone's been invited to this one, and the warehouse is both a recording studio and the kind of place Mike Hammer used to get himself trapped in, with bare beams and dusty floors, and one fan whirring way in the back where the red neon light from a First National City Bank shines through a window. Ahmet knows that for the Stones, New Orleans means black music. Black music is where they're from and they are scholars on the blues. Charlie Watts is one of the world's great jazz freaks, and this is his first visit to the city of Rampart Street and Bourbon Street, of Kid Ory and George Lewis. Ahmet knows that if the Stones go wandering down the French Quarter, they may catch some old character like Raymond Burke playing, but a legend, like a man called Perfesser Longhair, might be working out in Algiers, which is two hours away.

So with the ease of a wealthy man who has become wealthier by pursuing a business he loves, Ahmet makes some phone calls and rounds up Roosevelt Sykes, a fat, balding black man from Chicago who recorded 'Night Life' in 1936 and is known as the 'Honey-dripper'; 'Snooks' Eagelin, a blind black guitarist and singer, who many people think is dead; and Longhair himself, whose proper name is either Roy or Roland Byrd. Byrd is a black man of indeterminate age with a compressed narrow face and skin like fine parchment left too long in the sun. Ahmet first 'discovered' Longhair in an all-black town in the middle of the Louisiana prairie in 1948. Even then Longhair was famous for his songs and for playing the piano while blowing a mouth harp and working the drums with his feet. A frightened taxi driver took Ahmet and his white business partner out to a muddy field in the middle of nowhere, pointed them toward the lights, and told them to follow the music. It sounded like the entire Fats Domino band blowing and Ahmet had to fast-talk the black proprietor of the all-black honky-tonk into believing that he and his partner were from New York, writers for *Life* magazine, out to do a story. Why else would white men come to a place like this?

After the set, knowing that he was in the presence of an authentic primitive genius, his pants still wet from slogging through muddy fields to find him, Ahmet approached Longhair and said,

'We ain't from *Life*. We're from a record company. We wanna make records with you.'

To which Longhair replied, 'I signed with Mercury yesterday.'

Longhair did records for Erteg n and Atlantic during the fifties and had a hit with 'Tipitina.' Mainly he just kept on playing in small towns and black bars around New Orleans and in the country, as New Orleans became a big music town (Fats Domino, Clarence 'Frogman' Henry, Lee Dorsey) and then declined. With the rise to popularity of a young white piano player who calls himself Dr. John (real name Mac Rebbenack, a session man who worked on Sonny and Cher records) and his recording of an album of Longhair's kind of music, some interest in the old man has been revived.

Now he sits playing for the friends of the Rolling Stones. An old black man wearing a crushed hat sits behind the drum kit doubling up on everything, playing over the top, using only the snares. Longhair doesn't like most people who try to play with him and that goes for the drummer. Longhair's got these crazy rhythms that keep changing with no time signature that you can write down. 'Gotta Whole Lotta Lovin For You' follows 'Everyday I Got The Blues,' which is followed by the back-alley anthem, 'Stagger Lee'. 'I was standin' on the corner/ When I heard my bulldog bark/ It was Stagger Lee and Billy/ Two men who gambled late/ Stagger Lee threw seven/ Billy swore that he threw eight.'

When these old black men die, their music goes with them. As America changes into one big city joined by television signals and superhighways, its native artists, the black bluesmen, are going to vanish. The party is a flashback to a by-gone age. These old men can still boogie, and by midnight people are sweating and dancing, laughing and slapping five, sniffing coke off the backs of their hands, saying, 'My, isn't this a bitch?' and 'Ooo-ee, sure is hot.' Then they slug down some pink champagne and jump back on the floor to sweat it out. Richard Elman's there. So's Terry Southern. So's Ethan Russell. Everyone is getting down, and when Mick and Keith and Bianca sweep in, with Bianca looking as though she's just stepped off Tennessee Williams' front porch in a big hat with a net veil, a southern floozy's roadhouse red-checked blouse and a black shiny skirt, nobody has the time to worry how they are. People are taking care of their own business.

Then this old-time New Orleans street band struts across the floor, with a magnificent old black man in the lead, promenading in a black hat, white gloves, and a white-starred sash across his white shirt and black jacket with a stuffed pigeon dangling off one shoulder, people are up and walking in time behind the band, waving handkerchiefs, and bopping to that second line. Everything is fine! Hmmm my my my! Got to be!

These old cats have been making music all their lives without much reward, without ever becoming pop heroes or culture symbols. Even most blacks prefer the whiter sounds of big city R and B, or the polished urban blues of men like B. B. King, and these old cats don't even know who the Stones are. 'Mick Jagger? Which one is he?' one asks, as Ahmet writes out a check for him in the corner. They're just glad to be getting paid for the gig.

And somehow that gets through to everyone. It's like a syringe full of sanity that normalizes things and makes Texas seem like something out of the distant past. So that the next day, without much discussion or fanfare, everyone who was off is back on the tour.

Immediately before the plane is due to leave for Mobile, early Tuesday afternoon, June 27, Robert Frank sits eating breakfast. Grizzled. Unshaven. Razor packed away somewhere. Bags under his eyes. A waitress drops a dish cover and the sound clatters through his brain. He winces like a muscatel-soaked refugee from Skid Row. 'I have never,' he says quietly, 'been on anything like this before. I have been on trips with extraordinary people, but nothing that so totally excludes the outside world. To never get out, to never see anything... I am not used to it.'

Hotel corridors and hotel lobbies. Coffee-shop breakfasts and all-night parties and forty minutes in the afternoon to see the sights. The sharpest people don't even bother. Even within the S.T.P. party the Stones are again once removed from the outside world. After Texas, they become nearly invisible. They stay in their rooms until just before the limos leave, then sweep through the lobby and are gone. They dress in special backstage rooms where only the Inner Circle is welcome. The only time they're in plain sight is on the plane. They are total strangers in a strange

land, operating on their own time schedule, and after nearly a
month on the road, everyone around them is starting to count
the days until the four-day break that precedes the July Fourth
concert in Washington, D.C.

All they have to do is get through Alabama and they go on
vacation. The last time the Stones worked there, at Auburn University in 1969, the house was about three-quarters full, the hair
short, and the biggest cheer of the evening greeted an announcement that curfews for women had been suspended. But the
Stones have recorded some of their finest music in Muscle Shoals,
so Alabama is another place where they have spent a lot of time
without really seeing things.

Perhaps Alabama is a hard place for any outsider to know. You
come in with all these myths in your head and then see them
outside the hall, with stomachs bulging over their ammo belts,
.38 Magnums hanging obscenely off their hips, 'nigger' sticks
in their hands, baby-blue riot helmets covering their faces. Four
cops refuse to work inside the hall when told they will have to
remove their guns.

Earlier in the day Stan Moore meets with the local police captain. 'By golly,' the captain says in a high, whiney, funny cracker
voice. 'They tole me there was gonna be a colored boy to talk to
us.'

'Yessiree,' Stan says, 'I am *the* colored boy.'

'By golly,' the captain says, 'I think they're gonna take this
place apart. Stand on the chairs, and just take it apart.'

The promoter assures the police that if the kids do stand on
chairs, the building will not automatically fall down. The promoter is a colonel in the state militia and has a signed picture of
Guv-nah George Corley Wallace hanging in his office.

In the parking lot, the cops stand around in twos and threes,
nervously whipping and cracking their riot batons into the light
poles, jousting with each other like medieval knights getting loose
before a big one. 'I heah they been causin hell everywheah they
go,' one cop says. 'They bettah know we mean biziness heah.'

Over at the motel where the stage crew is staying, they've
drained the pool so that the longhairs don't foul the filtering
system. They're demanding that people come down to the desk
and pay in advance for local calls.

But the guy selling Sno-Cones in the parking lot has a beard, and he's tripping off some THC a kid from Louisiana laid on him. He says things aren't as bad as they used to be, but the cops come down on you whether you're black or white. The cop outside the stage door is fat and has grey razor-cut sideburns. He looks like a cartoonist's version of an Alabama sheriff and his given name is Joe Don. 'You can't like this kind of music, can you?' I ask him.

'Ah tolerate it,' he says kindly. 'Hell' ah been separated from mah ole lady foah more'n threee years now... you go somewheah foah a drank, it's all you heah.'

So it's not that easy to figure. One thing is for certain though. The hair in Mobile, a breezy little city across the border from Mississippi, is shorter than anywhere else on the tour. Kids have come from the entire southern tier of states, from Louisiana, Mississippi, Alabama, Georgia, and Kentucky, and the guys have their hair styled, one crinkle at the neck, one ripple over the ear, right on the borderline. It's hair that does not offend, that says, 'Hey, buddy? I work down at the garage. Do lube jobs on Saturday mornin and get black under my fingernails. So take your action somewhere else.'

Kids file respectfully down the street and obediently form lines in the soft, honeyed twilight. Kids in starched summer cottons and freshly pressed pants, kids in polished loafers, with Old Spice on their faces and Vitalis on their hair. The summer is about to open up in front of them, and some of them have come from as far away as Atlanta and Lexington. They pass by a row of peeling, ramshackle wooden houses without so much as a glance at the old black men in suits and ties who sit rocking on porches next to chipped white washing machines, waiting for the evening breeze. Little black girls in hand-me-down dresses scurry through the line and down the street, girls just beginning to sprout, with nicknames like 'Skeeter' and long skinny legs and pigtails.

At 220 Lawrence Street, three black women sit on the porch. One rocks slowly with a baby in her arms and pink rubber curlers in her hair.

'Do you know who's playing tonight?' I ask her.

'Mmmmmmmm-ehhhhh,' she shakes her head, wiggling shyly in the chair.

'Oh shoah,' one of her braver friends says. 'It's that Little Stevie Wondah.'

'My,' the one with the baby says. She smiles, and when she does, you can see that she's younger than anyone else on the porch. 'Stevie Wondah,' she says. 'Ah knew it was someone good.' Her arm jerks forward like an arrow loosed from a bow and she shakes a bottle of milk into her baby's mouth. 'Ah shoahly would lahk to go,' she says, touching a girlish hand to her curlers, as though to make certain they can be out by showtime. 'But ah heah they *awl* sold out.'

Backstage, the Assistant Mayor and Chief of Police of Mobile, Robert ('Call me Bob') Doyle ('It's a good Irish name'), has come to present the Stones with the key to the city. Keys to cities are something they have more or less stopped handing out, except to astronauts. But here is the assistant mayor in a grey suit, with a tie tack in the shape of a hand gun holding his tie in place, sonorously intoning, 'Some of mah consuvative frens have said to me, "Bob, what are you doin? Have you gone crazy?" ' The two newspaper photographers who swirled in with the assistant mayor go snap-crackle-pop with their flash bulbs to record the moment. The assistant mayor blinks, then continues. 'But ah say we got eleven thousand people out there tonaght and we got to make them happy too.' He solemnly hands out five gold keys and five leather-bound certificates to the Stones, who are standing in line like polite children on prize day at the academy. 'With that and a dahm,' the assistant mayor grins, 'y'awl can get a cup of coffee. Now ah'm goin home and lissen to mah Guy Lombardo records.'

The Stones are used to this kind of stuff, having been feted by mayors on their earliest tours, introduced to their giggling daughters, given plaques, then been told to leave town as quickly as possible. It's the kind of American tomfoolery they love, and no sooner do they get out the door than they start acting like the Monkees, biting the keys to check on their gold content.

Bobby Keys and Terry Southern have ignored the entire ceremony in one corner of the room, trying to out-Texas each other. First it's Crystal City, the spinach capital of the world, the town so funky it has a statue of Popeye in the town square, then it's Keys twanging 'Shee-yut' in an accent so thick you can ride a Palomino across it.

Terry responds with 'Fu-yuuuck,' but Keys walks off with honors by stringing, 'shee-yit fuuckdamn' together then striking a match off his thumbnail, country style, and shouting, 'Elsie? Elsie? You keep that dawg away from me now, you heah? Ah'll kill him if you don't, ah sweah.'

Southern looks at him with authentic respect when he finishes and even Keys seems a little surprised at what he's pulled out of the hat. 'Ah, yeah,' he says. 'Must be one of those black pills you gave me.'

'Shoo, boy, ah wouldn't trast you with one a them pills, you'd likely go cray-zee.'

'Ah am raght now,' Keys says. 'Outta my rabbitass mind.' He picks up a nearby bottle of Chivas Regal and takes a healthy snort. 'And about to get snot-flyin dronk too.'

Keys, a West Texas boy, from the mesquite and cotton country outside of Lubbock, has been on the road, more or less, for seventeen years. He has played his saxophone in Caspar and Laramie and Butte, in Twin Ridges and Helena, in dancehalls where fist fights spread like fire in a stand of dry timber. He has been in dozens of bands, ingested incalculable quantities of various chemical mixtures and come to believe in and live his own myth... the last of the all-out rockers.

As Bobby tells it, his life was changed that day they opened the new Humble station down the block in Slaton, Texas. Keys was eleven years old then and there was this skinny kid with glasses playing an electric guitar by the name of Buddy Holly. Buddy was in high school then, and from that day on, Keys knew he had to become a musician. By the time he was thirteen, he had a saxophone and was working Catholic weddings with someone named Stinson Baylen, who made most of his money as a plumber. Then he joined Tommy Hancock and the Roadside Playboys, who played clubs where they served real liquor. Keys was so young, he had to stay on the bandstand between sets.

'On mah thirteenth birthday,' Keys says, 'a bunch of mah frens took me to Devil's Lake, about twenty-five miles from Del Rio, Texas, and down to a whorehouse in Mexico. They got me drunk and bought me a fahv-dollah whoah. It was truly a red-letter day in mah life. Ah thought, hell, this beats shit out of Pony League baseball and the Methodist Youth Fellowship, of which ah was vice-president at the time. That got gone in a hurry.'

By the time he was fifteen, Keys had been hanging around outside the garage door watching immortals like Jerry Allison, Glenn

D. Hardin, Don Guest, and the great Buddy Holly pick and sing
for nearly four years. One day Allison called to say that Buddy
Knox, of 'Party Doll,' 'Hula Love,' and 'Think I'm Gonna Kill
Myself' fame, needed a sax player. Keys took the offer and spent
the next seven years playing six nights a week at clubs throughout the Midwest. Leaving right after shows, Keys and the other
four Rhythm Orchids would drive straight through to the next
town and pull into a rented motel room to clean up. You hung
your stage suit up on the bathroom wall while you took a shower
so the steam would take the wrinkles out. Your pants went in
between the mattress to get pressed and you used white shoe
polish to hide the grime around the collar of your shirt. Buddy,
the star, traveled separately, in his own Cadillac.

'Ah was always the youngest in the band,' Keys says. 'So ah
always had to drink more, take more pills, and get more pussy
to prove myself. Or else have to faght all the tahm. Lahk ah was
always the one who had to unload the truck, set up the lights and
the P.A. and then get Knox's suitcase out for him.'

After three and a half years with Knox, Bobby joined Bobby
Vee's band. Vee, who made 'Run to Him,' 'Rubber Ball,' and
'Take Good Care of My Baby,' hailed from Fargo, North Dakota,
and one day while Keys and the rest of the band were rehearsing
in a hotel in Moorhead, Minnesota, Fargo's twin city, this kid
came in, asking for a gig as a piano player. He said his name was
Eldon Gunn and he liked playing Hank Williams' stuff. Everyone in the band was into wide silk ties, high-collar shirts, and
Aqua-Net to keep their James Dean hairdos in place, and the kid
just didn't fit. So they told him to go home and practice some
more and come back when your act's together, and instead he
went to New York and became a folksinger by the name of Bob
Dylan.

Vee and the band worked the Dick Clark caravan, playing
behind acts like Freddy Cannon, Gene Pitney, Little Anthony
and the Imperials, Little Eva, Billy Stewart, Frankie Avalon,
Reparata and the Del-Rons. At the Teen-Age World's Fair in San
Antonio, Texas, in 1963, they were on the bill with an English
band named the Rolling Stones.

'Ah was amazed,' Keys says. 'They were the first band ah'd ever
seen who didn't wear uniforms on stage. Before the show, ah
remember Brian Jones sayin, "Look everyone else changes before

they go on." So they all switched their shirts around and they still weren't wearing the same thang. Then Jagger said, "Excuse us, but the fuckin amps keep goin out." Ah went, "Huhhh... ? He said fuck. Did you hear that? He said... fuck." It won mah heart foah-evah.'

Keys left Vee's band and went to Hollywood, where he lived on popcorn and Kool-Aid for a while then took the closest gig he could find, which was in Sioux City, Iowa. He played there half a winter, drifted to Denver, worked with an all-black band, then decided to give Hollywood another shot. He hooked up with Levon Helm, one of Ronnie Hawkins' old drummers, and began playing in a blues band with Leon Russell, Jesse Ed Davis, Gary Gilmour, and Jimmy Markham. One gig led to another, and a year and a half later, Keys met up with Delaney Bramlett, late of the Shindogs.

Delaney then met Bonnie, who'd been singing in bowling alleys. They found Bobby Whitlock, got a contract with Stax Records, and began forming a band. Keys joined, as did Jim Price, a Bible-reading Christian Scientist trumpet player from Texas. Delaney and Bonnie toured a lot, playing raw, funky rock and roll that attracted people like Eric Clapton, George Harrison, Ringo Starr, and Billy Preston all of whom sat in at one time or another.

Keys and Price left Delaney and Bonnie to join Joe Cocker's 'Mad Dogs and Englishmen' tour, an act consisting of thirty or so people that quickly became an authentic circus, with lots of talented people struggling for recognition and pushing for room on stage. Careers were created and destroyed in six weeks, and the full-length color 'documentary' of the tour reveals none of it. Not too surprisingly, Keys emerged as one of the few memorable characters in the movie and throughout the Stones' tour, Robert Frank feels him pushing to get his face and voice in front of the lens.

'Ah'll tell you about that Cocker tour, man', Keys says. 'We were given the idea everyone loves everyone, everyone works for everyone... but the things that were done to Joe Cocker during it... and especially since, are criminal. He has been used, abused, and stepped on, and he is such a beautiful cat, man, who ah love. On that tour, he was used to promote Leon Russell.'

After the tour ended, Keys began to do a lot of session work with the Stones, who discovered in him an incredible energy source, and an authentic link to the old rock and roll that Keith, in particular, feels heir to. On both the European and English tours, wherever Keys was there was a party, and sooner or later, they found something broken or had to call the manager to keep the noise down.

Being with the Stones gave Keys top-level stature in the rockbiz. Opinions as to how good a musician he really is vary, but his session rates became astronomical and people keep on calling him with work. Like anyone who comes from a town of less than seven thousand in West Texas, and finds himself being discussed on national television by Truman Capote, Keys' life becomes a mixture of the real and the calculated, the myth and reality.

'I love to play, man,' he says. 'That's what I am. Music is me. I go crazy on the road, sure, but what the hell, man, you might as well have a good time doin it. I like to stretch out a little. After seventeen years, I figure I deserve it... get high and what the hell... I live for today, man. That's all.'

Keys on the road is like no one else, with the possible exception of Keith, but when so many weird and twisted things happen, it's a life style worth considering. After the concert in Mobile is over, the plane returns to New Orleans and the band goes looking for something to eat in the French Quarter. The gurus of America, who come out at night, are most easily found in jails, parking lots, all-night laundromats and restaurants that don't close. At four in the morning, a high-stepping black man carrying a paper cup of beer comes into where the Stones are sitting.

'Evenin,' he says, looking the table up and down and giving no sign that he's recognized anyone. 'You people all *on* somethin, ain't you? I can tell. Ah'm a musician mahself. Blew a concert in be-flat this mornin myself.'

No one knows what that means, so Charlie Watts tells him to sit down and have a beer. 'Yeah,' the cat sighs. 'Dig it. Ah come down heah to play New Year's Eve and got so high ah ain't left since. Can you imagine? They even used to let you have real glasses to carry the beer down the street, but it's paper now. You can buy it on but you can't get no light bulbs, dig?'

No one does.

'Like this. They got a law on it. If your lights go out, you in the dark for the weekend but feelin' fine fine fine. On the otha hand, if you in Georgia you all right, more or less. Lightbulbs to spare, but no beer to be seen.'

'Who you play with, man?' Charlie asks.

'Aw, me? Play all kinds a shit. Philly Groove, the 'Fonics, "La-la means I Love You"... ah play with Isaac Hayes, man. Thirty-five pieces, two trumpets who can *read* and no filibusterin. Charts, you dig? You ever make it to the Apple, check out Orry's on 125th. Man will cut you some bad vines.

'Wot's 'ee talkin about?' Bill Wyman says helplessly. Charlie shrugs his shoulders and leans forward, fascinated.

'With Isaac now we open on this bald head in the spotlight, everyone thinkin it's Ike only it ain't. Chick who's gone clean shaven like him. The music comes in, da-*da*-da-*da*-da-*da*...'

'Wot's 'ee doin bass lines for?' Wyman says. 'Why do they all do bass lines?'

'Who's the drummer then?' Charlie asks.

'Shhh. Not now, man. I'm just gettin to the part where Ike comes in.' He raps it down for another fifteen minutes or so, smiling pleasantly, bobbing his head, laying down an open palm every now and then for a pound.

'Aw, man,' he says. reluctantly getting to his feet. 'It's been so fine bein wit you cats tonight. Wit musicians it's always *cool*. You kin always ree-late right away. You dig?'

'Haven't got a clue,' Wyman shrugs, going back to his clams.

'Well, I can't imagine who's going to be there,' Truman Capote says very quietly in the hotel lobby the next morning. 'Tuscaloosa's only three hundred miles from Mobile and school's been out for two weeks. You know, my grandfather was president of the university there for twenty-two years.'

'Peter and I are leaving, yes...but we will see you *all* in New York.'

With Capote gone, the tour has to look to itself for a new source of gossip and conversation and the leading subject is the doctor. In a time-honored tradition that has always surrounded the Stones, he is being sucked deeply into the vortex of the rock madness. People who usually get crazy near the Stones do so because of unlimited access to drugs. The doctor, however, is spacing out on ladies, who are only too happy to accept his invitation to go back to the hotel and meet the boys. For someone who's grown up in the antiseptic, slightly puritan suburbs of America, being out on the road with the Stones is like having the key to the candy store. It doesn't stop, and they come in all flavors.

Stumbling toward Nashville, with that four-day break shining up ahead like an oasis. The Tuscaloosa concert is jam-packed, with dope-smoking, pony-tailed kids who must have come out of the hills somewhere, but it's no more than a quick flash. The goal is to get out of Alabama and back to civilization without anything untoward happening.

The S.T.P. bus gets stuck in a snarl of traffic outside the hall after the concert. When Rudge tries to get a cop to help, the cop drawls, 'Ah doan give a fuck if you make yoah plane or not. You the same to me as anyone else.'

Incompetence. Rudge is surrounded by it. As heat lightning cracks in the blue-black sky and the bus stands mired, Rudge can almost hear the jet straining its engines for take-off at the little airport outside town. He shouts, 'Driver, use the other lane. I'll run out in front and clear it for us.' Rudge hops off the bus and runs pell-mell into the crowd. The bus begins inching down the street. Rudge leaps back on, smiling, and no sooner does the bus get free of traffic than the driver notes, 'Ah believe ah got me a flat.'

'No you don't,' Rudge says.

'This isn't happening,' Jo Bergman says, secretly glad because it's starting to feel a little like a rock and roll tour again.

'C'mannnnn,' Willie the baggage man says in that tone Manhattan taxi drivers use to explain illegal left turns to helpless pedestrians. 'You got plenty more tyres where that one came from. Keep drivin.'

'Ah believe it's gone to smokin on me,' the driver says quietly. He coasts it into a gas station by the side of the road and everyone piles out and sure enough one rear tyre is crushed and mangled and smoking like crazy and this is it. Rudge and his S.T.P. machine have been stopped dead. A breakdown in procedure. Stranded in an Alabama gas station. People start playing with the robotlike machine that dispenses the barbecue chips, looking at the grease rack and digging on how the weird green neon light distorts your face and makes it all runny and whoosh-y. Rudge takes one look at the pack of drugged somnambulists he's carrying around and runs off down the highway for help.

'Oh, wow,' somebody oh wows. 'We're okay now. The cops are here.'

Tyres screeching, red beams whirling, two Alabama State Police cars pull into the station. With S.T.P. immunity, as though they were hailing taxis outside the Plaza, everyone jumps in and the cars pull out for the airport. 'Think they'll legalize marijuana soon?' Robert Frank asks the cop who's driving his car.

The cop driving the other car has just come on to the midnight shift after spending the day pushing his rig back from Florida. He's got a bull neck, ox arms, razored sideburns, and weighs a good 240 pounds. Donald Nathan. Used to run to Los Angeles, make it in three and a half days, keepin eyes wide open, stickin to the back road so he wouldn't get weighed, forty-four thousand pounds of lumber at 107 miles an hour ooo-whee rammin it to the floor pushin the limit and they'd take him down in Texas regular for it.

Ole Donnie runs his wildcat rig all day then reports in for work on the graveyard shift as an officer of the law. A man's got to make some side money these days, he says.

'Bet you eat a lot of them white pills, hali?' someone says, getting smart.

'What?' Donnie says.

' I said, I bet....'

'Ah heard what you said, boy. Say it again and you be standin by that store watching me drive by. The poleese is here to help people. You remember that.'

Yessir, yessir, Yes Sir. We all gonna get our minds right real soon. We promise.

'Hey,' Gary Stromberg says helpfully. 'What kinda truck you drive? A Mack?'

The police cars storm into the airport and slam to a stop one behind another. Lightning is crackling, thunder booming, and great drops of rain are about to soak the green fields and red mud around the landing strip.

Rudge arrives last, hair streaming wet, in an open Chevy truck, having run into the first bar he could find for help. Long hair, funny accent. 'Excuse me, I've got a group of people who've done a concert and are stranded. I wonder could you help?' and half the place turned out to lend a hand.

The plane taxis into the rain and lifts off and it's as though some kind of victory has been won. Charlie Watts grabs Alan Dunn's ankles and together they go tumbling head over heels down the center aisle of the plane. High-school gymnastics at nineteen thousand feet and the next time Mr. Watts comes down the aisle he is looking very cool and dignified. 'Alan?' he says, with the aplomb of a young Ronald Colman. 'Alan? I say... apparently we've been asked to leave this place.'

The first half of the tour is over.

Book Two

Chapter Eight — JULY

Changes... Sure, I was completely mad. I go crazy.

MICK JAGGER

By this time in the tour, one month after it has begun, it's hard to pretend anymore. The thrill is gone. All of the things that were going to happen on the road have already happened at least a thousand times. The various celebrities have departed, not to return until New York. What remains before then is a solid month of gigs, of getting up on stage each night and making the fifteen-song set sound fresh, which is the basic showbiz proposition... go out there and break a leg, kid.. make 'em laugh or cry, get 'em off, no matter how many times you've done it before.

'You've done it and done it and done it and you still got fifty more dates to do,' Charlie Watts says. 'You get so well played in, I'm sittin there thinkin I've already played that lick and helped that number along and we haven't even come to it yet.' For the tour's final three weeks, Nicky Hopkins finds himself playing the same riffs every night, note for note, as though he were plugged into a piano roll device.

The boredom is everywhere. It greets you in the morning when you awake in yet another strange town and tucks you in at night when you try to come down from being wired and get some sleep. It is impossible to maintain your sanity or your basal metabolism on the road, and the changes that come down are invariably harder on the supporting S.T.P. personnel than on the band. Marshall Chess is on his way to losing twenty one pounds, Gary Stromberg thirty one. Chris O'Dell will become in the weeks to come—although it does not seem humanly possible—even thinner than when she came on the tour in Tucson.

At least the musicians know why they are there. Every night they climb up on stage and have thousands of people shout out their names, scream adulation at them and tell them for that one moment at least they are GOD, all that is important in the world.

'People who are going up on that stage every night can take a lot more of that shit,' Keith Richard says. 'First of all because they're getting constant exercise and pushing themselves to the limit and expecting it... but the people hanging around, watching the show and getting stoned, that's another thing. 'Cause there's no point of release for them. It seems to go on and on without there being a highlight to the day.'

After a show, in the empty 3:00A.M. hotel corridors of America, there's nothing to do but take another pill, smoke another joint, do another line, and try to find something to spend the night with. Ramada Inns, Holiday Inns, Sheraton Motor Inns, they all blur into one great antiseptic room with the pebbled carpet worn by the door and someone's scarf thrown over the bedlamp for atmosphere. No matter how high you get, it's still like being inside a bottle of Listerine, the plain green and clean white, plastic-coated, wood-finished walls and ceilings, the furniture with no sharp edges or too-bright colors that might disturb the inmates. The very space you occupy, with its restful institutional blandness, makes you eager for any kind of rush.

The doping intensifies to the point where people's faces begin to change shape, the skin tightening around their mouths and eyes and the flesh disappearing from under their cheekbones to give them that gaunt, wasted look so favored in high-fashion circles. Some people do no more than drink a lot of beer, smoke too many cigarettes, and take an occasional white to stay up. Others use the tour as an excuse to plumb the limits of inner space. In American 1972, the style is to mix your poisons completely, various drugs as well as large amounts of whiskey.

'I think it's completely wrong,' Jagger would say after the tour was over, 'to get totally fucked up and go out and play. I mean, I disagree fundamentally. The thing for me is to be as straight as possible. I'm not sayin I have to be completely straight; when I say straight I mean not fucked up in me head. Not that I wouldn't take a beer or get a bit drunk, but I never went on stage loaded. That is out of control. Never once. How could I?'

On tour, whatever you want is available. Five bottles of Demetol and a bottle of five hundred Quaaludes and now they're all gone; a quart-sized jar of coke just for an energizer; four Quaaludes to get to sleep, but if you start to speed on them drop a Placedyl—they use them for bad acid trips or nervous breakdowns; five hundred dollars of coke laid out in a four-foot line on a mirror and they did it all up; one guy keeps his stash in a rubber—calls it *real* prophylactic medicine, ha-ha.

Although the gap between performer and audience on this tour was firmly reestablished, a throwback to the pre-1967 days of flower-power equality, there was a meeting point in terms of drug access and abuse. For the first time ever, the children of America were able to cop, in their very own neighborhoods, the very same drugs that showbiz people had known about for years. Which made the 'Hey, man, try some of my shit—it's dynamite' rap dominate everywhere. Much in the way their fathers argued over the relative merits of Chivas and Cutty and forced the good stuff on guests, all the nouveau dopers wanted to impress the S.T.P honchos with both quality and weight. In order to reestablish the performer-audience drug-access gap and completely blow the minds of any 'freaks' who might wander on to the tour, the S.T.P.-preferred drug became amyl nitrate.

Amyl nitrate, or more properly amyl nitrite ($C_5H_{11}NO_2$), is described in medical dictionaries as being 'a flammable, clear, yellowish liquid with a peculiar, ethereal, fruity odor.' Amys act as a motor depressant and as a vasodilator in cases of angina pectoris. They ease the severe pain caused by the heart attack. In recent years, the medical profession has turned to more sophisticated means for dealing with heart seizures and amys have been taken over by those who use drugs for more quantitative purposes.

Known as 'snappers' on the East Coast and 'poppers' in the West, amys were the perfect hipster drug of the fifties. They could then be bought without prescription at most corner drugstores (a prescription is usually required now, though they can be obtained over-the-counter in out-of-the-way places) and employed during the act for those who desired extra acceleration at that all-important final moment. Amys are so noxious, carbolic, and obviously chemical that no one had thought to go on using them in any great quantity, until the tour.

Amys and coke, like tequila and grenadine or Kahlua and

cream, became the 'in' combination. So it was all you drank on top of all you'd smoked, whatever you'd snorted—some whites, a red, a shot—it was though there were not enough chemicals in all the world to blot out the pain of just being alive. En route first class through America, in another city, another day was about to begin. Getting fucked up seemed as good a way to relate to it as any.

You put the stage on second base and erect fences to keep the kids on the infield. You take the sound off the pneumatic lift platforms and put it on the scaffold. Drive the lift platforms back to the running track and put the arc lights on it and use them as light platforms with steel fencing to stop anyone from climbing up. Outdoors, you've got a double system for sound, so you get nice side fill. Comfortable...

At least that's how the Monck says you set up Robert F. Kennedy Stadium in Washington, D.C., for a July Fourth Rolling Stones' concert that will be attended by forty-seven thousand people. This is the four-day break everyone's been waiting for and while the Stones and some of the Inner Circle sit sipping rum punches and gin-and-tonics on a beach in the Virgin Islands, Monck is hard at work in Washington, doing his Woodstock construction number, sweating buckets in the sticky city heat to set up a concert that, on paper, makes Altamont look like a D.A.R. picnic.

Originally, Rudge and the boys wanted to play in the afternoon, with Mick dressed in a Revolutionary War uniform, and lots of fireworks and a genuine festival feel to the whole thing. But negotiations and conferences and hassles pushed the concert to the night of the Fourth, and it takes no great perception to see that in Washington, the nation's largest black city as well as its beloved capital, this means trouble. The prestigious *Washington Post* has assigned an entire bureau of people to cover it, and David Brinkely is in the press box. In back of everyone's mind is: If anyone is going to shoot Jagger, what better place than this? It's in the same general area where they did Wallace barely two months ago, and what's to stop some hard-faced Maryland malcontent who's had it up to here with all this hippie bullshit from opening up with a twenty-two? What's to stop some strung-out ghetto kid or white freak? What's to stop some good American from going plumb crazy on the day of his nation's birth, and killing somebody to celebrate?

So it is Monck's responsibility and Rudge's obsession to see that none of these nightmares become reality. Since one of the causes of the Altamont debacle is now generally conceded to have been the height of the stage (or, more properly, the lack of height, somewhere around three feet), the local promoters are taking no chances. Monck considers the ideal height for a deck to be from four-foot-seven to four-foot-nine. The Washington stage will be nine feet high.

On the front of the stage will be something called Robert strip, which is a row of number-twelve carpet tacks set at a forty-five degree angle, with the nails pointing toward the act. The strip is supposed to discourage idle hands and bodies from clambering up during performance time. On the night of the concert, Monck will rip up as much of it as he can and go to the trouble of telling the crowd the strip is not the work of the Stones' organisation, but it will still cause trouble.

Moreover, a device such as Robert strip is the worst kind of offence to a man like Monck who has showbiz credentials as long as each of his sinewy arms. Beginning at the Village Gate in the early sixties where he lit all the jazz heavies (and beneath which Bob Dylan beat Chip's typewriter half to death writing 'Chimes of Freedom' and 'Hollis Brown' in his apartment), Monk has lit the Newport Folk and Jazz festivals and the Fillmore East. With Miriam Makeba, he's worked in Kenya for Tom Mboya and then in Ghana with Kwame Nkrumah, then in Tanzania with Julius Nyerere. He has been more or less responsible for the stagecraft at the three watershed festivals of the sixties—Monterey Pop (where the culture surfaced and came to an end), Woodstock (where *The New York Times* decided it began), and Altamont (where the media gave up hope).

Now he traveled with as much immunity as anyone in America could muster, so far over on his side of the seesaw that he was touchable; so centered in his dedication to the band and the ideal of always putting on the best show that he *knew* how that nothing was impossible. While checking into the hotel in Washington, someone points out to the Monck that the decor of his room is, well, hotel standard and a bit tacky. Especially offensive, when considered in the light of an amy. Monck surveys the situation, sees what the observer means and unplugs a lamp and throws it out the window, five stories down into a courtyard. The manager comes quickly.

'Did you throw your lamp out your window?' he demands, trembling, on the brink of apoplexy. Hoodlums. Long-haired hoodlums.

'I want a lamp in this room,' Monck says, in a voice so respectable it would cause waiters at La Grenocalle to jump. 'Immediately.'

'I ah... look here, sir... we just saw a lamp....'

'Do you expect me to stand here and listen to your problems? There is no lamp in this room. I will require a lamp in order to be able to do the great quantity of work that faces me. Because you are the manager of this hotel, I am requiring your assistance by asking you to send a lamp to my room. Is that clear?'

'It is, yessir,' and although it is also perfectly clear that Monck has thrown the lamp out of the window in the first place, there is something about him that makes it not a crime to do it. He is very clearly one of those people who is above or beyond or just plain outside the law. No more than five minutes later the bellhop comes trundling upstairs with a new lamp.

Monck lives out his life in a beautiful Fabian dream of the way things ought to be. His idea of outside security at concerts is to hang giant speakers on the walls so that those without tickets would be able to hear. In order to lessen the anxiety with which the crowds approach the Stones' concerts, he once suggested that the band go on the road with a string of flatbed railroad cars and a midway. The midway would be set up outside a fairground where the Stones would stay for a week or so, playing often enough so that everyone who was interested in seeing them could do so easily, with none of the pressure that attends a one-night stand like the Washington gig.

A massive rainstorm the day before the concert does nothing to cool the city or make staging any easier. The hot humid East Coast summer bubble envelops Washington. Windows are open, cars cruise the streets with their radios blaring, and the kids camped on line outside the stadium have their heads pillowed on portable radios and cassette players. It's Stones Stones Stones and occasionally the song of the summer, the Cornelius Brothers and Sister Rose singing, 'It's too late to turn back now/I believe, I believe, I believe/I'm fallin in love.'

In the Stones' hotel, a briar patch of media people from New York and points East have flown in for the concert. Marjoe, the evangelist who shimmies like Michael Philip, is about, as are Ethan Russell, Annie Leibovitz, and an assortment of New York and London writers. Terry Southern is holding court. ' "Terrah," the great Faulkner said to me once at a dinner party in New York,' he tells Gary Stromberg, ' "Teraah? What *was* that sayin so favohed in the court of Napoleon? Ah, yes, now it comes to me... claret foah women, bohgundy foah men, and brandah foah heroes. Will you join me in another one?"....'

The doors to the stadium are opened in the afternoon. The hardcore kids have been waiting on the home plate side, figuring that's where they'll start letting people in, but instead they roll back a bleacher gate. The first few kids shuffle in, expecting to find the place half-filled already. Instead, it's empty. They find themselves all alone on the green well-manicured turf that seems to roll away for a good mile before it hits the stands. They bound, actually leap with joy at their good fortune, and then tear ass across the field toward the stage to get right down in front where you can see and hear better than any place else.

Which is not the way it works. With the stage so high and the crowd very drunk, there is a constant push toward the stage. It is the same desire to get close to the glitter that kept forcing the crowd forward at Altamont, the need to get near, to touch, to get a stronger hit off the energy. The push is so heavy that the kids all the way down front, fanaticos all, unshaven, funky, stoned from days of camping and waiting on line, are pushed so far forward they can't see a thing. Five hundred of them, denied access.

They begin trying to gain the stage. They climb on each other's shoulders and find it's possible to stand up there right in the spotlights, between the two monitors that allow Jagger to hear what he's singing. As soon as anyone makes a move toward them, they just let go and fall backward into the crush of people underneath the stage apron. Soon enough, kids find out that with a coat or a t-shirt under you, it's possible to support yourself on the Robert strip, except that your arms get kind of torn up. By the time the Stones come out, the front part of the white stage is blood red. The stadium looks like a painting by Hieronymus Bosch. Kids are heaving bottles and lobbing mattes of Japanese firecrackers and cherry bombs out of the upper-deck on to the groundlings below. A girl has the side of her face blown up. Chip gets hit with a bottle. Annie Leibovitz takes to ducking behind the amps every time Jagger dances over to her side of the stage.

It's frightening. All that energy, all those eyes, all those arms and voices and minds focused on one tiny, jumping-jack figure in a white rhinestone outfit. Because it's dark, Jagger can't see the house. He can't make the people get up and dance when he wants them to because most of them are too far away to see him clearly. They're also tired and drunk. Kids keep coming up onto the stage and getting tangled in the cables, crashing into the amps and being thrown off by the stage crew. It doesn't have the raunchy rock and roll feel it did in Chicago. It's out of control and terrifying, and the band rushes through the set with Jagger in a hurry to finish and get off.

When it's over, the Monck, for one, is more than happy to be moving on, into the unspectacular really-on-the-road section of concerts in Norfolk, Charlotte and Knoxville. Just before the 'out' is finished (the dismantling of the stage), a kid comes up to him and tells him something which he finds hard to believe… he goes over to a girl and asks her and she confirms it. The Monck learns that, as the band lurched through the set for the twenty-ninth time, in the tangle of sweaty human flesh in front of the stage, with their backs against the deck, two people made, what is usually referred to in politer circles as, love. 'Fucking,' the Monck would say afterward. 'Fucking… while I'm running around like crazy trying to make sure the lights are going to black at the right time.'

'We are about to hit the nadir of the tour as far as hotels are concerned,' Jo Bergman's newsletter warns after the Knoxville concert. 'We really did try… but due to circumstances, even Holiday Inns were unavailable, so we're stuck.' As the sine curve of offstage life reaches its low point, the music on stage peaks. In Norfolk and Charlotte and Knoxville, the set seems to fly from beginning to end, the musicians completely locked into one another and on time, like a championship team in its finest, most fluid moments. But only people who listen, like Ian Stewart, and the Stones themselves and their supporting musicians, are aware of the magic that's going down. Everyone else is either worrying about logistics or trying to find a way to get off.

'Being on the road,' Jagger will say, 'one's responsible to the band. You're married to them all and you're responsible for their health and well-being. What you do affects them and what they do affects you. If you step off the line and decide to take a year off, it affects everyone. If you take three months off, it affects everyone....'

After a decade of doing it, the Stones have evolved what must be the basis of any long-term marriage—a laissez-faire detente in which each partner is free to do what he likes within specific boundaries. In a place like St. Louis, where the blah level is right up at the ceiling, you need that kind of arrangement to keep individuals from going for each other's throats out of boredom.

'St. Louis?' Monck will say after the tour. 'Maybe you should say nothing happened in St. Louis. Oh, dear. Can you tell me what the hall looked like? If I could remember the hall. I remember Kansas City. Ah, whoa, wait a minute, it's coming back to me. Right. They had this horrible little bar with captain's chairs. They couldn't mix anything correctly. A gentleman from there sent me an "Eat More Possum" shirt which, when put in, the wash, all of the lettering came off. We put someone into the fountain outside of the hotel and the old ladies sitting around it paid no attention to us at all.'

In St. Louis, on the eighth day of July, the Stones try to make their ghetto move for ribs and barbecue only to have a limousine driver tell them, 'You crazy? No one goes to East St. Louis. People don't even walk there. They got snipers just sittin in the windows, waitin.' The band gets together with Stevie Wonder and together they rehearse an encore number consisting of 'Uptight' and 'Satisfaction' played by both bands, two drummers, horns-a-plenty and bongos, which is certain to kill 'em in New York.

People have taken to passing a butter plate of white powder in public, at restaurants, the theory being that if you do it with enough style and Ian, it is possible to snort anything without anyone taking undue notice. Jo Bergman and the Tac Squad get into a shaving cream and ice cream soda fight in the hotel drugstore. Not very classy, but it kills half an hour. But it's boring. One morning two S.T.P. dudes go out to do their wash. They get picked up by a chick who says she's a television actress. She does commercials, she says. Why don't you use my washing machine, she says. Let me make you breakfast, she says, and, uh, the machine is upstairs. By the time the guy with the laundry comes back from stuffing it into the washer, the actress and his S.T.P. co-worker are naked, with the guy sitting on her chest while she does him. So he rips off his clothes and does her. 'Wow,' he tells his friend when it's over, 'I thought you'd never get done, man. I couldn't take it much longer.' Then he does her a couple more times.

Her friends come over. They're seventeen years old and into shooting Preludin, which is speed in pill form that you have to mash up to cook and then strain through cotton. They've got a sixteen-year-old chick with them who cops for everybody by stealing prescriptions and robbing drugstores. An S.T.P. dude asks them how much they shoot. As much as they can get, they answer. Wow, he thinks, what a non-quantitative trip.

In St. Louis, Jagger stays holed up in his room, insulated. It is kind of a test of inner strength on the road to see how long you can take the confines of your own little cubicle before you break down and make a phone call to find out where the party is, which starts the merry-go-round all over again. Charlie Watts for one, even as long as he's been traveling, can't abide it. He'd rather be almost anywhere, talking to someone, anyone, than just locked in there, with the television on, alone.

Jagger is as good at hiding as you can get. Why bother to go out? Like, what for? Speed, shaving-cream orgies, and coke? On national television, the Democrats are trying to deny George McGovern the delegates he won in California while the Stones worked Winterland. Politicians are making jackasses of themselves in living color and Jagger is fascinated. 'This iss unbelievable,' he says. 'This is unn-real, inn't it?'

Sleepy and barefoot, in his room with the television on, Jagger is asked for some quotable statements. An interview is always an opportunity for him to perform.

'Ai've a terrible memory, y'know,' he says, yawning, 'and ai cahn't remember at all what happened on the las tour. A few gigs ai can recall... the Garden, Altamont, L.A., Chicago vaguely... it all blurs after a while.' He grins. 'Fuckin good audiences all the way on this one though. Bit a cryin for "Sympathy for the Devil" which ai've forgotten completely. 'Ow's that one go again... Yeah,

mebbe we could do a long version of it for Nixon or something...'

His wife, Bianca, has departed. 'Ah,' he'll say afterward, 'I find
it very difficult to travel with anyone on tour. Bianca's easier than
some people, but I'm just completely alone on tour. I just have to
be on my own.

'Lemme see,' he says now, trying to recollect, 'South was all
right, seein longhairs where there weren't any las time, though ai
doan know if that means a thing. We're all gettin tired now is
the truth. It's the gritty part where ya got to really pull yerself.
together...

'Madison Square Garden looks to be the big one, though I'm
not lookin forward any to Akron. The Rubber Bowl, is it? God!
By the time we get to New York...,' he shrugs and makes a gesture to indicate how hopeless it is to make forecasts, how even
Jagger cannot know what Jagger will be doing a month from
now. 'Maybe ai'il stand on my head, pull off all me clothing...
'Opefully, by that time, ai'll be completely mad.'

The observation is dutifully reported in *Rolling Stone* and a
month later in New York it will be picked up by the Daily News
and used to hype the final performance by the rock band that
even America's largest-circulation newspaper has somehow come
to approve.

Ohio follows St. Louis, and the strange time warp that is middle
America envelops the Stones. Wherever they go the crowds are
long-haired, suntanned, barefoot, in faded work shirts, with the
smell of grass and patchouli oil hanging over everything. And
yet nothing has changed. The police have their hair at the prescribed 1953 level and their heads in the Eisenhower administra-
tion, when torpor ruled the land and Patti Page was a pop star.

Someone puts a pipe bomb under the stage in the Rubber Bowl
and the four plywood panels that once were the deck become
toothpicks. No one's hurt. The Rubber Bowl is the home of
the Box Derby, a particularly ingenuous all-American event that
gives kids a chance to win money and scholarships by whoosh-
ing down a steep ramp at high speeds in devices of their own
making.

Only now these kids, who still go to the Burger King for a
couple of Whoppers and a choc shake so thick the spoon stands

up in it, and whose younger brothers build soapbox racers and whose sisters keep diaries, have replaced that illicit six-pack in the back seat with the nickel bat and the occasional red. And when several thousand of them mass outdoors, at night, to see a legendary band, in the presence of policemen who consider any chemical input outside of Miller's and Budweiser a felony offense, another kind of derby is certain to begin.

A few songs into Stevie Wonder's set, a pair of policemen move in on some dope smokers, make the mistake of moving in too deep, and find themselves surrounded. The kids, who are not too stoned to react to the prodding of billy clubs and orders barked from behind visored helmets, pull off the cops' helmets, beat them with bottles and knock them down, then throw away the bottles and move off before they can unholster their revolvers.

Calls for assistance come squawking out of the intercoms and walkie-talkies and forty cops with riot shields and clubs at the ready move to clear out the crowd. In a month's time, the Akron cops will accomplish the difficult but not impossible task of pushing around Grace Slick and Paul Kantner of the Jefferson Airplane and hurting one of their roadies, an act so outrageous that it causes a furor of shock and sympathy in hip San Francisco. It is a veritable throwback to the days when bands were hassled regularly by police, rather than treated like moneyed aristocrats.

From his position by the piano on stage, Monck sees the cops fan out through the crowd and begin beating people, indiscriminately. The violence spreads like a drop of oil in solution. He grabs the nearest microphone, orders Stevie's band to stop the music and booms, 'It is my suggestion that you allow the officers to move in as far as they feel it necessary. My requirement is that you allow them to pass. I strongly suggest that you do not raise a finger. When they are certain you are not a threat, they will leave the field. WE WILL NOW WAIT UNTIL SUCH TIME AS THE OFFICERS LEAVE THE FIELD.'

'RIGHT ON!' the crowd bellows, having found an onstage ally. Kids shaking fists, glaring, miniconfrontations all over the soapbox field as the cops continue to move to the aid of their wounded colleagues.

'*Gentlemen,*' Monck says, addressing the armed forces, 'the group is waiting, we are prepared to continue. WILL YOU ALLOW US TO CONTINUE?'

'RIGHT ON,' the crowd shouts on cue, as though from a soundtrack, as Monck continues to talk, doing a play-by-play of the police's every move, requesting them to leave while talking the crowd through a potential riot situation until the boys in blue withdraw and the show continues as planned, a minor Monck triumph.

'If you realize that someone requires something and you ask for it in their name,' Monck will say afterward, 'there is no "No." The Stones give me the excuse to be what I would have been anyway had I the substance or the literal cube of measurement to do it...' Which is the Monckian way of saying that if and when the Stones are concerned, enough desire and energy can accomplish miracles. It can even keep you involved through unending, drawn-out days of boredom.

Not everyone is locked in and holding up like Monck. Marshall Chess, who thought the tour was going to be one great joyride, who before it began felt like Mike Todd handling the storm of requests for tickets, is depressed. The tour is the hardest thing he's ever had to do. He's not eating when he wants to eat or sleeping when he wants to sleep. 'I have this thing,' he would say, 'this thing that I'm me. On the tour, I wasn't able to be me. I had to do what the tour wanted. But the tour was what Mick wanted, so that's what I was doing. For two or three weeks I could have handled it, but then it got heavy and depressed me... It was a drag.'

Chess is burning the candle at all ends, staying up all night with the band to party, then getting up early in the morning to field calls from New York about the progress of the film and the live tour album. He's losing weight and taking sleepers at night to come down from being wired. He's smoking one untipped Pall Mall after another, after having actually managed to quit completely during therapy.

In St. Louis, he gets an idea. He's seen the cover of a reissue of a Robert Johnson album that shows the man who is said to have sold his soul to the devil to learn the blues singing into a microphone in a hotel room. Perfect, Marshall figures. He has a ten-thousand-dollar mobile recording unit made up and delivered to Keith Richard's room to get him doing acoustic numbers late at night and pick up sound for a total aural documentary of what's going on. But the unit has to he shipped right back out to the

Coast to be put into a cabinet and more disaster will befall it when it gets to Detroit. It will never be used at all.

Marshall can't catch a break. He's dropped out of the swirling churning move that is the rockbiz in an attempt to gain some perspective on his own life, and if you don't play the game with your life, you get left behind. Marshall is no longer the boy who was programmed to be a record company president, whose bar mitzvah was attended by Jerry Wexler and Ahmet Erteg n.

'He has become laid-back, not so terribly paranoid and unfortunately cautious,' Chip Monck would say of him after the tour. 'There's no spark out of Marshall, there's no craziness and Marshall's craziness served the Stones. It might have eaten him up while it was servicing them... but... he has gone through an entire metamorphosis. He was a hustler, acquainted with the street... he was Chicago, the South Side... and the world of black records none of us really knew.

'Now I don't play with Marshall any more. There are no more games in his life. For him, he is in better condition. For the group, he isn't.'

After having gone to Jagger when he heard the Stones wished to start their own label in 1969 and presenting impeccable credentials, a lifetime's worth of knowledge about record marketing and sales gimmicks and angles, Chess went on the European tour that spring for only a week or so and then got so absolutely into the chaotic adventures and mad rambling that he, like Monck, began dealing from the top of the deck. A year later, Marshall and Jo Bergman ran the English tour. Marshall made a concentrated effort to get to know each of the Stones personally and because the effort was sincere, and because Marshall found himself getting off on Mick and Keith as the freest people he'd ever met, he was accepted. He got as close to the boys as any non-Stone ever did. After a while, it became apparent that he could not be them and, indeed, did not want to be. Somewhere in this set of very strong personalities, he was going to have to step back from the role of employee and find his own.

'Because when I go somewhere,' Chess will say, 'it gets to be a horror show. How's Mick? Where's Mick? What's he doing? It's sickening after a while.'

As a man who has put his time in, who has served and has a position close to the star, Marshall wants to be treated in the

manner to which he feels he is entitled. He is sensitive about
his edges and unwilling to relinquish the privileges of rank. It is
inevitable that he and Rudge will become adversaries who respect
each other but live in a totally divergent manner. So too with
Chip. Marshall tends to annoy him by trespassing on his turf; by
usurping his position at the piano during the Stones' set. Of such
things are showbiz disputes made.

Caught somewhere between the Rudge-Monck-Marshall split
is Jo Bergman, who has been in the rockbiz as long as the Stones
and has seen managers come and go—Brian Epstein, Andrew
Oldham, Allen Klein, Ronnie Schneider. Despite it all, she is
still emotionally involved, concerned about the Stones as people,
wonderfully crazy people. It is the craziness that Jo loves, and giggling away madly, she can tell you all about the time in Rome
during the European tour when the water ran out in the hotel;
everything was black, white, and green, and the police tied up the
baggage truck, issued a warrant for Jagger's arrest that only Anita
could translate (cursing in three languages), as Mick jumped over
the back wall and ran downtown for lunch.

But this time around there aren't that many funny stories for
Jo to remember. 'It wasn't fun,' she'll say afterward. 'And it wasn't
supposed to be. Be efficient, make money, and don't hurt anyone.
That was the given system.' For someone in as deep as she is,
five years in, who has suffered with the band since the days when
things were a lot less respectable and a lot more spontaneous, it
hurts. It has almost become a job.

As Rudge will say, 'So many people with the Stones get emotionally involved. They want to hang out and be with them.
The only thing I found out right away was the power they have
to completely eat people up. It's them, they're powerful, and I
fought that one right along.

'Because this business is a drug. I saw what it did to people
on the tour... the doctor standin in the bar tellin people about
what colour socks Mick wore in his room back in Kansas City.
The only thing I value about this business is my independence.
Without the right to get up and say "That's it; I'm going" I'm
useless...'

So as the S.T.P. caravan moves through the dog days of July,
with nothing so very exciting going on, the tension within the
travelling company begins to build. An internal storm is brew-

ing. 'Last time,' Jo Bergman would say, 'everything went wrong outside, so it was *us* against *them*. This time it was all so smooth that after a while it had to get hairy.' So smooth. Like a peaceful mountain lake that's so calm it gets on your nerves, so placid that it makes you want to pick up the nearest, biggest rock you can find and fling it as hard as you can. Just to make some waves.

FINANCIAL REPORT—MONEY TALKS, NOBODY WALKS

How is it possible to come this far into the journey without discussing the *raison d'etre* for the trip, the glittering pot of gold that lies in wait at the end of the rainbow road: money?

The S.T.P. minstrels are not Ken Kesey's Pranksters, out to blow the straights' minds by playing flutes on top of Day-Glo buses, nor are they the League, moving East toward spiritual enlightenment. They are Sunday Promotions, a New York-based corporation with accountants and lawyers, attempting to establish a blue-ribbon credit rating and come away with a healthy profit.

The Stones themselves are contracted to a Netherlands-based corporation called Promo-Tours. Sunday Promotions, the firm formed for the express purpose of running the tour, signs a contract to pay Promo-Tours so much money per concert, based on a guarantee or a percentage of the gross, whichever is higher. In most cases, it is the percentage, usually 70 percent of the gate, with the remaining 30 percent going to the promoter. Out of that, he must pay all his expenses and can reasonably expect to come away with around $5,000 profit per Rolling Stones show.

With tickets at $6.50 each, most concerts gross roughly $100,000, some more, some a lot less. In some places, the Stones work for 60 or 65 percent of the take. In a very small hall, like the Hollywood Palladium, they are there for a set fee. You pay Sunday Promotions, you get the Stones, you keep the gross. A top promoter, like Bill Graham, has yet another kind of deal, whereby Sunday Promotions pays his expenses and he works for a set fee, thereby minimizing his risk and guaranteeing a profit.

Originally, it is estimated that the tour will gross $2.9 million and that expenses will be somewhere around $900,000 before payment to Promo-Tours for the Stones' services which, for Sunday Promotions, is another expense. As it turns out, the gross comes closer to $3 million, with expenses close to a million. Before taxes, then, Sunday Promotions makes $100,000 in retained earnings. Should the company break up, the owners would then split the profits. Who the owners are is not clear.

Promo-Tours itself is said to be owned by a trust that the Stones own through their financial advisors. The reason the company is based in the Netherlands is that the Dutch have some of Europe's more lenient tax laws. Promo-Tours receives $2 million in payment for the Stones' services, minus 30 per cent, or $600,000, which is withheld for the Internal Revenue Service. That means $1.4 million in cash.

Out of this money comes the Stones' salaries, as well as Peter Rudge's, whose own company, Sound Image, is also under contract to Promo-Tours. All the other S.T.P. people and the supporting musicians are paid by Sunday Promotions, which disburses a million dollars in tour-related expenses.

After all the figuring is over, then, each of the Stones receives about $250,000 for the tour. This is a conservative estimate, and may be as much as $50,000 on the low side. Arriving in America on the twenty-eighth day of May, 1972, and departing on the twenty-eighth day of July, this works out to some sixty days (not all working days) at $4,000 per day, or $28,000 a week, more than twice what most middle-class family heads make in an entire year.

Still, in the rarefied strata of rock and roll heaven, the Stones do not really have that much money, especially after having ground it out for a decade. Just after their tour, Leon Russell goes out and works in *fifty-five cities*, grossing nearly as much with a lot less overhead. Neil Young embarks on a cross-country tour with a *ninety-ten* split of the gate.

Jagger and Keith have more than the rest of the band, for as the author-composers of most of the Stones' songs, they share the two penny mechanical royalty paid to the publisher and writer of each track on an album. Since the Stones publish their own music, they get to keep it all, which means twenty-four cents an album times a million copies (not all Stones' albums have sold that many copies, so this is an exaggerated figure) times twenty albums (again this is a rough figure; the Stones did not publish their own music for all their albums), which still equals a lot of money.

The other three Stones share in the artist's royalty on an album, usually 5 or 6 percent of the list price minus a production allotment. This comes to twenty-five to thirty-two cents an album, split five ways among the Stones, then once again for the producer. For example, 'Exile on Main Street' cost an astronomical $500,000 to make, with $100,000 of that going to pay for studio time in Los Angeles so that the tracks could be mixed and remixed.

If 'Exile' sells a million copies (which it doesn't, not right away—close to 800,000) at fifty cents each (it's a double album, two times twenty-five cents), the Stones will only break even. Which they don't. They make a profit on it because they have one of the stronger recording deals in the industry and get a bigger percentage than most artists.

Yet for all of this, or perhaps because of it, the Stones are weird on the subject of money. All of them were born without it. They are still young men who have made fortunes in their own lifetimes, primarily from the purses of their contemporaries, a peer group that up until a few years ago seemed most certainly anti-Establishment, if not actually anti-money. When asked, Charlie Watts will say, 'I ain't a millionaire and I've never been anywhere near it.' Wyman will note, 'I've got two homes and two cars and some money in the bank and that's it. With 86 percent tax on us in England, we'd have had to make a million pounds each in a year just to pay it plus what we owed Inland Revenue. Which we've never done. The Stones have sold up to fifty million units, and if I'd just sold a million albums by myself once I'd have more. I haven't enough money to see me through the next ten years much less my lifetime.'

Jagger will tell you, 'I made a thousand dollars on the European tour and no one believes me. They think I've made a million and they call us rip-offs and multi-millionaires. A thousand bucks each on that tour, which is fine wi me. I ain't worried and I ain't rich. Leon Russell's got more bread than I do. But I don't care, y'know? I don't think you can think about it. That about me bein a businessman is bullshit. I'm not interested in money. A businessman wants to be rich... and I don't.'

Nevertheless, the Stones like to go first class everywhere, up at the thin end of the plane as Ian Stewart once called it, where there is more room for your legs and they don't mind if you have a third drink.

As the boys grow older, they find themselves in the peculiar, but very real, artistic position of having to keep on working in order to maintain the life styles they have become so fond of. Having taken hold of the reins themselves and formed their own record label, having surrounded themselves with people who were determined to work for them rather than the other way round, after a decade of changing managers and of lawsuits, they find themselves finally on the brink of making enough big money to see them into their dotage.

A very real answer to the often-asked question of when they might break up would be... when they could afford it.

Chapter Nine

He was like Jimi Hendrix. He couldn't suss the assholes from the good people. He wouldn't kick out somebody that was a shit. He'd let them sit there and maybe they'd be thinking how to sell off his possessions. And he'd give 'em booze and feed 'em.

KEITH RICHARD, ON BRIAN JONES

Chip Monck has seen it coming and ten days before the band gets to Indianapolis on July 12, he approaches Rudge and suggests that Keith's friend Flex be asked to leave. Monck figures him to be an influence the tour doesn't need. Anything or anyone that interferes with the effectiveness of the principals when they get on that stage interferes with him, so it's come time for him to roll in on Flex and say, 'Motherfucker, you find me today with the authorization you hoped would never come down on you. Get out of here or I'm going to put a hole in your forehead.'

Rudge listens to him, knowing how overprotective Chip is, but also knowing that there's hardly anyone along who likes Flex, aside from the Inner Circle and the Film Crew. He doesn't work for Sunday Promotions, and aside from sweeping into dressing rooms looking pale and wasted in a black cape and taking a little sound every now and then for Robert Frank, he fulfills no apparent function.

Rudge approaches Keith with the matter and Keith tells him, 'He's staying. I'm payin for him and he's my friend and I need him. He's stayin.' There are all kinds of rules about the people who can and cannot come on the plane, but none of them apply to either Mick or Keith. They make their own rules. They are what the tour is about, and so when Rudge talks to Jagger about it, Mick says that as long as Flex stays clean and Keith wants him around, Keith can have him.

Mick and Keith are already picking up the tab for Chris O'Dell, who everyone in the Inner Circle really likes and considers a good friend. Having gone back to Los Angeles after spending the break with Bill Wyman and his lady in the South, Chris

was, presumably, back in the ordinary world for good. But after a
call from Keith, she caught the next plane to St. Louis, where she
actually got to play a few hands of poker before having to catch
a plane in the morning for New York. The Eclair that Jagger has
been using to film with is broken, and Chris has to take it East to
be fixed. When this is done, she flies right back into Indianapolis
and is on the road again. So if one friend can come along, why
not two?

'Friend,' the Monck says, 'the term is so fuckin loose. Keith
should open his eyes. As much as I love him... he should open
his eyes and become whole. I say that out of respect. The man is
marvelous. But his peripheral vision is not wide enough.'

It is Keith, more than Jagger, who tends to surround himself
with people who are usually in his employ, who wind up living
with him to take care of all the little things that need doing. Alan
Dunn has seen it happen more than once. 'You always get people
trying to live and play with them,' he says. 'There's a line you can
go up to... you start by bein an employee, but once you're over
that line, you don't want to work anymore and you're finished.'
With Keith being who he is, and believing always in letting it
happen, these people are never treated like employees. They're
always given access to whatever's going around. After a while they
cross that line, and things get loose, and chaos ensues.

At Keith's home in the South of France, a definite 'scene'
evolved, composed of people who would drop in to say hello
and then stay for a week. Mostly young, semi-rich and/or nearly
famous, and almost always physically attractive, they'd make
themselves at home drinking Keith Richard's white wine and
eating his food. Some nights when the lightning would crack over
the bay outside, sixteen, twenty-two, or some equally preposter-
ous number sat down to dinner, and one had the sense that at any
moment Dick Diver was going to pop out from behind a doorway in his tennis whites, as the hidden string quartet began the
music. All of it was from another era, when money was easier to
come by and the spirit of true celebration was upon the world.

Surrounded by his 'friends,' their chaos, his family, and his
music, Keith lived in the grand manner. At times, it seemed as
though the towering ornamental gates at his home served both to
keep the world out and those inside in. Flex passed through on
his way back from North Africa. Others came and went, bearing

gifts, offering business deals, hustling favors, and smiling until it came time to buy a plane ticket and move the party elsewhere.

Keith, who could so clearly see what had brought Brian and Jimi Hendrix down ('Ah, Jimi *le chat*,' a guest said one starry night, 'the most beautiful Sagittarius of our age, eh?') was himself prey to the same weakness. 'It weighs on you sometimes,' he would say, 'when you realize that if you weren't who you were, you definitely wouldn't be in the situation I'm in... imprisoned by other people's fantasies....' Around the star, there is always a subtle competition to see who can 'do' more—to make his everyday life easier and smooth away the details that root him to the earth so that he may be free to concentrate on his art.

'It's kind of a hangup to be treated like Prince Charles,' Keith noted on tour. Yet no one wanted to be awakened after a hot set and a long night to be asked some trivial question about the color of the drapes in the upcoming dressing room or the supper menu. Stones' people were expected to know what the boys wanted and to anticipate, without asking. Like acute parents who could tell exactly what their offspring would or would not eat, those closest to the Stones had to learn to think and act for them, in their name.

It's natural then for Chip Monck to point out these kids in Indianapolis. Monck has some kind of radar for dealers and dopers and he's noticed three white freaks and their women who've been popping up in city after city ever since Washington. They're always registered in the same hotel as the Stones and they walk around as though they're part of the tour. It is not impossible to know where the band is going next, but it is difficult to catch the hotel they'll be staying in in every city. Either these kids are doing a lot of detective work or someone inside S.T.P. is tipping them off.

They're dealers. With the itinerary being fed to them, they're getting to the cities early and dealing in the streets around the hall. By staying as close to the Stones as possible, they get to share in whatever police protection has been laid on for the hotel and they've already made thousands of dollars by peddling incense to kids who think it's opium.

'The liability is too great,' Monck tells Rudge. 'I wanna wipe these fuckers out.' For, as Monck says, 'If anyone joins this party with any thought other than the selflessness required in support of the artists, they'd better watch their fucking asses. 'Cause someone's gonna crawl up in them one night and beat them from the inside out.'

Prophetic words, especially in Indianapolis, a weird, two-night stopover if there ever was one. People get well-loaded the first night and Monck disconnects all the phones to insure their getting a good night's rest. When Bobby Keys wakes up in the morning, he can't get a dial tone, and this so outrages his road-weary sensibilities that he smashes his phone into bits until all that's left is the dial. Later, to prove a point, he orders one of everything on the menu.

The Stones have hired two local cops to act as special security to seal off the floor, and they set the tone for the whole scene. One is big and the other little. 'See this little man, heah?' the big one asks Chris O'Dell.

'Oh, yes,' Chris says wondering why everyone in Indiana has a cracker accent.

'He gets mean when he dranks. Now he's a good man all right, but when he dranks, he gets *bad*. Now tell me, what's wrong with these boys heah? I saw 'em take one out and run him in the field, he was so out of it. They takin a lotta drugs oah what?'

'They drink a lot,' Chris assures him, going into one of the rooms for something to calm her down. 'A lotta whiskey.'

'How 'bout that doctah? Is he really a doctah? He offered us some pills to help us stay awake, now we doahn't take no pills but little man he likes a drank every now and then.'

'No kidding....'

'Yeah. Who ah all these guhls 'round heah? Pretty nahce some of 'em. Little man said so himself; and he been married fifteen yeahs.'

'Wives,' Chris says, ducking into the room and then out again. 'Stewardesses. They fly in to be with them.'

'That true?' the cop says.

'Oh, yes,' Chris lies. 'Would I put you on?'

When the Stones come back to the hotel, the party revs up and Chris sees the little man with a glass in his hand. 'Uh oh,' she says, 'I think that little man's getting drunk.' By the time it rolls around to 3:00A.M. and things are getting fuzzy and warm with local ladies giving backrubs and talking about what Indianapolis is like as a year-round gig, the door flies open. The little cop rolls in, drunk out of his head. He flashes his badge at a room full of startled people and shouts, 'OUTTA HEAH! ALL YOU WIMMEN! OUT!'

'What the fuck?' Keith Richard says.

'These wimmen is dangerous. CLEAR 'EM OUT...'

The little man is promptly fired. Flex takes the opportunity to point out the dealers to Keith. Since they're using the Stones as protection, Keith reckons he should sound them out and goes to visit them. They're flattered that a man of his stature would come to call and they stand there and brag about how they've ripped kids off in every city, which is a mistake. If you're gonna deal, *deal. That's* the rockbiz code. If you're gonna rip people off, stand alone.

These cats don't even have the dignity of outlaws. They're petty crooks and poor hosts to boot and Keith leaves, not wanting to have anything to do with them. It occurs to Flex that the dealers are now not under anyone's protection. He gets hold of Willie the baggage man and Leroy the Stones' bodyguard and tells them that he's going to handle these kids who are putting the Stones in danger. So they accompany him to their room, not really knowing what's going on, and when they get there, Flex starts coming on heavy, threatening them with two big men, one as white as the other is black, backing him up.

'You been followin us around,' Flex says. 'You been gettin information about where we're headed. And, as Willie stands there listening, he realizes what this is. A New York City street number. Flex is shaking them down.

'I want a thousand bucks from you,' Flex says.

'We ain't got no money,' one answers.

'Bullshit. You got thousands from selling incense opium, right?'

The kids hem and haw and mumble, but nothing changes hands. As soon as it's over, Willie goes to Rudge and tells him what's going down. A guy traveling with the S.T.P. caravan is shaking down dealers with the Stones' security as muscle. If these kids turn around and blow the whistle on him, everyone is in trouble, and for no reason, since the Stones personally have had nothing to do with this one. Rudge decides to move on these kids. Along with Leroy and the local cops, he goes to their room, gets the door opened, and throws all their luggage into the lobby, with Leroy making sure they understand they're to leave the hotel and stay away.

The situation gets the S.T.P. hierarchy so freaked out they put another security man on the job. He is also black, has worked in the rockbiz for a long time and knows the Stones since their last American tour. Along with Stan and Leroy, he becomes one of a small platoon of very tough and together black men standing watch over the Stones.

The next day Willie tells the new bodyguard, 'Flex gotta go. We coulda done it in Kansas City if we'd been thinkin... have one of the promoter's boys put him on a bus and then the plane leaves and he's not on it. An they don't have to face Keith....'

'Why don't I grab him?' the new bodyguard suggests. 'Throw a sheet over the mother's head, tie him up and leave him in his room with a "Do Not Disturb" sign on the door.'

'He'll die in the room,' Willie says. 'He'll suffocate.'

'We'll call 'em from Detroit and tell them to let him go.'

'Nah,' Willie says, shaking his head. 'It's no good.'

But something must be done. Willie and the new bodyguard know that Rudge wants Flex gone. Since Jagger doesn't care one way or the other, they're free to act. Keith will be a problem. No one wants to face him when he finds out they've thrown a friend of his off the tour. Maybe it can be done while he's on stage. But it has to be done. It's imperative. One of the Tac Squad boys passionately tells Willie, 'Even if I lose my job... we've got to get rid of him.'

Sometime early in the morning of the Stones' last night in Indianapolis; around 5:00 A.M., Robert Frank is on his way to Flex's room for some tapes. A groupie and a member of the stage crew are crawling naked around a bed discussing whether or not it's feasible to fuck under the influence of smack, and Robert wants to film it.

He finds Flex looking paler and more hollow-faced than usual as Willie stands packing his bags for him. The bathroom is full of towels smeared with shit and Flex is just standing there looking wasted and mumbling, 'Got to go... to the airport... got to... right away.'

Robert knows something has happened and that it has to do with drugs, but he doesn't know what. He can't ask because Willie is there big as life and the two of them have already tangled once. 'Airport' Flex mumbles, 'right away.'

'Hey,' Robert says kindly, 'don't go. We need you to take sound when Danny can't.'

'Gotta leave.'

'At least stay around until Detroit.'

'Right away.'

And that's all Robert is going to find out about it tonight. He takes the tapes he came for and goes into the hallway where he sees the new bodyguard. 'What happened to Flex?' he asks him casually.

'How should I know?'

That's funny, Robert thinks, that's a funny answer. Because he must know. Then he goes down the hall to film and doesn't think any more about it.

What has happened is that the new bodyguard asked Willie to bring Flex to see him. Willie did just that, not knowing what was going to happen. As soon as the door swung shut, the new bodyguard rolled Flex on the bed, whipped out a pistol and put it to his forehead and said, 'If you scream, I'll blow your brains out.' Then he began beating him, pounding heavy punches into the bones of his chest so that the black and blue marks began welling up immediatcly, each blow landing with the sickening wet squash of fist against tissue.

'Now you leave this tour. You leave it now. You hear me? You been hanging on too long. And when you leave, you don't know my name. And you leave *now.*' Head lolling to one side, spittle dripping slowly out of one corner of his mouth, Flex gagging for breath and begging, 'No more, no more, please.'

All the punches are to the chest and ribs so that it hurts to walk or breathe but nothing shows. When Flex gets back to his room, he has to use the bathroom towels to wipe himself clean, having let go as he laid there getting beaten on the bed.

'Just go home,' Willie says. 'Now that it's done, better just get it over with and leave.'

By the time Mick and Keith rouse themselves for the plane ride to Detroit, it's early afternoon. Flex is gone. Robert Frank tells the doctor what he saw last night and the doctor calls the airport and they page Flex. He comes to the phone and moans, 'I got worked over... I can't come back,' and the doctor runs and bangs on Keith's door.

'What's happenin?' Willie asks, with the disinterested air of a man who knows nothing.

'It's very bad,' the doctor says. 'I can't talk to you now.'

'YOU GODDAMN MOTHERFUCKER,' Keith screams when he's told. 'WHAT THE FUCK DID YOU DO?' He comes out of his room and grabs Willie, who's loading the luggage for the plane. 'WILLIE! What's going on?'

'Keith, what do I know what's going on?' Willie says.

'You know and you're gonna tell me.'

'C'mannnnn, Keith... I got a fuckin job to do.'

'WILLLLIIIEEE!' Keith screams. 'I'm puttin your ass against the wall... Tell me what's goin on here.'

'I ain't got time for your nonsense, Keith,' Willie says, going into Jagger's room to get his bags. 'Hey,' he tells Mick, 'you better look out for your friend Keith. He's goin crazee.'

A friend of Keith's is missing and no one will tell him what's happened. By this stage of the tour, his temper is not very long to begin with, and all he wants to know is who did it and why, but all he gets are blank looks and people saying they don't have the time to talk to him.

The limos pull out for the airport. In the first car, Keith tells the other Stones as much of it as he understands, which is that someone has done Flex, but no one will say who. The rest of the band is confused because they know the way Keith lives and the people who surround him at times; there's no way of knowing what's really happened.

Peter Rudge has flown on early to Detroit so there's no one to handle matters or cool them down and the plane ride is madness. 'What happened?' Keith demands of Willie after take-off.

'Whadda I know what happened?' he says. 'You know as well as I. So whadda you buggin me for?'

'If this gets around, Willie,' Keith threatens, 'every band in England will know about it. You'll never work again...'

'Keith... I don't give a fuck. I'll go home right now. I dig ditches, you know? I work. I'm a worker. I don't need this shit. You goin after me like that in the hotel...'

'Ah, Willie, I didn't mean nothin by that....'

'Keith, I don't know what you mean.'

There's a circle of people around Willie and another around the new bodyguard. They've picked Flex up at the airport and he sits silently near the doctor, who's examined him and can testify that he has been definitely tomahawked.

'Just tell us what happened,' Jagger says to the new body-guard.

'You wanna fire me, go ahead,' he says. 'I'll leave. Pack mah case now. I'm ready.'

''S not what I asked you, man,' Jagger says. 'Ai wanna know what happened.'

'You got complaints? Take mah job.'

The new bodyguard is playing it the way only someone who has come from the street can. He is staring straight ahead, not speaking, totally denying all the charges with his face and his body as well as his eyes, the way generations of black men have sat mute in the basements of police stations.

'You know,' Bobby Keys tells Willie, 'That guy back there says you're a fucking liar... I wouldn't let anyone call *me* a liar.'

'Hey, Bobby... cut the bullshit, will you?' Willie says. 'What am I, easy to beat down on 'cause I'm low, man?'

Robert Frank is standing in the aisle listening, getting angry. Two people have taken the law into their own hands and pulled a Gestapo number and now people are pleading with them for the truth. He's fed up and disgusted with this rock and roll sickness that makes everybody who gets near it crazy.

'You prick,' he says, loud enough for Willie to hear.

'Why, you old cocksucker,' Willie says, getting to his feet and coming at him in the aisle. 'Don't you *know?* I'm from New York... you're from New York. When this thing's over, I go back to New York. You go back to New York. They go to England... we'll be there a long time... you think I can't find you?'

A few crew members get in between the two of them and move them to separate ends of the plane, but that's how it goes for the rest of the trip. Sporadic outbursts, flaring arguments, shouted accusations. The new bodyguard sits stoically through it all like some great black statue.

By the time the plane lands, no one is making much sense and a stream of angry, babbling people greet Rudge, who is unaware that anything happened in the few hours he's been gone. 'We got a little problem here,' Jagger tells him and he and Rudge confer and decide that things are so blown out of proportion, only a general 'truth' meeting is going to clear the air.

The Film Crew is furious. Flex was one of them before the incident and what has come down since has made them all angrier. They demand justice. Detroit is a poor place to try and smooth anything over, much less be just. The town is a tough place to play, what with street kids, Ann Arbor radicals, inner-city blacks, and a police force that is no one's idea of a peace-keeping force. Willie unloads the baggage from the plane into a Rent-A-Truck and has it driven to the hall to deliver that speaker-cabinet Marshall has ordered. The kids massed outside Cobo Hall see the truck come rolling down the hill toward the entrance and they swarm on it, pounding at the sides and hammering at the handles, screaming, 'We're gonna take it right through that door.'

Jesus Fuck, Willie thinks, they're gonna hijack the truck. 'Get outta here,' he shouts, 'MOVE IT.' The driver floors it, and it's not until they get to the hotel that they discover the kids have opened the back doors and ripped off the sound unit, which is now a neat ten-thousand-dollar loss. Willie doesn't know that the guy who built the cabinet installed a phoney limiter inside of which there is a silver vial containing three or four grams of coke as a little present. Half an hour before the show starts, the cabinet is found in the street, completely stripped. A few minutes later a kid comes to the stage door with the limiter in his hand, saying, 'Look what I found laying in the street.' Having found more than he knows, the kid gets to see the show for free.

But Willie is hassled. First the truck and now this meeting. A meeting over Flex. His S.T.P. badge, his wallet, and all his papers were stolen by the kids who broke into the truck. Now he's got to go and get yelled at because the new bodyguard cooled out a kid who had no business being along in the first place.

Before the meeting, Flex walks up to him and says, 'Look, Willie, I wanna talk with you.'

'Ach!' Willie says disgustedly. 'What's there to talk about? Huh?

'You here with the Stones? You at the show? That's what you wanted, ain't it? That's the important thing for you....'

The Stones, the Tac Squad, and the Film Crew plus the three principals—Willie, Flex, and the new bodyguard—are present at the meeting. The tour party, a body in motion, for the first time will have to police itself and the meeting quickly becomes a trial with Jagger taking power and emerging as both the grand inquisitor and presiding judge. Robert Frank is not allowed to film what happens. Only a few people speak, and the man who holds everyone in his hand is the new bodyguard, who does not speak at all. He sits like a noble black savage brought in chains to a court whose jurisdiction he does not recognize, secure in the knowledge he did what he was hired to do—protect the Stones. People ask him questions and shout with frustration, but he sits there unblinking, his face betraying no sign of emotion.

'Well, what's it gonna be?' Jagger asks him, in the faintly disgusted tone he uses to get through the heaviest situations. 'If you did it, you're gonna have to go. If Willie's involved, him too.'

'If you did it,' Keith implores, '*say* you did, man.'

But the new bodyguard will not cop to a thing. Nor will Leroy, who also knows. Leroy has spent night after sleepless night guarding these people. Leroy saved their asses in Seattle. He stood outside the front door at the Playboy Mansion in Chicago, monitoring the flow. He's had to wake Keith up in the mornings, and watched out for him and Bobby Keys when they stayed back to party with Stevie Wonder in Tuscaloosa. Like Dilsey in Faulkner's *The Sound and the Fury,* Leroy has taken everything these white children have to give and still kept on. He understands where the new bodyguard is coming from, and why he did what he thought he had to do.

Keith doesn't even know why he has a bodyguard. 'I always feel it's stupid,' he says, 'but I put up with it because people involved with it longer than me say it's necessary. Shit, they're always nice cats to have around, to get their story, where they're from and what they've been doing....' The new bodyguard is sure of what he's done. *He* knows.

Cross-arguments start and little waves of tension ripple across the room. 'Why do I have to go through shit to ride in the mobile after every gig?' Marshall Chess asks.

'Because *nobody* goes in the mobile except musicians,' Alan Dunn says: 'You know that.'

'I think I belong in there.'

'You don't and if I say you don't...'

'Awright,' Jagger says flatly. 'This ain't gettin us *no*-where. We just wanna know who did it. If you done it, just say you did.'

Robert Frank is watching and he can't believe they have to beg this guy to admit to a crime.

'No one's gonna be sent home or nothin,' Jagger says. We just wanna know the truth and then we can clear the whole thing up.

'All right,' the new bodyguard says finally, and the attention of everyone in the room zeroes in on him. 'You all talked. Now it's my turn. This man... ,' he points to Flex, 'was in mah thing. My job is to keep you outta trouble. So, I'll say it and make you happy. I whipped the boy. I ain't proud of it. But it had to be done. This man was shakin people down in your name. If it had been Stan Moore, or Leroy, I'd have done the same, shook and slapped them around. You put it in mah hands. You call me anything you want when it's over 'cause that don't faze me a pound. I'm gonna make sure an get you through.'

It stops everyone cold, a confession without remorse or guilt. It's so out front that people start to think, well he *was* only doing his job, and since no one much likes Flex anyway, it's easy to forget that he's been beaten black and blue. Why punish a man for acting on an impulse that was in a lot of people's heads anyway?

The Film Crew wants everyone involved thrown off. A plague on both your houses. Serve justice by sending everyone home and continue without them. But Rudge and Jagger know that if they throw the new bodyguard off, they not only cut their own security by a third, but run the risk of enraging a man who has already shown the ability to take decisive, punitive action when he thought the situation warranted it. So what's to stop him from coming after the tour?

'We're not gonna send anyone home,' Jagger says. 'Maybe if this had happened in the first week or somethin it would be different, but we've awl come this far already. 'Cause both sides are wrong. X shouldna done what he done. And neither should Y. One man was doin his job though and the other wasn't. Shake hands and we'll get outta this room.'

'All right,' the new bodyguard says slowly. 'I'll shake his hand.'

'Oh, man,' Flex moans from his chair across the room. 'Can you come over here, please? It hurts too much for me to get up.'

As they shake hands, Robert Frank thinks that this really is too much. Here's a guy who's been humiliated and destroyed, letting the bodyguard hug him. No one will stand up for Flex. He's Keith's friend, but when it comes down to hard facts, the Stones have no friends. Not on the road. Not any that don't work for them. Flex failed in his role, and so whatever happens to him is justified.

'I'm sorry it had to be,' the new bodyguard says as they stand there, 'but you asked for it, and you'll get over it.'

He will. Keith says it would be better if he didn't go into Canada with them, but he can come back in New York for the final concerts and, as Willie said, 'you're with the Stones, ain't cha? That's what you wanted, ain't it?'

'He did his job, didn't he?' Charlie will say later of the new bodyguard, 'and his job isn't very pleasant. But you need those people. America's bigger, so you need them. That's the funny thing about America... the way he's paid to do that.... almost like a gunman. America's a bit paid, inn't it? But my America isn't like that and my friends in America ain't like that. So I don't know. I ain't American.'

It's what happens when you're a tourist. Get too close to the natives and one's likely to bite your hand off and then smilingly inform you that it's just a local custom. The Stones are tourists with a vengeance, who'll go home well paid for what they do. No matter how air-tight the spaceship they travel in is, the madness that's on the streets and in the cities has to seep through sooner or later.

The incident is closed. If the interests of justice haven't exactly been served, those of business and common sense have. The tour will be kept in motion. When Willie makes an impassioned little plea at the end of the meeting, no one really listens. 'I'm gonna tell you somethin,' he says, pointing to Peter Rudge. 'You got to respect this man over there. No one's helpin him. You're all one against the other... you don't care... I'm leavin.' Willie is a good company man who believes in being loyal to the person he's working for, in this case Peter Rudge. But nobody else wants to pull together... so forget it.

People go over to Willie and talk to him. Charlie says' 'It ain't me, Willie, is it? You ain't mad at me, are ya?' and Charlie's so charming about it all, Willie has to laugh. Of course it isn't him. Then the Detroit cops find the kid who stole his bag and Willie changes his mind and decides to stay. He drives straight through to Boston to await the Stones for the last week that will wrap the whole thing up.

And that's it. Over and done with. 'Well, ai don't really want to talk about it,' Mick Jagger will say afterward. 'Not unless you wanna spend half an hour talkin about some borin story. I cahn't remember it, really. There was a bit of a kangaroo court, yeah, someone had done something, whatever it was, all these little things go down, and someone else had gone too far in redressing the wrong. I wasn't gonna sacrifice the tour for it. I wanted to keep it goin and that was the decision I made. A lot of people disagreed with me and a lot of people didn't. But really, the thing is... I don't remember a thing about it.'

Chapter Ten

I suppose all of us in public life are performers in a way...
                    MAYOR KEVIN WHITE OF BOSTON

Everyone is tired. The goddamn plane has taxied up and down the runway at full speed twice and then slammed on the brakes and come whistling and screeching to a jarring, swerving halt. Some kind of liquid is pouring off the wings and Jagger has that 'oh, Christ we're gonna buy it this time' look on his face. He'll inform anyone interested that the take-off and then the power turn are absolutely the most dangerous parts of any plane ride. Today the Electra can't even get off the ground.

The Stones have just spent what you might call a taxing weekend in Canada. On Saturday, they played Toronto's Maple Leaf Gardens only to find the local police had decided to make a real show of strength at the concert. For some reason, three rows deep, a hundred yards' worth of cops sit at picnic tables directly outside the dressing room, munching on chicken dinners. 'What the fuck are all those *pigs* doin out there?' Jagger says in the dressing room, loud enough for the cops to hear. 'Peter?' he shouts. 'What's a bunch of police doin roight outside the dressin room? Eay? Ai fucking doan want them there... oh, shit, man...?' And when the band goes out to play, someone says that the temperature on stage is a hundred and forty-seven degrees.

That seems a bit exaggerated, but still it's so hot some people stay in the dressing room during the set, rushing as they are on amys. They hit a chick with one and she does a stiff-legged backward faint, smashing into the concrete floor head first. Gary Stromberg laughs. He figures she's doing a number. 'Put an amy under her nose to bring her to,' somebody says. 'Maybe you should cut back on the amys with her,' the doctor says after he brings her around.

And when the band comes offstage, Keith takes three steps toward the dressing room and falls dead away. Gary Stromberg laughs. He figures he's doing a number. They manage to revive

Keith and decide to keep him in Toronto for the night to rest. Heat exhaustion.

Sunday is a day off, spent in Montreal. The hotel is finally back to European-class standards and there is the feeling of having returned to civilisation. That night the party is in Keith's room. Everyone is in a different dimension, another state of altered consciousness, with Robert Frank sitting on the floor reading the Gideon Bible and Chris O'Dell trying to work out what is 'bron grah-vee.' Ribs with 'bron grah-vee' have just been delivered, but they sure do taste just like... ribs with brown gravy. With brown gravy. A-ha.

On the bed lies a very beautiful girl who's come along from Toronto. She's high-fashion beautiful, with high cheekbones that don't quit, but she has this habit. And an unpronounceable name. Just now she seems to be asleep, with the telephone in her hand. Maybe she isn't asleep though, because Keith keeps filling her in on what's going on every now and then.

'Keith?' Chris O'Dell says, 'she's asleep.'

'Hey, bay-bee,' Keith says. 'Wake up. We gotta call your mother.' The chick speaks Serbo-Croatian or something. Keith and Bobby have gotten into taping phone conversations, and one with her mother in the native tongue is the one they have to get. But the chick keeps nodding out. So Chris takes the phone and gets information, but when she asks the chick for her last name, it's something like 'Roszniekiweickzneicki,' which no one can spell. So they put the receiver into her hand and tell her it's information.

'Yeah, bay-bee,' Keith says, 'your mother. You got to talk to her in that language.'

'Hello?' the chick says into the phone. 'Is this information? Yah? Venn does the next train leave?' Then she nods out.

Later that night the phone rings in Peter Rudge's room. He picks it up, talks for a while, then begins making phone calls. 'Rudge-O here,' he tells Gary Stromberg. 'This is rather important. Could you come down to the hall? We've been bombed.'

Some person (or persons) has placed one to three sticks of dynamite underneath one of the trucks. Fortunately, it is the one that holds steel loading ramp, so all it does is blow a four-by-eight hole in the bottom of the truck, disintegrate the ramp, and destroy all the cones in the speakers. The driver, who usually

sleeps in the rig, is off somewhere, which saves him from at least
a heart attack, if not actual death. All of the windows are broken
in the apartment buildings on the street facing the Forum where
the truck is parked.

The street is roped off. The police are making diagrams and
gathering shards and pieces and a very French Sergeant de Detec-
tif is in charge. Rudge persists in calling him 'captain.' Someone
says to him, 'Certainly this is the work of one of your French
separatists.'

'OH NO, M'SIEU!' he replies with classic Gallic outrage.
'*C'est une* American draft dodgeur. Zey are all over. Zey come up
here with *impunity*.'

Not long after, a laundry truck pulls up on the street and two
uniformed guys wheel a big hamper into the Forum. Anyone
who watches 'Mission Impossible' knows these guys are in on it
and the hamper contains explosives, but the cops just watch.

Then the calls start coming in. The bomb at the Forum was
just the first of four timed to go off at intervals during the day.
They wake Jagger up to tell him about it. 'Who did it?' he asks
sleepily. No one knows. 'Well,' he yawns, 'why the fuck didn't
they leave a note?'

But he's shook. The French separatists, it is well known, are
crazee. They'll stop at nothing, and all day long he keeps referring
to the incident uneasily, worried that they plan to pull something
off at the show. But the show itself goes off peacefully, the bomb
squad having turned the building upside down more than once.
Outside the hall, the kids and the cops get down to it and four
teen people are injured, thirteen arrested, and a TV news cruiser
set on fire. UPI, in an inspired piece of fiction, reports that the
Stones leave the Forum by means of a helicopter that takes off
from the roof and circles the crowd announcing, 'THEY HAVE
LEFT THE BUILDING: GO HOME' in both French and English.

Now the plane sits at the Montreal Airport unable to take
off. The air-conditioning doesn't work while the plane's on the
ground, so it's hot as hell and boring. The only thing that keeps
people from falling asleep is Chris O'Dell. The Tac Squad puts
her in charge of morale while they go off to find commercial
flights. First she does a little tap dance down the cabin aisle. Then
the footballs come out and the Stones and the S.T.P. dudes go out

on the runway. The English guys are kicking the ball around like Spurs and Manchester United on a good day while the Americans dodge and dart and fade back into the pocket to throw long passes.

Chris grabs hold of the emergency bullhorn you're only supposed to use when the plane goes down into the North Atlantic and starts cheering, 'Richards, Richards, he's our man/If he can't do it, Jagger can/Jagger, Jagger....' Naturally no one who's English knows what the hell she's yelling about but the other ladies on the plane join her to form a trio of post-psychedelic pom-pom girls. 'Our team is red hot/Your team is all shot...' until the airport security men tell everyone to get back on the plane and stay there.

After two hours on the runway, the pilot gets the airspeed indicator fixed and the plane taxis into position and makes it into the sky. It looks like the show is going to be late tonight. Halfway through the flight, the pilot asks the person in charge of the Stones' party to come to the cockpit. He tells Rudge that Logan Airport in Boston is fogged in. The Stones' advance man, who is already there, has set things up for the Stones to land in Bedford, Massachusetts, but the pilot doesn't know it and he tells Rudge they're going in to Theodore Francis Green Airport in Warwick, Rhode Island. Which is the first mistake.

In Boston, the concert city, Kevin White is walking the streets of the South End. It's been quite a week for the mayor. As the Stones sat through their truth meeting in Detroit, he sat by his phone and waited for George McGovern to call back and confirm that, yes, he was to be the Democratic party's nominee for vice-president.

A forty-one-year-old man,with salt-and-pepper hair, a politician's face, a long stooping walk, and that characteristically dry New England phrasing, White seems to be a perfect counterweight for rural, smiling South Dakota George. White is Irish, Catholic, liberal, the father of five children, a tennis player and voracious reader, a personable shirtsleeves kind of guy who can *project* as well as deal in the back rooms. He's a new-old politician who will attract the city vote and not alienate the coalition of traditional interests McGovern will need if he is going to put the hurt on Richard Nixon.

But when the call finally comes, White is told, 'Kevin, it's not you. It's someone else. It's Eagleton of Missouri.' 'You were my first choice,' McGovern is quoted as saying 'I wanted you. But the Senate killed us.'

Three days later, at a Puerto Rican Day celebration in Blackstone Park in Boston, there's a lot of celebrating and some drinking and the cops come to arrest someone and do it the wrong way. The crowd goes to the streets, and they have to call out the Tactical Police Force. Thirty-five arrests are made, twenty-seven people are injured, and a police car is set on fire.

All the next day, rumors as thick as the hot, humid air fly around the South End. Cops have called kids 'spics,' and beaten old men with soda bottles until their faces were masks of blood. It is the classic urban ghetto riot pattern, the night's flames are fanned by the day's rumors, and when the sun goes down, the crowd gathers again. They firebomb and loot two stores, and when the fire engines roll up to fight the blaze, they fling rocks and bottles at the firemen.

The next day, as the Stones sit on the ground at the airport in Montreal, White goes into the streets with his police to show the people that their mayor cares. In the tradition of Bobby Kennedy and John Lindsay, he walks the streets of the area in shirtsleeves, talking to people. During the day, he is advised by an aide that the Rolling Stones will be playing Boston Gardens that night. Over a hundred policemen with dogs and the entire TPF will be on duty there. White makes a mental note to stop by to check the situation out.

One floor below the city desk of the *Providence Journal,* in the photo lab, Andy Dyckerman is putting some pictures in the developer. He's halfway through the three-to-eleven shift on what has been a quiet day so far. A call comes down to say there's a report that the Stones are coming through Green Airport. A reporter is already on his way there and Dyckerman is to meet him.

Thirty years old, with fairly long hair and a mustache and a withered right hand, Andy Dyckerman has been a newspaper photographer for nearly ten years. He is also a Stones fan. He digs to play their music at parties and for awhile even thought about going to Boston to shoot the concert. A poster of the Stones used to hang in an honored place in the dining room of his home.

So he gets in his car, which has official Rhode Island Press Photographer's license plate number 36 on it, and drives to the airport where someone tells him that a charter plane has just landed across the field by the weather station and the fire department. Sure enough, there is the Electra with the stuck-out tongue painted on one side. A bunch of people are milling around in the open area in front of the fire station's bay doors. Their luggage is heaped in piles on the concrete. Contact.

Two hours on the ground in Montreal and now this. What is the procedure for landing in places you weren't supposed to land in, Rudge wonders. Half the people on the plane don't even know they're not in Massachusetts. They've gotten so used to rolling off the plane and into the limos, they just assume it's going to happen again. But it's not, unless Jo Bergman can find a bus company in the *Yellow Pages* that will take them the fifty miles to Boston.

It's already eight o'clock and the caravan has to go through U.S. Customs before they can split. Rudge has bullied the two local Customs men into an improvisational trip whereby he reads people's names off the manifest and they come up with their own bags. If anyone is holding, all Rudge has to do is not call them or have them waltz up with someone else's bags. In fact, the Customs guys are so blitzed, every S.T.P. person could come up carrying the same suitcase and they wouldn't notice. They've never had to deal with anything like this before.

There they stand, the Stones' Touring Party, peaceably spacing out on the neat rows of helmets hung on hooks, on the coiled hoses and the runway stretching away all concrete and empty into the distance. Across the pavement comes Andy Dyckerman, with a camera case over his shoulder, a 35-millimetre camera around his neck and a flash attachment in his hand.

'Uh-oh,' thinks Stromberg, an anxious photographer. 'Can I help you?' he says, moving out to intercept him.

'*Providence Journal*, Andy Dyckerman,' Dyckerman says. 'Like to take some pictures.'

'I wish you wouldn't, man,' Gary says. 'We're going through Customs and we're late already.'

'If you could just move off to one side?' Stan Moore adds, coming up to help.

'I have a right to be here,' Dyckerman says calmly. 'This is public property and I have the right to take pictures on it.'

'We're clearing Customs, man... look, it's been a rough day and everyone is uptight. I'm tellin you that if you bother these people, it'll be trouble....'

'I have a perfect legal right to take pictures,' Dyckerman insists.

'And I've got one to stay with you and make sure you don't,' Gary says.

Stromberg, whose brightly coloured outfits, long hair, beard, and aviator shades make him look like a high-class Hollywood dealer, is acting the cop in this little drama. He knows the Stones don't want this guy popping that flash-gun in their faces and it's up to him to protect them, no matter what.

'It is my *right*,' Dyckerman insists, 'to be allowed to take these pictures.' And so saying, he brings his camera up to his eye and lets fly and the flash goes POP!

'Okay, that's it,' Stan Moore says, taking him by the wrist and moving him away. 'You been told nice; maybe you didn't understand. No pictures.'

Dyckerman is angry. These people are interfering with the freedom of the press. They're on public property and they're public figures and there's no reason he shouldn't be allowed some pictures.

'What is it with this little guy?' Robert Frank asks Rudge. 'Why don't you let him take his fucking pictures and leave?'

Anyone who knows the Stones can sense it coming. A confrontation. Someone wants something they are not prepared to give and sooner or later someone will have a guitar or a bottle swung at his head or his camera grabbed and thrown out a window.

Dyckerman goes looking for help. The airport police say they're busy. So are the state police. Go find a Warwick patrolman, they tell him. 'Yeah, yeah,' a fireman who's phoning police forces says into the phone, 'we got the Rolling Stones here and a photographer who says he's been assaulted.' Dyckerman finally locates a Warwick police sergeant and has him accompany him back to the crowd. Stromberg takes one look at the cop's face and thinks....

no help here. This cop don't know who we are, but it's for sure he don't like us.

'I ain't lettin you take pictures,' Stromberg tells Dyckerman flatly. 'And if he says no,' Stan Moore adds, 'it's no. And I'll enforce it.'

Dyckerman tries to shoot a picture, the flash pops, and Stromberg and Moore slide in front of him like a collapsing zone defense on a basketball court. He turns toward Bill Wyman and they follow. People trail him wherever he goes and at one point Jagger creeps up in back of him, sticks out his tongue and makes a face, daring him to shoot it. What a great picture, Dyckerman thinks. But as soon as he gets his camera up, Jagger ducks away behind Chris O'Dell.

The sergeant stands watching all of this, a bunch of adults playing hide-and-go-seek and freeze tag, until Stromberg makes a direct appeal.

'Officer, we're in Customs here... tell this man he has no right....'

'All right,' Peter Rudge says, finally coming over to intervene. Let's be sensible. Sergeant? Mr. Dyckerman? How many pictures do you want?'

'I can't say,' Dyckerman says.

'Just tell me how many you need and I'll clear it with the band and we'll have it all over quickly. They were supposed to be on stage half an hour ago. You can take what you need and leave. Sergeant? Am I being reasonable?' Rudge asks rhetorically. He *knows* he's being reasonable. And the sergeant seems to agree.

'I don't know how many I need,' Dyckerman says, refusing to give an inch to these people. 'I want to stay here and take as many as I have to...'

'Hey, man,' Stan says. 'This man is allowin you five or six. Whyn't you take 'em and be happy and then split?'

'I don't have to...'

'Sergeant?' Rudge implores, with a pained look on his face. 'Sergeant? Are we not being reasonable?'

Another plea is about to leave Rudge's mouth when Dyckerman turns and tries to skirt the wall of S.T.P. people in front of him. He's spotted Jagger off to one side, protected by Chris O'Dell. 'Turn around,' Chris tells Mick like it's a game, 'he's coming.' Out of the corner of her eye she sees Keith. Keith has been sitting placidly on the bumper of an old truck with his black satchel, his three-and-a-half foot scarf, and a belt over his arm. Dyckerman's little broken-field run takes him right into Keith's path and the next thing anyone knows Keith is up and with one looping motion, he swings everything in his hand at the photographer. The sound of the belt hitting the camera is audible and Dyckerman shouts, 'Ouch! He struck me,' more out of surprise than anything else.

'That's it,' the sergeant says, disgusted. 'Put that man under arrest.'

Two cops bend Keith's arms behind his back and slap a pair of cuffs on him and propel him toward the paddy wagon which is parked on the other side of the building. And it's not a game anymore. Chris checks that he's left his black satchel behind.

The cops aren't moving Keith fast enough to stop Jagger from getting to them. 'Look, man,' he says running over. 'Loik, what you doin? We got a show tonight and there's a whole lotta people waitin. So come *on*, man....'

But the cops don't break stride or even show that they're interested and Jagger pushes in closer and shouts, 'If you're gonna charge him, okay, but arrestin him is gonna be a bigger hassle for you than us. Know what ai mean? It's a stupid fuckin thing to do, arrestin him...'

'Mick, don't...' someone says. 'Mick...'

'Stoopid fuckin....'

'Arrest this one, too,' the sergeant orders, and they put Keith in the wagon and come after Jagger with their cuffs. There's pushing and shoving and Jagger, who has no love for cops or uniforms to begin with, is playing it to the hilt. The cops are small and he figures he might even be able to get away with knocking one over. It's hot until Leroy pushes into the circle and says, 'Ease up, honkies, I'll put the cuffs on him mahself.'

'Three of ya,' Jagger sneers. 'Three of ya to arrest....'

Robert is filming and Danny's taking sound and Rudge and Stromberg are right on top of it all, talking and gesticulating. Marshall Chess sees them put the cuffs on Jagger and comes running across the pavement shouting, 'You stupid motherfucking assholes,' so they oblige him too by slapping the last pair of cuffs on him and shoving him inside the wagon, where Keith has been sitting peacefully watching it from the beginning.

What is this? Rudge wonders. Marshall has just run right across the airport into the paddy wagon without stopping. Across the airport and into jail. It's unn-real.

Robert Frank has his camera up, he's filming, but the light is bad and he's hoping they'll turn some kind of dome light on inside the paddy wagon so he can get Keith and Jagger framed in the doorway. He's grappling to hold on to his position close to the door and the cops are doing all they can to move him out. One grabs him and twists his arm. 'Don't break my fucking arm,' he shouts as they bounce and push him into the wagon. Under arrest.

A few minutes later, almost as an afterthought, they tell Stan Moore they're going to have to arrest him too because Dyckerman says he was assaulted by him before they got there. As an ex-cop though, they let Stan ride in the police car. Up front, with the officers.

More out of curiosity than anything else, Kevin White goes to visit Boston Gardens. One of his aides attempts to explain what is on stage. The air, the mayor notes, is heavy. The noise is unbelievable, and after a short while he leaves, not really understanding any more about it than before he went.

On the ride into the police station the boys in back of the van concentrate on breaking a roach into tiny pieces. Keith Richard hears a cop in front radio in, 'We're bringin 'em in now. Four wops and a Jew.' Which is strange, Keith thinks, only one of us is Jewish, and the rest not woppish-looking at all. Why, Keith reflects, with his customary sense of style, it's the cops who are wops. Indeed. He's hardly ever seen two more woppish-looking gentlemen in his life.

All hell is breaking loose at the airport. 'You'll regret this, sergeant,' Rudge promises the arresting officer.

'Paparazzo!' normally peaceful Charlie Watts flames, 'I'd 'ave 'it 'im meself'

'You little cunt,' Nicky Hopkins says through clenched teeth.

'Absurd,' Wyman snorts.

'Y'awl bettah take me in *now*,' Bobby Keys tells the cop, "cause soon as you leave, ah'm gonna bust that little gertz raght in the mouth.'

'Me too,' Jim Price says angrily.

'So save yoahself a trip,' Keys says, 'and take me *now*. Ah assure you the very minute you split ahm gonna open his face foah him.'

Bobby is furious. His best buddies have been slapped into the back of a Black Maria and driven off for the hoosegow and he can't even get himself arrested. A set of authentic jailhouse rock is going on and he can't sit in. But he's doing everything he can to change that. He's gotten Jim Price angry and together the two of them are cursing spitting mad, but no matter what they do, they can't get popped.

Rudge is in his glory. Battlefield conditions. He's operating on three phones, one to the promoter in Boston, one to the Stones' New York lawyers, and one to a local lawyer named Joe Galluci, whom Rudge finds by letting his fingers do the walking through the *Yellow Pages*.

Rudge gets hold of Galluci and asks him to come to the police station. He tells the New York lawyers to fly up to Boston and stand by. He gathers together all the unarrested musicians and persuades them to board a rickety old yellow school bus bound for Boston. He's all ready to go downtown himself and deal with the coppers when he notices that one Robert Keys is not on the bus. He is, rather, on the runway, shouting, 'C'mahn you pigs, ah'm still waitin...'

'Bobby,' Rudge says, 'the bus... the bus.'

'Ah ain't goin nowhere without mah buddies,' Keys declares.

'Bobby, please,' Rudge pleads. 'We'll take care of this. If you wanna help them, get on the bus. Please. You're not gonna help anyone this way.'

And after another five minutes of arguing, cajoling, and pleading, Rudge packs Keys on to the bus, which rolls out for Boston.

When it becomes apparent that the Stones are someplace other than the backstage area of the Boston Gardens, Monck begins delaying the show. Stevie Wonder does not go out until eight-twenty, with instructions to play as long as he likes. He does close to two hours and then an encore.

'Stevie,' Monck says to him in the dressing room, 'I need twenty-five, thirty minutes more.' Stevie goes out, does one more song and then splits. For nearly seven weeks Chip has treated him with relative disinterest, not even bothering to personally call the lights for his act, and that's how it goes in the rockbiz. Monck doesn't even bother getting angry.

'Ladies and gentlemen,' he tells the crowd. 'Let's hear it for Stevie Wonder.' He does two or three of those, aware that he now has no one to bring on. For the first time in nearly two months, there are no five Rolling Stones in the dressing room warming up. 'Please be advised,' he tells the crowd, 'that we've got an equipment failure that will take at least thirty minutes of work. We apologize for the inconvenience.'

Backstage and in the office of the hall manager, the phones are humming. The Stones are in jail; they must be released. The Gardens is faced with the quintessential showbiz riot situation... a house full of people and no act.

After leaving the Gardens, Kevin White makes one last tour of the South End and then goes home. One of his aides calls him there and explains there has been a new outbreak of trouble down on Brookline and Washington streets and also that the Rolling Stones are under arrest in Rhode Island. If they don't show, no one knows what might happen in the Gardens. The mayor gets dressed and goes down to the hall.

At the hall, Monck is getting impatient. If the Stones are busted, he wants to tell the crowd exactly that and offer them an option: those of you who can wait, groovy. Those of you who don't want to stick around, go home; it's going to be a long night. But they won't let him do it. They're afraid that if the kids hear that the Stones are in jail they'll rip the Gardens into splinters and sawdust. So Monck goes back onstage and says, 'Ladies and gentlemen, I'm glad you're Boston and not New York. But Boston is about to have a problem. You're going to wait another hour.'

'Booooooooooooooooooooooooooooooo. Eat it man. Fuck yew. Bring on the Stones.'

'The Stones' plane has been delayed. I can give you all kinds of bullshit, but let me play more music for you. Talk quietly. Don't punch anybody and give me twenty-five minutes and I'll see if I can't come up with some more information for you.'

In the police station in Warwick, the phone rings. 'There a Mr. Rudge here?' a cop asks.

'Right here,' Peter says, biting a finger.

'Ah, Mr. Rudge... it's, uh, the Mayor of Boston... sir.'

And there is a very respectful silence that spreads through the station house as Rudge goes to the phone and says, 'Yessir... I understand that, sir... we do, sir. No sir, I promise I can get them there, sir. Yes, sir. Sir. Yes, *sir*. You may call me back here, sir, yes.'

When he hangs up, the sergeant he threatened in the airport just looks at him with regret and doesn't say another word all night. Then the phone calls really start to roll in. Mayor White for the police chief. F. Lee Bailey, the Stones' New York lawyers, the newspapers, the wire services, the radio stations... the Governor of the State of Rhode Island. White explains to the police chief that he wants him to release the Stones, on a matter of public safety so that they can play in Boston. 'And can you give them a police escort too?' he asks, as though it were normal for police to give motorcades to people they've just arrested.

In their cells, the prisoners are unaware of the activity going on in their names. After being driven to the station, they were told to remove ties, shoes, and belts ('As though,' Keith Richard says, 'you're gonna hang yourself for bein arrested for screamin at a cop'), and each placed in small, dark four-by-six cells. The only light comes from the corridor and there's a hard slat bench to sit on. Keith is in the first cell on the right, then Jagger, then Chess, then Robert Frank. When they lead Stan Moore in, there's a chorus of 'Hey, man! They got you, too? What you doin here? What is it with these cats?'

'These people are crazy,' Marshall says sorrowfully from his cell, shaking his head.

'Can't I get in with my friends?' Stan Moore asks the cop. 'We got plenty of room,' the cop tells him. 'You can have one of your own.'

Then he slams the door shut and bolts it, and Stan, who has spent eight years as a cop and detective and eight more as a government security man, sinks down and thinks Jesus, the Man finally got *me*.

There they sit. Criminals. Desperadoes. This is where the road has brought them. Where is the party Marshall went looking for? Where? Is this how America treats its visiting rock royalty? Is it? With the chain and the padlock and the mug sheet?

'Say, bro?' Stan asks this guy across the hall from him. 'What you in for?'

'Aw, they say I killed a chick,' the guy says, and everyone gets quiet 'The chick wanted some shit so I give it to her. I didn't tell her how much to take. OD ain't my fault.'

'Christ,' Chess moans. 'Mick? Did you hear that?'

Mick who, man?' the guy asks.

'Jagger,' Stan says. 'Mick Jagger.'

'You kiddin me?' the guy says, afraid to believe it. 'Mick Jagger ain't in *here*, is he?'

'Ain't but a few doors down,' Stan says proudly.

'Honest to Christ?' the guy swears. 'I can't believe it.'

'Hey, Mick… say hello to this guy.'

'Yeah,' Jagger says from the shadows of his cell. 'How you doin, man?'

'Jeezus,' the guy swears. 'I can't believe it. Honest to Christ! Me and Mick… in the same jail.'

'Shit, bro,' Stan says, 'I'll get the man to come down and say hello. That is, when they cut us loose.'

With the word out on radio stations and rumors starting to spread outside the Gardens, what happens if the kids inside learn of the Stones' arrest by word-of-mouth. It'll be splinters and saw-dust time.

'You see that guy standing over there?' Monck's stage manager asks one of the mayor's aides. 'That is Chip Monck, the foremost microphone worker in the United States. You saw the Woodstock movie? That is the voice of Woodstock.'

The aide is suitably impressed and well aware that they're going to have to take some action soon regarding those kids out there, so he introduces Monck to the mayor and, in his best Rhett Butler tones, Chip booms, 'Good evening, sir. We do have a problem, don't we?' Monck tells the mayor that he himself is originally from Wellesley and therefore, more or less, a part of the constituency. Monck knows no fear. Before the night is over, he spends forty-five minutes entertaining the crowd by reading most of *Jonathan Livingston Seagull*.

The mayor is but another facet of the wonderfully surreal movie that is unwinding around him.

'I'm gonna pull the detail,' the mayor says, meaning that he

needs his police in the ghetto, where the stores are burning
again.

'By all means,' the Monck concurs. 'Didn't Woodstock show
us all that they are eminently capable of policing themselves?'

All of this showbiz stuff is a bit strange for the mayor and here's
this Edwardian-looking character, who's charming as hell and has
the chutzpah to suggest that he, the mayor, go out on stage, out
there, and tell the fifteen thousand assembled that their idols are
under arrest.

'May I say that they will feel warmly toward you if you tell
them the truth,' Monck says. 'There may be an occasional "fuck
you" but as a rule, I usually thank them for the courtesy and continue.'

White has to laugh at that one. After all, someone has to tell
these kids the truth. He's called the MBTA and they've agreed to
keep the trains and buses running for two hours after the concert
ends—whenever that may be—so everyone will be able to get
home. He's asked Rhode Island to let the Stones go, and Rudge
has assured him that if they get out, they'll be able to work so
there's nothing much left for him to do but inform the public.

But in the back of everyone's mind is the possibility that if
White goes out and blows it, the kids will sweep over the stage
and tear off his tie, box his ears, and set fire to his suit. They have
come to see the Stones, not their city's number one authority
figure, and it could be a disaster all the way around. Still, White
sees something in Monck's face and manner that makes him trust
Chip, and together the two of them walk on stage.

'Ladies and gentlemen,' Chip says to the crowd, which is solidly bored, tossing frisbees back and forth, sucking on joints
rolled in wheatstraw paper, reading comic books, exchanging soul
kisses, drinking wine, dropping reds, and eating candy. 'This is
not my usual pleasure. There is someone I have just met who I
would like to introduce to you. Ladies and gentlemen... the most
honourable Mayor of Boston, Kevin White.'

'FUUUUUUUUUUUUKYEEEEEEWWWW, KEVIN.'

'YAAHHHHAAAAAAAHHHHH. GO HOME, STIFF'.

With his tie just a tad down from the collar of his white shirt,
in his shirtsleeves, White stands before the microphone radiating
uneasy integrity, like Hank Fonda in *Twelve Angry Men*. About
8 percent of the audience bothers to look up at him, the rest go

on tossing, sucking, drinking, dropping, smoking, kissing, and eating.

'Listen...' he begins.

BOOOOOOOOOOOOOOOOO. BRING ONNA STONES. BOOOOOOOOOOOOOO.

'Listen. . .

'BOOOOOOOOOOOOOOOO.'

'SHUT THE FUCK UP!' Monck, the crowd control expert, shouts at the hecklers. White is so surprised he nearly falls off the stage, but, like the true politician he is, he recovers in time to start speaking.

'YOU WANNA KNOW WHY AYE'M HEAH?' he asks, in that dry New England accent, and that gets their attention once and for all. 'THE ROLLING STONES WERE BUSTED IN WARWICK, RHODE ISLAND, ABOUT TWO HOURS AGO.'

'FUCK YOU FUCK YOU FUCK OFF THE PIG MAN FUCK YOU.' A slow rolling wave of jeers and catcalls sliding down from the balcony like an avalanche of runaway garbage. Kevin stands there, waiting patiently, valiantly, for it to die down. When it finally does, he hits them with the punch line.

'BUT AYE'VE CALLED THE GUVENAH OF RHODE ISLAND AND GOTTEN THEM OUT AND THEY'RE ON THEIR WAY HEAH NOW.'

'YAAAAAAAAAAAAAA, KEVIN KEVIN, RIGHT ON KEVIN, RIGHT FUCKING ON KEV.' People bellowing, tearing apart their vocal chords to sound Kevin's name. A horde of stoned-out kids stomping and cheering. Good old Mayor Kev got 'em out. And Kevin White, a man not unused to the punishments and rewards of public life, gets a taste of what it must be like to be a Rolling Stone and hear people scream like that for you every night. It occurs to him that this may be it. Fifteen thousand people howling his name and he may never hear it like this again in his lifetime.

'BUT NOW,' he trumpets. 'AYE NEED YOU TO DO SOMETHING FOR ME. AS AYE STAND HEAH TALKING TO YOU TONIGHT HAHF MY CITY IS IN FLAMES.'

Monck and the stage crew exchange glances. Wow. What an image! White has picked up on the energy and he's riding it.

No way they have to worry about him any more, the man is in charge. He is performing.

'AYE'M GOING TO TAKE SOME OF THE POLICE AWAY FROM HEAH. AND AYE WANT YOU TO DO ME A FAVOR. AHFTAH THE CONCERT ENDS, GO HOME. WE'RE KEEPING THE MBTA OPEN FOR YOU UNTIL AFTAH THE SHOW. AND WHEN IT ENDS, PLEASE GO HOME. DON'T GO RIDING AROUND. DON'T GO TO THE SOUTH END. JUST GO HOME. I APPRECIATE IT. THANK YOU.'

Huzzzzzzzzah for Kevin, the rock and roll mayor. One last great slapping-five hurrah for a performance that would have made Frank Skeffington proud. And it's only because the mayor has to get back to the South End that Monck doesn't call him back for an encore.

In Warwick, the phone calls continue. The number of kids massed in the street in front of the station house is mounting to Beatle-esque proportions. One by one the prisoners are brought upstairs, mugged and finger-printed, three sets, local, state, and FBI. By the third one, Keith notices, you can pick up some technique and give it a little extra roll that helps define every last whorl and ridge. The cops by now know what they've got themselves into and they're being nice to everyone. One tells Keith, 'Forget it. No one ever got out of this jail after eight o'clock at night.'

But that does not take into account Galluci. Joe Galluci steams into the police station wearing Bermuda shorts, black socks, a white t-shirt, and a cigar. Rudge's phone call must have pulled him away from the TV set, because he's brought along the wife and kid, who are acting like it's a Sunday party rather than a criminal proceeding. Mrs. Galluci is talking politely to whoever looks like he needs a word of encouragement. Stromberg is on the phone trying to locate a helicopter in which to reach Boston. Galluci goes behind closed doors with the chief and when the doors open again, the whole thing is settled.

'Hey, Pete,' he says to Rudge. 'One thing. You got any pictures of the group? Jeez, the kid would love a picture.'

'Stan Moore?' a cop with a clipboard sings out in the jail corri-

dor. 'Let him out... Robert Frank?... Let him out. Michael Jagger?
Let him out... Keith Richard?... Let him out. Okay, that's it.'

'Wait a minute,' Marshall Chess says. 'You got Marshall Chess
on that list?'

'Huh?' the cop says. 'Nah. I don't see no Chess.'

Marshall's hanging on to the bars of his cell, like a real con. He's
been pacing ever since they got there, Death Row material, unable
to sit or relax. 'What the fuck's going on here?' he explodes. 'You
don't have a Chess on your list?'

'Yeah, oh yeah.... on the bottom. Awright... let him out too.'

'Hey, Mick?' Stan Moore says to Jagger. 'How 'bout sayin hello
to my man down here?'

'Sure.' Jagger says, coming down the hallway to pay his respects
to a fellow criminal. 'How you doin, man?' he grins. 'They got
you in here too, hah?'

'Jeeeeeezus ta Christ,' the guy moans. 'It *is* Mick Jagga. What
you doin here, Mick? Hey Mick, can I have your autograph?'

'Sure,' Jagger says, laughing helplessly. 'What you want me to
put it on?'

Rudge has three thousand dollars in cash with which to stand
their bail. For Jagger and Chess, both charged with obstructing
a police officer, it's fifty each. For Stan Moore and Keith, both
charged with simple assault, it's fifty each. For Robert Frank,
charged with assaulting a police officer, a felony, it's a hundred
dollars. Frank, already infuriated by the whole thing, hits the roof
when they hand him back his camera. It's been opened. 'God-
dammit,' he screams, 'you opened the fuckin camera.' His yelling
rouses the chief, who says don't worry, it doesn't matter anyway.
Frank can't have the camera, it's 'evidence,' the weapon he alleg-
edly used to assault the sergeant with at the airport.

Andy Dyckerman, who was having a quiet night down in the
photo lab before this all began, has been watching in horror. After
Keith was arrested, he assumed they'd let him go and that Stan
Moore would be the only person he'd see at the station house.

In the days to come, after the wire services have carried the
news that the Stones were busted in a tiny town in a tiny state
because of a local newspaper photographer, loyal Stones' fans
from all over the country will send him hate mail, letters asking
him if he'd have acted the same way toward Lawrence Welk,
young girls telling him they hope they never get as old and mean

as him (thirty). Dyckerman will even turn one letter over to the FBI. The underground press in Boston will brand him a 'Galella' and the word *paparazzo* will occur and reoccur.

By the time it all dies down, Dyckerman will have become authentically gun shy. The Stones have come and gone, touching his life briefly, but in the future no matter what kind of assignment he goes out on he will take care to ensure that no conflict occurs. He will do everything in his power to go on living a quiet and normal life, in the house where a poster of the Stones once hung in the dining room.

Outside the station, the crowd has gotten so big that the cops decide the only way to get the Stones out safely is through the basement garage. Everyone leaps into the only two limos that could be located and they take off behind a motorcycle escort. The cars have their wheels out of line, which means that over forty-five miles an hour, they bounce like crazy and slew all over the road. And the State of Rhode Island police escort is intent on maintaining a flank speed of sixty. The newly released prisoners and the Tac Squad and Stromberg are getting shook and jangled into Boston. Jagger seems intent on getting the show done. Keith looks exhausted and depressed. Red lights flashing, streetlights gleaming on helmets. At the state line, the Rhode Island cops give way to Massachusetts police. At the city line, two cars full of Boston plainclothesmen and five motorcycle patrolmen take over.

Under arrest as recently as an hour ago, the Stones are now sweeping into a major city like a conquering army. And the city is in flames. Out of the right-hand windows, all Jagger and Keith can see is this orange glow. Wowwww, everyone flashes, the kids have gotten so pissed off with waiting they've finally done it... taken the torch to the home of the Bruins, Celtics, and various ice shows and turned it into a raging inferno, and now it's burning like the Reichstag. From the radio some DJ is shouting, 'If I was doin security, at the Gardens now I'd say,' and he launches into an extravagant German accent, 'yoo vill stey in yore zeats! Vee haff poleese on zee right undt zee left undt if yoo stend, yoo vill be shott!' and then he plays a German march.

Limos speeding through the hot, humid city streets as the Puerto Rican ghetto goes up in flames with German martial

music blaring from the radio. Too outrageous to be real. Gary
Stromberg's looking over his shoulder for the movie camera.
Boston Gardens is covered with kids. They hang from fire escapes
like human cobwebs, peer hopefully out of doorways and windows, crowd the streets. Three of them have gone to Mass General already with dog bites from the police canines, and when the
limos roll in, the kids realize who it is. This tremendous cheer
'YAAAAAAAAAAAAA' goes up. The Rolling Stones are free
again. 'YAAAAA THE MAN CAN'T BUST OUR MUSIC.'

Marx Brothers style, the Stones ran up through an old hotel
and into the Gardens' dressing room. Chip has been doing a
blow-by-blow description of their progress toward the arena and
now he announces grandly, 'Ladies and gentlemen... Mick and
Keith are in the building,' and the place explodes, kids slapping
five and pounding on their seats, as though it's the greatest thing
that ever happened. It's after midnight, which means they have
been in the hall for nearly five hours, plus however long they had
to stand in line outside.

Jagger is shuffling in place to get warm; they tune quickly and
Chip says 'Ladies and gentlemen... The Rolling Stones,' and the
starlight beams from the Super-Troopers pick them up on stage.
Charlie kicks in the downbeat and an electric rush of compressed
energy and anticipation flows across the synapse that separates
stage and audience. For one long moment they're all one, all
criminals, all outlaws, with the Stones playing music only for
the people who have sprung them. 'Oh brown sugar,' kids howl,
'how come you taste so good?' They pick up the 'yeah-yeah'
chorus as Bobby Keys blows a furious circus solo. The horns are
punching and kicking holes in the melody, the drums are booming and everyone is out of the dressing room to watch. Off to
one side of the stage all the red S.T.P. badge holders are dancing
like everyone else. By the middle of the set though, it catches up
with them. The Stones are visibly exhausted and less than sharp.
They do an encore and it ends after two. The people go home
feeling they've seen more than a concert, they've participated in
an event. It's a throwback to the older days. Remember when the
Stones got busted? Yeah? Were you there too? Far out.

After the concert, the Stones' New York lawyers hold a briefing
to tell people what they can and cannot say. Any kind of serious
arrest or felony charge will make Mick and Keith's delicate immi-

gration status even more tenuous and keep them from coming back to work, so Stromberg gets on the phone trying to get his version of the incident into the newspapers.

Stromberg hasn't really slept in nearly a week, and there are black hollows around his eyes that even his glasses don't hide. His grinning laugh is getting ghostly now, and even Rudge, always a pillar of strength, has taken to counting the days until New York. Once they made that turn south from Montreal, Rudge figures it's got to be downhill. Bombs, arrests, whatever, they're going to make it into New York City one way or another.

The next day they invite Mayor White back to the dressing room to present him with an autographed tour poster. The Mayor comes and accepts the gift graciously. 'Their dressing room was quieter than my headquarters on most nights,' he will say afterward. 'There was a certain unpretentious reticence and shyness that I didn't think was put on. I liked them as individuals and I was amazed by their performance. One appreciates the power of a group to hold a crowd of that size. Eventually though, their music won out over my eardrums and I left, still not really understanding it. As to my association with them, I expected some political flak from Rhode Island and elsewhere. Surprisingly, not that many people caught the whole event. Some considered it cornball, some didn't. The Stones were appreciative. So was I. Let's say I did what I could... I'm not quite Mayor Daley, but then I'm not a Rolling Stone either.'

Before that second concert begins, the Mayor of Warwick holds a press conference. For one, he wants to be governor (which he gets to be). Second, he's upset at the relatively small amount of bail some of the Stones' people were released on, specifically Robert Frank's hundred-dollar bargain-basement felony. And last of all, he wants to make it perfectly clear that the City of Warwick itself has nothing to do with arresting and jailing the Rolling Stones, as a matter of public policy, so will all the people who have been flooding the switchboard at City Hall, with phone calls please cease and desist so the government can return its attention to serious matters.

That night, before the Stones take the stage at the Boston Gardens, over the small, but well-respected state of Rhode Island, the skies go gray then black. Lightning tears through the cloudbanks and the thunder rolls. A fullblown summer storm starts dumping wind and water. From Warwick to Woonsocket, the state goes dark. All of it, as though ordered into Interdict by the Church. No TVs, no radios, no record players, no friendly light when you open the refrigerator. Nothing. The State of Rhode Island has been plunged into a medieval darkness. And it stays that way until the Stones walk offstage in Boston at eleven-thirty.

Blame it on whomever you like.

Chapter Eleven

After Boston, it's getting harder and harder to get the band out on stage for the set. Once Stevie finishes up, everyone *knows* that it's time but there seem to be a lot of little tasks that need to be done before everything is just right. Like tuning and tuning and then tuning some more until Chip's voice finally booms out in the hall, and they've got no choice. Philadelphia and Pittsburgh are no one's idea of thrilling places to spend the third weekend in July, and what with everyone thinking about New York, they're like a final affront, the last obstacles on the path.

The knowledge that there are but a few sale days left until it is all over is driving people to find weirder and more outrageous things to do. Like Stromberg and the Monck. Ever since Detroit, they've been hiding little things in the bowl of rose petals Michael Philip scatters on the audience at the end of 'Street Fighting Man.' Just for a giggle. In Detroit, a chicken leg was considered daring. By Philadelphia, they've hidden a great chunk of raw liver in there, and when Jagger hurls the petals in the bowl into the house, some kid returns the favor by hurling the liver right back onto the white stage, where it squishes and sloshes around in a bloody slipstream.

For the next show, they get hold of a pig's foot replete with hoof, knuckle, striated muscle tissue, bloody drippings, and stick *that* in the flowers. But Jagger has gotten wise to the game and he tells Leroy to check out the flower petals before the show, which he does, thereby preventing some Philly kid from going home with a welt on his forehead, saying, 'I'm tellin ya straight, ma! Mick Jagger hit *me* in the head with this pig's foot!'

Weird City, all the way around. On the bus ride into town, one of Stevie's horn players, a heavy-set bopster given to rolling his eyes back and forth in moments of madness and shouting 'Berserkness' as though there were no other word in the universe that could properly convey the insanity of the movie going on inside his head, cracks an amy and says, 'Let's hit the bus driver.'

Locked into rush-hour traffic with a bus full of people and an arthritic old man behind the wheel, what better time to give the old codger a rush he won't soon forget? The horn player actually gets halfway down the aisle before saner heads prevail and pull him back to his seat. 'Let me hit him,' he begs, eyes rolling. 'He'll dig it. I know he will.'

It is altogether fitting that at this time Renee joins the tour to make her bid for rock immortality. Renee is a fresh-faced girl from Grosse Pointe, Michigan. She is nineteen years old, attends secretarial school in New York City and, in a crowd, could pass easily as your ordinary, industrious, God-fearing working girl. She considers herself a writer and while on tour she tells everyone that she is taking notes for an article which she later decides not to write.

With no one giving much of a damn about anything except getting to New York in one piece and then home at this point, Renee comes on like a cool breeze off the hot city asphalt. She is some kind of change.

Back at the large midwestern university she attended for a couple of quarters, she read all about groupies and thought, God, those chicks have guts. She couldn't believe some of the things she read about the way groupies and rock stars acted after the concert was over. Being a good groupie was as righteous as anything else. It was an established role, and the Stones had even gone to the trouble of inserting the Butter Queen of Dallas, Texas, into one of the songs on 'Exile on Main Street.'

Armed with a slip of paper on which a friend has written the name of someone who is supposed to be working on-stage security for the Stones, Renee comes to Philadelphia to see the concert. The name she's been given is phoney, but it's a beginning. She goes to the backstage door with it, talks to a lot of cops, waves the slip of paper about, and keeps repeating that she has to see this guy. Someone goes inside to fetch Stan Moore. Renee tells him the guy's name and Stan says, 'Never heard of him.'

'Well, can you check on it for me?'

'Look, lady,' Stan says, 'I'm head of security, so I should know, right?'

'Okay, man... sorry to hassle you.'

She retreats into the Spectrum and watches the Stones. 'How *spontaneous* the Stones' music is, she thinks. Keith's guitar tears through everything, making you feel as though you're seeing the band play together for the very first time.

When the set ends, she charges right to the front of the hall and sits down by the stage. A cop comes over to her and says, 'Guess what? You'll have to leave.'

'Joe said I should stay,' Renee tells him, 'and he works with the Rolling Stones.' Renee doesn't know who Joe is but then neither does the cop. He looks at her face for a long second, shrugs, and says, 'Okay. Stay as long as you like.'

A couple of the guys in the stage crew are checking out the equipment and Renee gets talking to one of them. He has the security guy let her past the wooden barrier that separates the kids from the professionals and the next thing she knows, she's riding away from the Spectrum in an S.T.P. car. My God, she thinks, settling back into a soft leather seat, this is exactly what a groupie would do. I'm being a groupie. Far out. So whatever this guy wants me to do, I will. Because I got myself into this and I'm not going to sit here being a prude.

Marshall Chess is in the front seat of the car she's in and Chip Monck is in the one in back. People keep opening and closing the doors at every red light, shouting things out the windows and smashing into each other at intersections. Someone crawls out of one car onto the hood of the one Renee is in and makes faces through the windshield.

It's all very crazy but Renee doesn't have much time to dig on it. She's in the back seat being initiated into that groupie thing. 'It wasn't too much, y'know,' she'd say afterwards, 'just a little blow job. I played it by ear. It wasn't the first time I had done anything like that. It was just the first time with a perfect stranger. Marshall couldn't stop laughing.'

By the time the cars pull up at the hotel, Renee has won a place in the hearts of the crew. They take her in past the security guards and she finds herself walking down a carpeted hallway, at the end of which is—*Keith Richard himself.* Keith's leaning out of a doorway in a red shirt looking *so* cool, just checking on some of the talent coming his way. 'Hey, you with the red shirt,' Renee hears Marshall shout to him. 'Get back in that room. You wanna get raped?'

'Aw,' Keith smiles, 'I'm just a juvenile delinquent.' Then he pops back into his room and closes his door. God, Renee thinks, is he far out!

The roadie takes her to his room to finish up what they started in the car. They have to do it in the bathroom because the guy's roommate is supposed to be very straight. The roadie leaves after it's over, and Renee sits watching a movie with his roommate. Then he gets up and locks the door. Renee has no idea of what the etiquette is as far as groupies and roadies are concerned and she doesn't think much about it. She just goes ahead and does it again.

Afterward, the roommate says, 'I've got to go to sleep now. That really wore me out.'

'What?' Renee says. 'That little thing? I mean, really? Go to sleep, man.'

Even though the guy says she can stay in the room, she gathers her stuff together and walks out into the hallway.

There's this gorgeous cushiony chair out there. She settles down in it and watches a bunch of real live, hardcore groupies at work. Girls with expensive clothes and false eyelashes, burnt-sienna hair, and glittering three-inch fingernails. Renee can hardly believe how beautiful they all are.

'We gotta get Keith,' one says, in an accent that combines the worst in glottal stops from the West Bronx and South Philly.

'Yeah, yeah,' a friend agrees nasally, 'he's *so* tough.'

'Bring him down,' another says, 'we wanna *tawk* with him.'

'Yeah. Wow. Keith, wow, he's so tough.'

Renee is sitting there digging on it all when out of a hotel door pops Michael Philip Jagger. The girls all go ahhhh, they try to ahhhhhh stay cool. They immediately light up cigarettes which is standard procedure when you're trying to pretend you don't know who Jagger is and that it's only a cosmic coincidence that finds you standing within whispering distance of his hotel room in the early hours of the morning.

Mick looks them over, then stares at Renee as if to say, 'What is this little orphan doing here?' Then Jagger frowns. Oh God, Renee worries, what have I done? He's going to kick me out. But all he does is close his door and go back into his room.

Renee settles into her chair for a long quiet night out in the hallway. Tomorrow, she figures, I'll go back home. It's been quite a trip already.

When down the hallway comes Gary Stromberg, with a lady in tow. Gary stops and flashes a questioning smile at Renee. The chick with him tugs at his arm and he keeps on walking. Another S.T.P. guy comes down the hall. He smiles at Renee and tells her his room is a lot more comfortable than the hallway and that she can stay there if she wants. 'Wowww,' she breathes, 'you'd let me stay in your room, man?' The groupie grapevine, always a mine of misinformation and mangled half-truths, has informed her that the guy is married. It's part of her code not to fool around with men she *knows* are married so after the guy makes a few fumbling passes, she tells him how she feels, and he lets her go to sleep.

'I really loved him for that,' she says afterward 'because he understood. I guess because he was English. That's what I was told—only an Englishman would feel that way. Of course, I've met a few nasty Englishmen since then. Very nasty.'

The next morning, Renee meets a chick who is really a groupie.

She's spent the night with only a roadie and feels kind of bad. 'She wasn't what you'd call a real high-up-there groupie... I guess I had reached the heights without even working at it. I hadn't even paid my dues yet.'

That afternoon, she goes down to the spectrum to see the show, although she doesn't have tickets. She stands at the back-stage entrance for an hour or so, taking to cops and watching them ride their horses. 'Let's split,' she says finally to another girl, 'I'm goin home.' But then this cop comes up and gives her some tickets. So she goes into the show and it's... terrible. The Stones are really tired and Mick is hardly moving at all. Renee decides to go home as soon as it's over.

But on her way out she gets caught up in a school of groupies who have been everywhere and done everyone. One of them says she's the daughter of a famous groupie. Another is telling stories about the time a well-known rock star threw up on a bed.

A guy from a record company comes out with a pass to the second show in his hand and after some jiving, he gives it to Renee and leads her backstage and all of a sudden, with surpris-ing ease, there she is—in the dressing room. God, Renee, she thinks to herself, you've got to remember this. All these famous people... God, there's Bill Wyman within two inches of you.

Renee, in her lilac outfit with the lilac stockings feels like the lilac lady. The dressing room buzzes and hums around her. A guy who looks like Mick Jagger but only thinner and prettier comes in. Renee immediately falls in love with him. Chris O'Dell scurries by. Chris of the blond and curly hair, the Pisces Apple Lady Renee has heard so much about from the other girls hanging around the hotel.

Chip Monck's golden voice booms from the P.A. and the show starts. Renee goes out to watch from the side of the stage, dancing a little bit every now and then, feeling nice, when a guy she's never seen before comes over and asks her, 'Hey, what's your moral code, man?' By this time, she's smoked a little and sniffed some, and all she can do with the question is laugh at it. 'Like... what is... your moral... code, man?' she repeats.

'Come with me,' the guy says, knowing that he's found the person he was looking for. 'See that sound truck over there?' he says. 'How would you feel about giving the engineer in it a blow job?'

'You're nuts,' Renee giggles. 'You're crazy. No, I couldn't... I... no, I can't... well, I don't know.' Renee figures that the last thing they want around the tour is some stupid bitchy little chick saying, 'No, no, no.' She considers the proposition for a moment more and says, 'Sure. You're doin me a favor by lettin me listen to these concerts. Why not? It's not gonna kill me. I'm not Miss Prude of 1972 so why pretend to be? But I want to look at him first.'

They take her into the sound truck and someone says, 'This is the chick that's gonna do it.' Renee looks across the sixteen-track console and sees the engineer, who as it happens is young, dark, and handsome. Okay she thinks, O-kay! This isn't some ugly guy. This is cool. No problem.

'The lighting is really bad,' Robert Frank says from behind his camera, 'but let's do it anyway.'

'Yeah,' the engineer keeps on saying, 'let's do it anyway.'

'All right,' Renee says, with some authority, 'let's do it.'

With the engineer at the console mixing 'Midnight Rambler' and Renee facing him in a chair, she makes her film debut. She even opens her eyes once to look directly into the camera, something a film star ought never do. Marshall Chess, again present, is laughing so hard he has to use the floor to keep himself from rolling out of the truck.

'Cut.'

'Hey,' the engineer protests, 'let's finish it up, huh?' After all, this is *cinéma vérité*, right?'

'I wanna see the show,' Renee says.

'Go on then,' Robert says, 'you're a good girl.'

After the show ends, Renee leaves the Spectrum with the record company guy who got her in. She doesn't know if he's going to take her back to the hotel or not. To tell the truth, by this time, it's all a little confusing. It's hard to know who to say yes to and who to say no to. Well, Renee thinks, it doesn't really matter. I'm just another piece of ass on this tour so what's the difference? Back at the hotel, she and the record company guy get that little piece of business over with in a hurry and then they take a shower. The guy tells her he has problems with his wife. She takes advantage of him because he's so nice.

'You are nice,' Renee tells him.

'That's the problem,' he says, getting angry.

'Okay, you're a bastard then.'

He sends her to get some whiskey from another room where she meets the doctor. He tells her, 'Come back later. There's a party in Keith's room.'

An hour later, Renee knocks on the door and is let into the inner-inner sanctum. A couple of chicks are sitting on a bed and all the doors are open, and Mick and Keith are walking in and out. Like blah, Renee thinks, when is something going to happen? A whole new set of groupies sweeps into Keith's room and the rest of the band sidles in. Jim Price is there and Stevie Wonder and everyone seems to be pretty mellow. Except for Keith.

Keith looks wild. He's up and walking, impatient and upset. Wow, Renee thinks, this guy has got to be straight. He's having as bad a time of it as I am. He's really human and he's not getting into this stupid stuff at all. All those crazy clothes he wears are just a front, a mask. Because all he's thinking is, 'This is such a drag. I want to get home to Anita.'

Just another late night S.T.P. hotel-room party, with Bobby Keys playing his tapes of that night's concert and Mick in the corner jiving and laughing with Stevie. After a while, they begin clearing the room. Oh God, Renee flashes, I shouldn't be here. I don't have anyone I'm with. She leaves and spends the night in a room down the hall that's being used by all the people who haven't managed to score someone famous for the night.

When she wakes up in the morning, all the money is gone from her pocketbook as well as her red tights. She's been ripped off. Stranded and penniless in Philadelphia on a hot, muggy, spaced-out morning. With her brain full of static electricity and old banana skins, she does the only logical thing—she freaks.

Panic. Out and out terror, and the only solution that occurs to her is this black guy who came on to her at the party last night. He asked her to stay with him but she said no, without really knowing why. Prejudice maybe. Whatever. Anyway, now she needs some help. So she goes and knocks on his door.

But he isn't going to do anything for her unless she does something for him. Wow, she thinks, do I have to do it again? Again? Groupies sure are nothing if they don't put out. After it's over, they take a shower. He gives her twenty dollars.

'Gee, thanks,' Renee says, 'I'll pay you back in New York.'

'I'm really glad you said that,' the guy says, 'I wouldn't want you to think I thought of you as a whore.'

'Whooowhee,' Renee says, 'I wasn't even thinking about that, man. But now that you mention it, okay. I don't really care, but whoowhee...'

Renee splits and is walking down the hallway when she sees Margo coming the other way. Margo and her good friend Mary have been around the tour for a couple days, too. Margo says, 'Come with me. We've got to get Mary out. She spent the night with Bobby Keys.' Well, Renee doesn't really know Margo except from what the groupie grapevine says about her, that she's a pathological liar, but she follows along to Bobby's room. They knock politely on the door and wait. No answer. They bang the brass knocker. Nothing. They try the doorknob. It's locked. They start pounding and kicking on the door.

'What ya want?' comes a sleepy voice from within.

'There's a chick named Mary in there,' Margo says. 'We wanna see her.'

'Ain't no one here by that name,' the voice moans. 'Can't you see ah'm asleep?'

The two of them turn and walk away. Up the hallway comes

Robert Frank. At breakfast the black guy who'd loaned her the money had asked, 'Say babe, how do you feel about orgies?'

'Well,' Renee had said, after thinking for a minute, 'I was in one once with some friends. Like it was, "Let's all strip and fuck" so we did. And it was fun, 'cause it was with friends.'

Her answer has gotten back to Robert and now he says, 'We want a chick to fuck someone on the plane for the movie.'

'Oh, wow,' Renee says, 'I'll do it. Am I going to be the only chick? Ask Margo and Mary too.'

'We'll have to check with Mick and Alan and Peter first.'

'Well, if it happens,' Renee says, 'okay. I don't mind.'

Robert takes the girls to meet Peter and Alan. They're such cool, laid-back guys. Peter is so friendly you can't resist him. When Margo says to him, 'Peter, we've heard some *really* nasty things about you,' he just squints at her through the cigarette smoke and says, 'Like what?'

'Like this Peter,' Renee says, walking into the bedroom, where he sits talking on the phone, closing the door. Rudge just laughs and goes on talking.

Out in the front room of the S.T.P. command suite, Margo and Mary are discussing who should be allowed to go on the plane. It's an honor of the first order and an even more coveted prize right now since they're both under the impression they're being taken along to fuck the Stones. 'It's *got* to be me,' Mary insists, nearly breaking into tears, 'Bobby wants it to be me because of last night.'

'Get fucked,' Margo says succinctly. Two or three more turns of the argument and they're at each other's throats.

'Shhh,' Robert says, trying to smooth things out. 'We'll use all three of you if Mick says it's okay.' They call Jagger and he gives his permission. So it's set.

Wow, Renee wonders to herself. What have you gotten yourself into now? You're nuts, man.

The next thing she knows she's riding to the airport in a limousine containing Margo, Mary, Robert Frank, Danny Seymour, Jim Price, Mick Taylor, and Charlie Watts. As the car pulls into the terminal, there are rising girlish screams from outside. Mick and Charlie exchange weary smiles, as though they've been through it before.

Everyone gets on the plane and Renee takes a seat up near the front. 'Go to the back,' Robert directs her, but all of a sudden she is feeling very nervous and extremely uptight. She needs time to think. What *has* she gotten herself into? Margo and Mary sit down across the aisle from her and start making really, bitchy, cutting remarks. On top of what she's feeling, it's just too much. 'You two better shut up. and leave me alone,' Renee explodes. 'If it wasn't for me, you wouldn't be here, *if* this is where you want to be.' Blessed with an unnaturally loud and piercing voice, Renee's outburst is heard up and down the length of the plane. Everyone shuts up.

A few minutes after take off, Margo goes to the doctor's seat and says, 'Doc, I've got a heart murmur, wanna hear it?'

Of course he does. She's wearing a little sweater that she's got to take off and naturally she's not wearing anything underneath. Someone comes back and lifts Mary up onto his head and pulls off all her clothes. Gee, Renee thinks, this is really something.

Everyone comes to the back of the plane to watch. Mick Taylor is playing bongos, Keith's shaking a tambourine, Jagger is wailing away, doing his 'Oh don't do that—Oh don't do that' rhythm. Bill Wyman's young son happens to be on the flight and Bill's taken him up to the front end of the aircraft and interested him in looking out the nearest window.

Although she's had only a whiskey sour, Renee feels like she's peaking on acid. She's flashing and rushing and unable to focus on anything. Both Margo and Mary are completely naked by now. Bobby Keys has a drink in his hand and he's shouting, 'Get some orange juice. Get me somethin wet I can throw.'

They turn Mary upside down and start eating her. 'Any minute now, Renee,' Renee says to herself 'and it's gonna be happening to you.'

Jagger is laughing as hard as he can. The girls are getting bounced and passed around. Two cameras are turning. Renee gets up to walk away.

'Where you goin?' Bobby Keys asks her. Renee looks at him and all of a sudden he becomes a guard at the prison gate. God— she's a prisoner and he's her jailer.

'I didn't come for this,' she says weakly, 'I want to go up front.'

'Get back there and *strip*,' someone shouts, 'or I'll do it for you.'

Even Bobby Keys, who has participated in some of the tours stranger extracurricular activities, has reached the end of the line on this one. Bobby is offended. What the hell are these chicks doing naked in the back of the plane? They belong in a hotel room. Someone grabs Renee's arm and she screams, 'Let go of me, cock-sucker.' She wrenches free and looks up and one camera is on the girls, the other on herself.

'Oh God, leave me alone,' Renee cries, pushing her way up to the front.

No more than ten minutes later, most of the noise and all of the action has subsided. Renee finds Robert and says, 'I'm sorry I couldn't go through with it... but it just wasn't my trip.' Margo and Mary are still naked, sweaty and sticky with orange juice. Margo is wearing Renee's good corduroy jacket on top, backwards.

'That's okay,' Robert says.

'Hey,' an S.T.P. guy says, 'why don't we do it now?'

'It's okay with me,' Robert says, looking at Renee.

'Let's wait until Mick and Charlie leave so there's no audience,' she says shyly.

The S.T.P. guy helps Renee off with her clothes. She takes off his boots then gives him some head, but the guy can't get it up. She tries to fuck him sitting down but that doesn't work either. They pull all the armrests out of the seats and try again, but it's still no good. Renee goes down on him some more. 'Get *down* on it, girl,' someone shouts and Renee can hear the cameras clicking and turning.

After what seems like a very long time, Renee hears someone say, 'We're gonna land.' She's still naked and unable to focus. Bobby Keys stands next to her with a drink in his hand. 'Can I have some?' she asks.

'Not after what you been doin, man,' he says.

'You cocksucker!' Renee says, outraged. 'You wouldn't even give me a drink?'

'Here,' he says, handing it to her. 'Keep it'

'God it's empty—at least take back the glass.'

No sooner has she handed it back than the guy she's spent the flight rolling and tumbling with grabs hold of her and says, 'We gotta do it again. I *have* to come.' He's soon dripping sweat all over her. The plane comes skidding to a halt at the end of the runway and still the guy is going at it. Someone sticks a pass to the concert on her rear end, and the doors open and all the people leave and still...

When it's finally over, she slips into her top and her pants and carries her shoes down the stairway. Both Mick and Robert are out there filming her and the entire S.T.P. contingent has had to sit in a bus, waiting for the scene to climax. Renee walks down the aisle of the bus and takes a window seat. 'God,' she thinks, 'I'm in Pittsburgh.' In the dressing room backstage, an S.T.P. dude comes over to her and says, 'Madam?'

'Just one of the girls,' she says airily.

'Madam,' he repeats, 'come with me.'

He takes her into the tuning room where she sits down and talks to Bill Wyman, who she describes as a 'nice older man.' 'Okay, madam,' the S.T.P. dude says, taking her by the hand and leading her into a bathroom. 'I want you to do your thing so I can take a picture of it.' Volunteers stand in the bathroom, waiting.

'No, no, no,' Renee laughs. 'You're crazy. I can't do that.'

'All right,' one of the volunteers says, 'let *me* take the pictures.'

'Why don't you all eat each other out and *I'll* take the pictures,' Renee suggests, making her exit.

After the Pittsburgh concert, she goes back to New York. Margo and Mary make it to the city too. They both run out of money after the tour ends and go to work as naked dancers at a midtown peep show. Then Margo gets into making porno flicks and Mary starts turning tricks.

'They shouldn't even have been on the plane,' Renee says afterwards. 'They're not even real groupies, man. The Stones should have had the Butter Queen, Suzy Creamcheese, or Cherry Vanilla there.'

'God. Since the tour ended, it's been so great for me. I went to Madison Square Garden to see the Faces and to Max's Kansas City with T. Rex. I saw the J Geils Band at the Capitol Theater and I even met the engineer from the sound truck again. He took me to watch Edgar Winter record. This very crass, famous musician was there and he said, "Hi. why don't you suck my dick?" They all expect me to do something wild now every time. T. Rex asked me to go to Florida with them because Gary Stromberg told them all about me. Even Chip Monck smiles when he sees me and says hello.

'I think that everyone is a groupie in one way or another if they like music. It's just a matter of who your heroes are. I grew up digging Chuck Berry and Howlin Wolf just like the Stones did. I think a tour makes it easy on a chick. She doesn't have to bother putting the make on anyone. Everyone knows what she's there for. She's there just to say yes.'

Tales from Rock and Roll Heaven

IF YOU WON'T, BABY, YOU KNOW YOUR SISTER WILL

The contemporary music fan is the most fickle animal in the world. If you don't ball him, he'll ball someone else. So the next time you come back, you better look good, with a new hair-do, because there are ten others who'll give it to him, for the money and the popularity.

BILL GRAHAM

It is spring in Brooklyn, Easter vacation, and all the kids are out of school. I am thirteen years old and Murray the K is throwing one of his semi-annual rock and roll shows at the Brooklyn Fox. Each show lasts nearly two hours, features twelve or thirteen acts doing two or three hit songs apiece with the back-up band doing its best to make it all sound just like the record. Five shows a day and sometimes seven and, in between, as filler, there are films about the Navy's Blue Angels and turtle-hunting on the Malay Archipelago.

The whole point of going to the Fox is to see at least three stage shows - an act which requires stoic patience, Zen concentration, and a lot of dangerous trips to the bathroom. In fact, the entire project is extremely hazardous, entailing actual meetings with the young kids of the inner city, the blacks and Puerto Ricans of downtown Brooklyn, who would most certainly beat you up on the subway, on the line outside the theater, stab you in your seat, ask you if they could 'hold a nickel' by the candy counter and/or stuff your head down the toilet. Still, to see Del Shannon, the Capris, and the Shirelles in the glow of those hot blue stage lights was worth the price of admission.

To each show came droves of fifteen- and sixteen-year-old

black girls. They'd line up outside the theater at 7:00 A.M., then spend the entire day inching closer to the first row. They wouldn't go home until way after midnight, not until they were red-eyed from crying and smoking countless furtive cigarettes, exhausted from the hundreds of kilowatt-hours of energy they'd screamed out at those on stage.

The majestic Fox, a red plush Gothic cathedral of a movie house, filled to the smoky brim with these tough-talking black girls, with purple ribbons in their braided hair, black and white saddle shoes, cigarettes in their mouths, and red-and-black letter-men's sweaters with three black circles on the arm and lettering on the back that reads 'JACKIE WILSON FAN CLUB.'

At that time, Jackie Wilson was *the* man. From 'Reet Petite' on down to 'Lonely Teardrops' he had a string of hits unparalleled in the world and he was *bad*. The highlight of his act was when he'd slip off his shantung silk jacket, hook it casually on one finger, flip it over his shoulder with an insouciant grin, then do this little kick and whirl that sent him spinning in a circle in time to the beat. Guys in schoolyards all over the city worked on that move for hours because if you could do it, you had Jackie. But a month or so before the show at the Fox, while walking into his apart-ment building in the early morning hours, Jackie had been shot in the side by what was then described as a 'jealous female fan.' Jealous females seemed to be a downright hazard for the stars of early rock. Sam Cooke was shot to death in a motel by one, although people said there was a lot more going on there than that.

Still, Jackie's being wounded was a major calamity, and a down-right crisis, and Murray the K kept right on top of the situation, feeding the people bulletins on his health. As Easter approached, and time for the great show grew near, Murray actually began suggesting that Jackie himself might make an appearance on stage one day to demonstrate that he was up and walking and back in circulation.

After what seemed like hours of the Ronnettes lifting their skirts higher than anyone had ever done before, of the Mello-Kings pulling off shoulder stands and forward rolls during 'Tonight, Tonight,' Murray took the mike on stage to say that it was his privilege bee-a-zay-bee (which was the way he talked) to present a man who, though he was still recovering from his wounds, had absolutely *insisted* on coming up to thank all the wonderful fans who'd sent him get well cards and letters and prayed so hard for him. Here he was, JACKIE WILSON.

The girls stood up, clapping their hands, making a fluttering sound like the beating of wings. Jackee, they cried out, their voices sweet and clear, Jac-kee, Jac-kee.

Jackie Wilson stood on stage, visibly pale. He was unshaven and wore no tie and looked like a man who had indeed recently caught several slugs in the vicinity of a vital organ and was only beginning to come around. He began a few words of thanks, mumbling, as talking was not his thang, y'see, just bein a singer an all, y'see, here to say thanks y'awl and do ya see?

The girls screamed, ooooohed, ahhhhed, nudged each other in the side with their elbows. They squirmed in their seats, feeling Jackie's power between their legs. They stood up and shimmied. One or two called out, high and sweet, SING, Jac-Kee, SING.

Jackie smiled weakly. The voices grew in strength. SING, Bay-bee, SING, C'MON, Jac-kee. They waited and waited for the downbeat that would start 'Lonely Teardrops,' that would send Jackie whirling in a circle and have him dropping to his knees.

As Jackie stood there, trying to get a word in, the pure sweet voices began to drown everything out. Like a Greek chorus, the voices rose imploring, begging, beseeching, until even Murray the K realized he'd bitten off more than could be chewed comfortably and exclaimed that Jackie was not, Jackie could not, Jackie conclusively *will* not be able to sing today so how 'bout it, folks, how 'bout a final hand for Jackie before he leaves.

But no one is listening. The little girls, possessed, howl for what they want, for what they have to have. JACK-EE, OH BABEE, SING. And as Murray waves to the band to hit it and Jackie hobbles off, those sweet black contralto voices keep on crying out for what they cannot have—SING, JACK-EE, SING.

In the very band that Murray the K waved to, on the other side of the curtain, sitting on stage and looking down into the snake pit of mewling, puking kids was Bobby Keys, not yet twenty, but already on the road with sax in hand.

Thirteen years and three thousand miles from the Brooklyn Fox in the fall of 1972, Bobby Keys is playing behind Joe Cocker in the San Francisco Civic Auditorium. Just two and a half years before, Cocker had filled the Fillmore East to capacity on Good

Friday night and sang as well as a man can, with thirty other people onstage singing and playing with him.

Yet on this night, Cocker seems a man so lost that he is constantly betrayed by objects, by mike heads that flip over the wrong way when he touches them, by cymbal stands that fall to the ground when he walks past. His paper cup of whiskey is always just out of reach so he has to bend and stretch for it, thereby introducing the very real possibility that he will fall down once and forever.

Slurring and screaming words to songs that long ago ceased to have any meaning for him, with a voice that rasps like a file, with a finger pointed to the sky at the wrong time for emphasis and his left hand flicking madly at nonexistent curls, Cocker moves like a battered sinking man. Apeneck Sweeney on a rock stage.

Some in the crowd begin to move out and leave for home, but many more stay. A few shout, DRINK UP, HAVE ANOTHER DRINK, but many more applaud each number and then demand the obligatory encore.

'OB-SCENITIES,' Cocker mumbles into the microphone. 'Bobby Keys,' he says, attempting to introduce the band, Bobby Keys... and ah, uh, Bobby Keys...' Spilling one drink, taking up another stooped over and muttering, he lurches through two more numbers then makes his way to the drum kit where he sits beating methodically at the cymbals with his fists until someone mercifully brings down the lights. The next day, the promoter's people talk about what a crime it is to send a man out on tour and not take care of him. But someone else says that if Joe had actually fallen down, just let go and collapsed, people would have dug it all the more. They could have identified, this guy says, because nowadays everyone digs to get fucked up.

SING JACK-KEE SING. If you don't, there sure are a whole lot of guys behind you who will.

Chapter Twelve

New York is New York is New York. Till you do it there, it hasn't happened. They could have sold the Garden out for a year. They are the biggest draw in the history of Mankind. Only one other guy ever came close—Ghandi.

BILL GRAHAM

Ah, thank you Stones for giving New York the best of you. You put us first on your list by making us last on your tour.

ALFRED ARONOWITZ, 'NEW YORK POST'

MICK IS LOVE TO 20,000 AT STONES BASH.

'NEW YORK DAILY NEWS' HEADLINE

Any schmuck can rent a black limousine for eleven dollars an hour now. The capitalist situation is people in awe of something successful. They love the fact that he [Mick Jagger] has it all, all the chicks, the clothes, all the houses, the things you're taught to work for. A point about the Levi society we all live in now is... you can have all the money you want and still be happy.

BOB GIBSON

By all accounts, the ninth circle of Hell is a fine and private place when compared to midtown Manhattan during the last week in July. The last week in July is the most desperate time, the low point, when the summer seems to stretch away on either side like a great expanse of burning desert waste. The asphalt cracks, the great buildings drip sweat from whining air-conditioners, people seek a hole to die in. Those who have fled for the summer are long gone. The cool days of September that bring relief are light-years away. The spirit of the mad dog is everywhere.

Black men stumble into traffic on Waverly Place, thumbing their noses at buses and wailing private litanies. Taxis screech to a halt on Lexington Avenue at three in the morning, their riders leap out of the back seats, curse, grapple, and exchange punches, then hop back in and ride away as the light goes green. In Brooklyn and Queens, in the small, dark, air-conditioned corner bars, the patrons drink another Rheingold and try to get the Mets game in a little clearer. Tomorrow morning the subways will again be full of white nylon shortsleeved shirts, beads of perspiration, hair.

The Night Evelyn Came Out of the Grave is playing at neighborhood theaters. In Bed-Stuy, a horde of cops go to arrest a young girl wanted in connection with a stabbing and two plainclothesmen get shot with a twelve-gauge shotgun. A sniper exchanges fire with police in the Bronx. Both Gibson and Stromberg are in town for the final Stones' concerts and they have problems elsewhere. The drummer of a band called White Trash that they handle lies in a coma in a Chicago hospital after being brutally beaten for having long hair.

A twenty-year-old black freshman walks into the office of Dean Henry Coleman at Columbia University on Morningside Heights and shoots him in the head, the chest, and the jaw. 'Head of Columbia shot' an announcer headlines on an all-news radio station, and in his suite at the Sherry-Netherland where two cheeseburgers cost fourteen dollars and shrimp salad goes for five and a half, Bob Gibson worries. Christ, he wonders, have they gotten Clive Davis?

Michael Philip Jagger will be twenty-nine years old on Wednesday, July 26, and God, in his infinite wisdom, has arranged an eclipse of the moon as a light show.

Stromberg sits reading a newspaper that says 'MORE HEAT ON MCGOVERN TO DROP EAGLETON.' 'Sure is a lotta crazy shit goin on,' he says quietly to himself.

'Yeah,' Gibson agrees, looking to see if anyone is taking notes, 'but you can't dance to it.'

New York had been waiting for months. Whatever the price was now, New York would pay it. The Stones would get everyone off. Everyone. They had to. It was in the contract.

Like incessant children with strident voices demanding attention right now!!! the phones are ringing. At the Sunday Promotions office at Madison Square Garden, at the hotel where the S.T.P. stalwarts are based, at the fancier hotels scattered throughout midtown where the Stones themselves and the supporting musicians are sequestered, at Gibson and Stromberg's suite, the phones are ringing. People *need* tickets, they *have to have* press passes, the New York imperative governs everything; do you understand this is essential, a matter of the *highest priority*, no matter who's calling.

At Atlantic Records, Mario the Big M picks up the phone time after time, says 'What it is!' which is his excuse for hello, then sighs and says, 'Man, you got to *know* how it is down here. I'll do what I can for you. Lemme check it out and get back to you, but if Ahmet say no, it gonna be no...'

'Peter, Peter!' Jo Bergman calls to Rudge at their office in the Garden. 'It's Jerry Rubin. He's on the phone and he wants tickets for tonight's show. What should I tell him?'

'Tell him to steal them,' Rudge says, without looking up.

The world is collapsing around Rudge. The Film Crew is not allowed backstage at the Garden because they're not union. The cops there don't want to take orders from Stan Moore because they don't know him and he's black. Even though Garden Security has been told in advance that Stevie Wonder and his band are coming, what their license plate numbers are, and the information that Stevie Wonder is *blind* f'God's sake, they refuse to let him drive into the building. He has to walk up Thirty-Fourth Street like everyone else. Bomb threats have been received at the hall and in the hotels, and Rudge knows this is where the Angels are going to have to do it if they're coming. It's their last chance. Everyone who's been traveling under an assumed name changes it again and Keith Richard becomes Count Ziggenpuss; Bill Wyman and Astrud, Lord and Lady Gedding; Mick and Bianca, Mr. and Mrs. Shelley. Wyman is warned not to eat any of the food in his hotel because it might be poisoned.

Jagger is in the suite where Richard Nixon usually stays when he comes to New York, and the room next door is being used to screen all arriving packages and birthday gifts. Even normally placid Mick Taylor is put out. 'They told me I couldn't go out shopping or order food from room service for fear there might be poison in my curry or something. So I ignored it all and did what I wanted.'

They're using the mobile home that's transported the Stones into the halls for months as a decoy one day, then as the real thing the next. On one of the runs into the Garden when the camper actually has the Stones inside, a New York City policeman orders it to halt at the entrance way. The very tired driver refuses, so the cop pulls out his gun and points it straight at him, and at Jagger, who is directly behind him. The driver makes a little noise in his throat, pins the cop against the wall with his front bumper then drives on past, waiting for the sound of bullets ripping into his back tires.

At the first show, it's obvious that the final concerts are going to be both a conclave for all the heavies left in the rockbiz as well as a return to the days of Dallas and Houston when the dressing rooms throbbed with celebs. Truman Capote is back, wearing a buff jacket and a felt jungle hat with a leopardskin band. 'Who are you tonight?' Charlie Watts asks innocently, 'The sheriff?'

Richard Elman and Annie Leibovitz have returned. Dick Cavett is present, wearing a fringed buckskin jacket. During the show, Capote is the only non-Stone who gets on stage, dancing peacefully in one corner as Cavett shouts 'Go! Go!' and laughs from down below.

Backstage, blood is pouring out of the back of a kid's head. The rent-a-cops are cursing with street accents. They're from Hunt's Point and Flushing, guys who read the *Daily News* every day for the *Jumble* and chew Muriel cigars into wet and moldy ruin. Yet here they are working security at a rock concert. When a kid who is being thrown out takes a swing at one of them, a private cop blackjacks the kid until he is unconscious, then works him over some more by the elevator.

'Leave him alone,' a crowd of S.T.P. people yell. 'Quit it.'

'Who said dat?' the cop demands, whirling around.

'It wasn't right what you did,' Alan Dunn says and the cop curses him and makes a move to open his head. Willie jumps in and shoves the guy and Jim Price materializes from somewhere and says, 'Calm down... calm down.'

'I am calm,' Willie screams. 'But you,' he shouts, pointing to the cop, 'you blackjacked that fuckin guy. Now blackjack me. Meet me in the street alone and we'll see how good you arc with a blackjack.'

The guy goes completely crazy at that and tries to get at Willie. More people jump on him, and Alan Dunn is among them, breaking up the fight in which he was originally the intended victim.

'Fuck yas,' the guy keeps shouting. 'Fuck yas.'

'You cheap bastard,' someone yells. 'You're in good company.'

'Throw this man out,' Price says calmly from around a cigar. 'He's berserk.'

It's all Laurel and Hardy with shouts and fists, and as soon as the Stones go on, the floor starts moving. Five stories up in a steel and concrete arena on Eighth Avenue and there are earthquake tremors running through the place. The Garden is staggering on its I-beams and poured-concrete foundations, and the light bridge in back of the band is bouncing up and down in the middle.

New York is media turf, and to accommodate the raging desires of the press, Atlantic Records has arranged a press reception after the concert at the Four Seasons. A ticket is a hot commodity. Anything that gets you within shouting distance of the Stones is worth money.

The party is to take place in two large banquet rooms, one replete with fountain and palms, the other with long tables set with wells of cheese souffl and crackers. Between the two rooms is a corridor built for Orson Welles to track in. As the night wears on, the long, narrow hallway fills with a collection of vampires, lizards, fuzzy-winged fruit bats, and three-toed sloths, the strange nocturnal creatures who make up the pimpled fringes of the rock press and PR establishment.

The regulars are doing coke in the corners off the tips of Buck hunting knives, the brand the rockbiz prefers. There's nothing good to drink and nothing much to eat. The bartenders pretend they don't speak English and the good stuff is locked away under the counter. 'You rotten fucker' someone curses, as the bartender first ignores him for fifteen minutes, then brings white wine instead of a whiskey and soda, then takes it all away before he can taste any of it. 'You Brazilian wetback. Bring that back! I'll have your job for this!'

'*This* is what rock's all about,' Gary Stromberg says stonily at his table, lifting up a rock and looking at it. The circle of people around him nod in agreement. 'I've got no nerves left,' he says. 'Where do I go from here? Every sense has been juiced to its full potential.' Someone claps a hairy hand over his face and cracks an amy under his nose. A burnt-cotton carbolic smell drifts through the Four Seasons. Amys litter the floor, waiting to be stepped on.

Stevie's horn player greets a record company president with two yellow roses in his hand. 'Smell these,' he says kindly, taking care to snap open the two amys hidden between his fingers as the guy bends over. Then he watches as the guy's brain falls out of the front of his forehead. BERSERKNESS.

Rock writers and famous critics stand around trying to pretend they've chosen a respectable profession to spend their lives in. All of them are waiting for the guests of honor. The Stones. Where are they? Is Mick coming? Nervous glances at the door to ensure they won't slip in unnoticed and once they're in, how best to say hello? Grown men acting like adolescents, like feverish pre-pubescent girls, discussing where Mick gets his rings and the things he wears around his neck.

Clad in the luminescent suit in which he began the tour, Keith Richard wanders over to the only person he recognizes at the party and sinks into a chair.

'How you doin, man?' he says quietly. 'Bit wearyin, ain't it?' He gestures with his head at the crowd in back of him and five people follow his glance, wondering what he means by that.

Keith looks lost. There are dark shadows beneath his eyes. His skin is the colour of cheesecloth and drawn tight against the mask of his face. The Inner Circle has been put asunder and scattered in various hotels, and although some people check out of their hotels and into Keith's to keep the party going, it's over. It's not the same as being loose and looking for craziness on the road. Keith keeps to himself, hiding out in his room, brought down and depressed. The energy he's been husbanding to get him through the tour is gone. He's making it to the shows and then crashing for twelve or fourteen hours, spending most of his time asleep. 'New York was so awful,' Chris O'Dell will complain later. 'After all that time, all of a sudden you were by yourself. You were nothing.'

'Right now,' Keith says, looking around helplessly, 'is when you realize you're a product.' Just then a lady looms up out of the haze. She can't hold on to it anymore, she's more than a little stoned, she's got that bright red, New York lipstick smear that says... Berlin in the thirties baby/How about some unnatural sex in the hall closet? She pants, 'I just wanted to say... I thought you were so good in the movie....'

'What movie?' someone asks.

'*The Long, the Short and the Tall,*' Keith says.

'*Bridge on the River Kwai,*' someone else says. 'Yeah. You blew up the bridge, man. You were beautiful.'

'Really,' she pants. 'Thank you. Thank you. For what you gave me. It was wonderful.'

'I swear,' Keith says, in that same steady monotone, 'I never fucked her. I swear.'

A low grumbling roar swells up from the other side of the room. A circle of people fall and stumble into the room, all of them facing Mick Jagger and his wife, Bianca, while attempting at the same time to enter a crowded party by walking backward. Popping flashbulbs, and the kind of hysteria one associates with Marilyn Monroe and Liz Taylor. It's taken Alan Dunn three hours to persuade Mick to come to the party and now that he's there, he just keeps walking, moving steadily, until he is out a side door and riding back downstairs in an elevator before anyone knows what's happened.

After he leaves, there's a moment or two of silence. The star of the evening has been driven out of his own party. But since regret has never been part of the New York life style and is certainly not an emotion anyone would give vent to at a cocktail party, the cracking, sniffing, and drinking soon begin again. By the time the waiters take away the food and shut down the bar, it is early in the morning. The last guests go stumbling toward a wide marble stairway that looks like a Selznick reject from *Gone With the Wind.* Although the bars are closed, bottles appear from the backseats of private limousines. A photographer and a record exec square off in front of the place and work off some excess energy by bouncing each other off the pavement. Taxis cough monoxide fumes as their meters tick away dimes and quarters.

'I want you to come do a radio show,' some guy says, putting the arm on Stromberg, 'I've got a chick for you.' Gary agrees and is on his way out when he sees Terry Southern, who has also come back on the trail, holding on to the bannister. Catatonic, Stromberg thinks, one step in either direction and he's gone. 'Terrah,' Gary says, 'ah're you, boy? C'mawn. We gonna do a radio show.'

'Wonderful,' Terry says.

It is 4.00 A.M. In the studio, the show's other guest is already on the air. Jackie Curtis, one of the city's leading transvestites, is wearing a chiffon dress, a blond wig, and half-day's growth of beard. She has a tattoo on one arm and good biceps, and has already called her answering service on the air and made an appeal for someone to pay her rent.

The show's host is attacking the Stones for being one big rip-off, and as soon as Stromberg and Terry sit down, Gary gets into explaining how the kids all across the country have turned out for it and ticket prices have been kept as low as possible. A rational line of thought if there ever was one. Which at this hour has absolutely no validity. No matter what anyone says, Jackie Curtis keeps bringing the conversation back to Mick Jagger's cock, which she is pleased to note he carries on the left side. Without a doubt, she says, he is still one of the great crotches in rock and roll and she sees no reason why she shouldn't get to play Jean Harlow opposite him in the film version of *The Beard.*

Whenever he is asked anything by the host, Terry pauses. Then he starts talking and stops. He gets a sentence or two out on the subject in question and then veers into the events of years past, remembered conversations, tangents that fascinate everyone. By the time the show ends, it's light outside. One day down, two to go.

In order to convey the total mind-destructive effect New York has on the S.T.P. caravan, consider Markus, one of the stage crew. A quiet country boy who lives in California, growing zucchini and taking care of his lady, he has maintained his sanity for two solid months. Whenever the extracurricular madness and shouting begins, he slides into the nearest wall and becomes invisible. But in New York, even he loses it.

First off, there's his room at the S.T.P. hotel. None of the staff has English as even a second language. The air-conditioning works just well enough to allow you to keep the windows shut against the grimy heat, but not so well that you can count on breathing regularly. The lobby is full of large groups of grinning Japanese gentlemen hung with Nikons, who are in transit from the Empire State Building to the Statue of Liberty.

The hotel is the absolute worst excuse for a living space since the Black Hole of Calcutta, where at least the rates were a little more commensurate with the service. The only policy they enforce effectively is their refusal to allow longhairs in the lobby unless they have room keys. A thin line of hard-eyed, squint-faced, hotel dicks forces the close friends and relations of these lucky few to wait across the street for them, undoubtedly fearing that to permit more than one longhair in a room at a time is to invite drug conspiracies and political calumny.

Markus checks into the hotel and opens the door of his room to discover they have assigned him an authentic closet, done in red, blue, and white, with the total effect that of being inside Betsy Ross' casket. It's a hundred degrees inside and out, and he can't eat, and when he drinks the tap water, he pukes. It's the height of filth and you can't call for help because the phones are busy all the time. Which leads to the now standard S,T.P. act of rebellion... Markus jerks the phone cord out of its socket, stomps the receiver into pieces, then goes down the hall to call room service.

'Room service?' he says, 'I've destroyed my phone. Get me a new one. I've got business to take care of and I ain't got time to hang around. Right, I sure am sorry all right, but I'll pay for it.'

What? What did you say, sir? You broke your phone? The assistant manager comes up to look into this. People are not permitted to break their phones in New York City. The hotel's head policeman informs Markus of this. There are things that can be done to phone breakers. It's a federal offense. By God, it should be. This incident may be a blot on your record for the rest of your life, they tell him. After a lot of this sort of palaver, Markus convinces them that he had a minor breakdown of sorts. They agree to withhold criminal action and find him a new room which, as it turns out, is on the thirteenth floor. They would have a thirteenth floor.

Thoroughly unsettled by now, Markus decides to go drinking with some of the stage crew. Not to one of them plastic, East Side singles swamps. Some place bad. If you're in Hell, might as well see the sights. Some place *real* bad. Badder than Harlem. Some place like the Bowery.

'You sure this is where you wanna go?' they ask him as the car turns off Canal Street on to Mott.

'Bad,' Markus keeps saying, 'it's got to be bad.'

'Bad enough?' they keep asking.

'Not yet,' he says, until he spies this old guy lying in a doorway with no shoes on. His feet are swollen and his toes poke out of red socks like dead soldiers frozen at their posts. There are scabs all over the guy's face and his whole body is kind of blown up, waterlogged. 'This is it,' Markus says, 'now the worst bar.'

The worst bar is filled with cripples, with the toothless, one-eye-missing, sonny-kin-ya-buy-an-oleman-a-drink street people. Long-gone, glazed eyes and stubbled faces, drinking from quart bottles of Ballantine Triple X ale as Johnny Cash's 'Ring of Fire' plays on the jukebox. The S.T.P. boys get as blind drunk as anyone else on beer and bad tequila. On the way uptown, they hang their dicks out the car window and piss.

Everybody's got it. Edge fever. Apple Madness. Rock shock. End-of-the-road psychosis.

'A-ha,' Gary Stromberg says to Dick Cavett as he walks into the Stones' dressing room before the Tuesday afternoon show. 'It's the George Plimpton of rock.' Dick smiles politely and edges toward the banquet table. Like everyone else, he finds himself waiting for the Stones on their turf. Because his late-night talk show is said to be in danger of going off the air, and because the Stones are hot, he has come to boost his ratings and give the nation a backstage look at the rock world.

Stromberg initiated contact with Cavett's people, who invited Jagger to come and sit down for a full ninety-minute interview. Just Mick and Dick for a solid hour and a half, which might be great TV but is completely out of the question. Jagger hasn't the time for that kind of thing and, besides, it's unthinkable for a star of his magnitude to wander that far outside of his own frame of reference.

The mountain must come to Michael Philip. So Stromberg invites Cavett to come out on the road, to Boston and Philly, where he'll be able to film and tape all the stuff he needs backstage and at the hotel. But Dick, too, is a star, and a busy one, and he hasn't the time to go gallivanting, so a compromise of sorts is reached which thrusts Cavett into the heart of the New York maelstrom in order to get an hour's worth of product.

Dick is accompanied by a full ABC camera crew who go about setting up their equipment and taking light readings. Chip Monck runs in and out of the dressing rooms, oblivious to it all in a red-and-blue Montreal Canadians' hockey jersey, saying 'Yes? Would you please? Can you? A Kahlua and cream? And a cardiac needle, I think.' Princess Lee Radziwill sits quietly in one

corner of the room next to Andy Warhol, who looks pale as death
and perfect in a seersucker sports jacket and faded jeans. Today's
Daily News and *Post* are scattered on a table and both papers are
full of articles and pictures on the Stones.

The TV lights ignite into life as the boys themselves slouch in.
Soon enough, Dick has the microphone out and he's interview-
ing Bill Wyman. They chat pleasantly about this and that, with
Wyman smoking a joint wrapped in filter paper in plain view of
America.

'Are you a chain smoker?' Cavett asks politely.

'No,' Wyman grins, 'not at all...'

'It looks like you're going to burn the filter there,' Dick notes,
as Wyman takes a deep drag and says, 'No, I won't. I assure you.'

Cavett's interview with Mick takes place in a spare dressing
room that has been set up like a little studio. Dick seems a bit
nervous and Jagger is there in body only. That fragile, spooky
quality he shares with most finely tuned race horses is away and
galloping. He's all over the place verbally, smiling, mugging, shaking his head at some questions, wisecracking his way past others.

'What's your weight?' Dick asks. 'Someone outside wanted to
know.'

'Ten kilos,' Mick says.

Mainly he is jittering, qualifying everything he says, which is
Jagger at his most maddening, saying, 'Yeah a bit yeah all right
yeah a gas actually hard to say a bit exhaustin but I'm ready to do
it again,' and so on. What goes down on tape is two very wired
individuals trying to talk to each other in the obvious presence of
a camera.

At the edge of the circle of lights and cameras, Dick's clipboard
assistants, male and female, check the second hands on their
watches and make notations. Someone mentions that Cynthia
Sagittarius is outside, waiting to get in, and one of the assistant's
eyes light with recognition. 'Oh,' she says, 'bring her up. Please.'

In the month since we left Cynthia by the side of a road in
the South, fame has reached out its sweaty palm for her. She has
been enshrined forever by *The New York Times* Sunday Magazine,
which uses her name in the title of their tour story. 'As Cynthia
Sagittarius says—"Feeling... I mean, isn't this what the Rolling
Stones are all about?" ' Big black letters on white newsprint and
some of Cynthia's friends start mumbling things like 'star' and

'elitist.' After all, Cynthia's not the only person who's been following the Stones around for two months, nor is she the most daring. Hell, Jo-Anne had herself smuggled across Lake Michigan by motorboat with the Coast Guard in pursuit in order to get to the Toronto concert. Now, that's dedication.

Still, Cynthia is persevering. Much like Benny Profane of Thomas Pynchon's *V,* she has spent the last two weeks yo-yoing up and down the East Coast from gig to gig. By the time she steps off the elevator onto the Garden floor, the TV crew is set up for her and waiting. The ABC lights and the ABC color camera and the ABC assistant grabs her by the shoulder, gives her a But-how-are-you-dear hello and marches her over to her mark. A second later the lights blaze crystalline bright and in slips Mr Cavett with a microphone.

'Ah,' he says with a wry grin and a dip of his head, 'so you're the famous Cynthia Sagittarius, eh?' Dick's delivery combines the dryer elements of Fred Allen's voice with Groucho Marx's rhythm, 'and you hitchhike to every performance, eh?'

'Oh,' Cynthia says, wide-eyed. The lights are so bright on her face they wash out her freckles, the microphone is by her mouth and waiting, the cameras are turning, the people are consulting their watches and waiting. 'Oh,' she says, 'I can't.'

'Okay, okay,' somebody says. 'Hold it.' The cameras stop.

'Dear?' the assistant explains, 'Dick just wants to ask you some questions.'

'A minute spot is all we need,' someone else clarifies.

'Go ahead,' Gary Stromberg grins.

'C'mannnnn,' Willie coaxes, 'you can do it. Remember all those sandwiches I gave you.'

A semicircle of people stands waiting. What the hell? The kid comes out, does her schtick, then the lights go off and you cut to the commercial. Everyone wants to be on TV.

'You see,' Dick explains kindly, shifting from foot to foot 'we performers are so conditioned that when the light comes on we begin. So maybe if we can try it again.'

'Oh,' Cynthia says yet again, looking around, 'you've all been so nice to me.' She looks at Cavett, the lights and the camera, and her face breaks down and she starts to cry. 'That's what's so terrible. You've all been so nice to me and I can't...' She starts to blubber, 'I can't.'

'Okay,' Dick says, motioning for the crew to back off. 'We're sorry,' he says to her, 'we didn't mean to upset you.' All his assistants give each other that palms up, eyebrows raised gesture that says.... Whatta you know? Somebody who don't wanna play the game.

And having thrown away her chance at being famous for at least fifteen minutes, Cynthia wipes her nose and dries her eyes and resolutely marches into the house to see the Stones for possibly the fortieth time in the past two months, the only person in America to come into contact with it all and emerge untouched.

As the band moves out of the dressing room toward the stage, Peter Beard says, 'Have a good show.'

'Yeah,' Willie says. 'Hit 'em high, hit 'em low.'

'A good show?' Keith says to himself. 'Good luck chaps, all the best,' he mumbles, hitching his guitar to his shoulder and going out to wait for the introduction. The Stones stand in back of a double curtain, stage right, surrounded by a circle of bodyguards, an ABC cameraman or two, Rudge, Dunn, Robert Frank and Danny, all of whom have come as far as they can go. On the other side of the curtain, the buzz and hum of the crowd is clearly audible. The curtain blows back and forth gently and Jagger shuffles in place, bells tinkling, Charlie spins his drumsticks in never-ending circles. Then Monck makes the announcement, the tidal-wave cheer wells up, and they step through the curtain alone, to begin another performance.

After it's over, with another one still coming up that night, Peter Rudge looks like a very sick man with a lot of problems that no one can solve. As though it would hurt him to smile, as though the effort itself was too painful to contemplate. 'Please,' he tells everyone in the dressing room, 'please. No one onstage tonight except the band. No one at all.'

God,' Peter Beard tells Charlie Watts, 'the combination of some of the African rhythms with your music would be fantastic. Why, look at Picasso. He was great, but the African thing made him greater. "Women of Algiers"... it's that fusion I'm talking about.'

'Well,' Charlie says slowly, 'Ai loik the concrete nudes meself. The great feet an all.' Charlie's wife Shirley sits by his side, listening. Marshall Chess is in and out, worrying about the Film Crew. He's taken to wearing thick, white-framed sunglasses that hide half his face and make the pretense of looking together irrelevant.

'It's the actual charge of the rhino that's most thrilling,' Beard says. The band has left for the stage, but the dressing room is as full as it was before. Stevie's horn player comes offstage after a hot set, soaked with sweat, with that familiar carbolic odor hanging over him like a cloud. He's got a new trip. A syringe with no needle in it that he jabs into your arm just as he flicks your skin with a fingernail so that by the time you look down there's this grinning madman holding a syringe in your arm, shooting you up with God knows what. It's a major horror and the first time he hits Keith with it, he's tuning, about to go on. Keith looks down, sees what's going on, stiffens up and starts to go into shock until the guy pulls it out, holds it up and says, 'BERSERKNESS, huh?'

'After this tour,' Stromberg says, pointing to the horn player, 'he's going into medicine.' As if on cue, there's a snap-crackle-pop and two people get hit with amys in a corner.

'Christ,' Marshall says, 'I remember the first time I got hit with one. I was on the phone talking percentages and someone called my name so I turned my head. POP! "Hold on," I said... POP!

"Hold on, geez"... for twenty minutes, I said, "Hold on." I was rushing. Phew. I got my nose burnt that night. That's bad shit, man.'

'Doc, doc,' the horn player moans, slumping in his seat, 'gimme a heart attack, I need an amy.' Stromberg giggles madly. 'Hit the doc,' someone suggests.

'Nah, no challenge,' the horn player says. Spying a priest on the other side of the room, he actually gets to his feet, pulls another of the little corncobs out of his jacket pocket and advances on him.

'No,' Stromberg screams, 'NO. He's from Our Lady de Santana, it's a rock and roll mission.'

'So's mine... let me hit him.'

On stage, the Stones are doing one of the best shows of the tour, a rocking bitch with one song exploding right after another, the musicians tight and on top of each other. The crowd is solid New York, they think they're the hippest and the toughest, but they look a lot like the kids in Indiana and Ohio. They scream for much the same things. With the greater anonymity of the

Apple comes the desperate need to cry, 'I AM.' Some of the outfits are very outrageous... top hats and breechcloths, black leather and chain belts, black fingernails and lipstick, rouged nipples... a good proportion of the house look like they've been dressed by Hermann Goering, while the rest have bare feet, cut-down jeans and long blond hair, the Levi look of the sixties.

'*Come on down/Sweet Virginia*,' Jagger sings, as Keith and Mick Taylor sit perched on stools behind him with acoustic guitars in their hands and soft blue lights shining.

Backstage there glides a chick in red satin hot pants. Half her ass is out for inspection, and a fake fox fur is looped over a no-bra net top that features her nipples.

'Just drop your pants and there you are,' a record exec says, nodding in her direction.

'Yeah,' someone says, 'shoulda seen her when Zeppelin was here. Her and her girlfriend done this number on the rubdown table with one of the boys. He said to the security guard, "Hey, you want some of this?" Little fat guy, weighed three hundred pounds, he threw off his hat and billy club, one starts lickin his balls while the other gave him head. I was dyin... "I couldn't come," he says twenty minutes later, "I was too scared."'

'Talk about scared,' the record exec says. 'Hey, Doc, I come down with this pimple on the outside of my joint... now couldn't it be something other than what I think?'

'It's possible,' the doctor says. 'It might be a dry ulcerated lesion caused by a spirochete.'

'A dry... ulcerated... lesion, huh? 'Cause I got one after this chick and her friend went down on me at a concert here a month ago. But it went away, so I was wonderin... Hey, you wanna try her? She and her partner, they work together. Lemme call her over. She'll like you...'

'And actually,' the doctor says clinically, as the chick approaches, 'just soap and water will kill the spirochete.'

One final show to go, the show that Chip Monck has been waiting for since the tour began, the night that it will all peak. Monterey, Woodstock, the concert for Bangladesh, all the shows the Monck has lit and supervised, will pale in comparison to this one, *the* show of the rock era.

Onstage, total chaos must reign. Monck has rented an elephant for seven hundred bucks. ('Chip! Seven hundred?' Rudge groans.) The elephant is trained to walk up steps. At the end of the set, it will come out on stage, bump Jagger, then bow and present him with one perfect long-stemmed rose. Everyone will then sing 'Happy Birthday.' The elephant will pat Mick on the ass and leave. Beautiful. Makes the seven bills seem a mere bagatelle.

No elephant, the Garden says. Elephants are for the circus. What happens if the beast gets enraged by the unruly crowd, runs wild, and horribly mangles a brace of teenyboppers?

Okay, the Monck concedes, no elephant. But there must be things to drop on the people from the ports in the ceiling. This is an official Monck trip—ending tours by dumping wild and assorted goodies on the band and the audience from the roof. Like beach balls. Or balloons. Or confetti. Maybe even flour. 'I'll need an airplane engine and an eight-inch air duct for the confetti, but we got five hundred pounds of it so there should be enough...'

No beach balls, says the Garden. No balloons. The kids will start throwing them at each other and a riot will ensue. No flour. Flour burns when you drop it from that height. Maybe confetti. Maybe.

Hmmmmm, the Monck wonders. The problem with dropping inanimate objects out of the ports is that the people in back of the stage, the ones who most deserve a treat, will be denied. So, uh, let's drop uh, let's drop chickens. CHICKENS! The idea unfolds in Monck's head like a tulip blossoming in a series of time-lapse photographs. Chickens indeed. What could be better than a flock of squawking chickens in mad flight as the Stones whomp and kick their way through 'Street Fighting Man'?

But the problem must be researched. Monck and Stromberg obtain a chicken and throw it out of an upper-floor window in the Sherry-Netherland. It makes it a good two blocks down Fifth Avenue before settling safely onto the pavement and disappearing. Chickens do fly. Monck goes to the Bronx and buys five hundred chickens at a dollar and a quarter each. He has to look extra hard for ones with wings but he gets them, and then goes back to report proudly to Rudge on his success.

'Chickens?' Rudge moans. 'Five hundred? Chip, you know me

and chickens. What happens if they come down and claw people's eyes out?'

'Yes,' Chip admits, 'that might be a problem.' Also, the people might begin tearing them apart and eating them live, geek-style. 'What we'll do,' Chip says, 'is dip their little toes in a vat of warm paraffin. That way they'll have little booties on and they won't be able to claw the people.'

When the Garden hears about the chickens, they seal off the roof.

It's more than a mere difference of opinion regarding the hows and whys of stagecraft that separates Monck and the Garden's Staff. It's the quintessential conflict between the free spirit and the organization. To the Garden, rock and roll is but another set of gate receipts, and if you lie down with the businessmen, you wake up wearing gray flannel. These are the people who were going to run the whole tour, but now the Monck can't convince them to permit the great pie fight. of all time on stage. Chip is thoroughly defeated every way he turns.

'Amys,' Gary Stromberg tells Chip, trying to cheer him up. 'We'll lay them all over the floor and hire a caterpillar to drive over them and crush 'em and imagine! There'll be twenty thousand people rushing at the... no. Huh?'

Poor Chip. New York, supposedly the crown jewel in the tiara, is turning out to be a rhinestone. A cheap, fucking rhinestone. The tight-money people are in control and all Monck can do about it is punch one or two out, curse a lot, and scheme.

It is with Chip Monck's sense of frustration that most of the S.T.P. heavies enter their final day on tour. New York is definitely winning. Thomas Eagleton seems certain to get the axe from Smiling George. Dean Henry Coleman is going to live. Bobby Ramirez will be dead in a few days. Gary Stromberg goes to Tiffany's to buy some trinkets and refuses to give his right name to the salesclerk. He doesn't want to be bothered with a lot of junk mail.

At the Sherry-Netherland, a girl introduced as the Downer Queen of New York is talking about Seconals and Mandrax and how a car door happened to slam on her finger in London. 'We were high,' she explains.

Robbie Robertson of The Band needs four tickets, and Columbia and Paramount called earlier today. The phones are ringing all the time and the demand has escalated into screaming hysterics—listen, you bastard, you know who I am?

It is quieter in Michael Philip Jagger's suite. Just the birthday boy, Commander Rudge, and Robert Frank. Robert is totally exhausted. More so in his head than physically, but still he has managed to schlep his camera and tape recorder up to Mick's room by himself. Danny's not working today. By New York, Robert is jokingly referring to Danny as the 'second Keith,' a phenomenon that regularly occurs with people who get too close to Mr. Richard. When Robert arrives in Jagger's suite, Mick is more than glad to see him. Within the S.T.P. community, Robert has won nearly universal affection as a man of integrity. He has proved himself every inch of the way, and not only do the Stones accept him, but they respect him, which is a rare phenomenon.

It's a shame that he can't begin to film now, because for the first time, the Stones are vulnerable. Their resistance has been worn down and since they like Robert so much, there would be no switching off of lights when he walked into a room with his camera, no avoiding the microphone. The truth is all around now, itching to be recorded, if only he can get himself together enough to do it.

'Film, but no tape recorder,' Robert is told, as Jagger and Rudge sit on the bed, calmly going over the figures for the tour. Two and half million, $700,000, expenses over budget, more than we had hoped for after taxes, a real clean gross, and so on and so forth. Robert is once again amazed by the way Jagger compartmentalizes his brain and concentrates on the financial reports, then goes out to perform before twenty thousand screamers in the Garden.

Jagger is twenty-nine today, the age at which Nijinsky performed for the last time in public. Madison Square Garden, where he will celebrate the occasion, is in a state of siege. From Nutley and Passaic, White Lake and Swan Lake and Ellenville, from Forest Hills and Corona, over the Throg's Neck and the Whitestone and through the Midtown Tunnel, by subway and bus, the crowd has come and is walking, pushing, and shoving in the streets from Thirty-First to Thirty-Fourth, on Seventh and Eighth Avenues.

There's a full block of street sellers and buyers, quoting, 'Ticket? Ticket? Who wants a ticket? Seventy-five.'

'Hey, man, fuck you, it was fifty a minute ago.'

'Check around. Seventy-five, man. I don't make the price. You gotta pay what it costs.' They're haggling like Arabs in the marketplace, with the only commodity available Stones tickets.

The cops stand behind wooden barriers with polished billy clubs in their hands, eyes hard. If this is the end of the world, you won't see it in their faces. They're bored and doing their jobs, New York City's Finest to the bitter end.

'Hundred and fifty for a pair of tickets,' the very stoned driver of a blue Pontiac with Jersey plates keeps saying out of his window, as he inches through the crowd of t-shirt sellers and souvenir peddlers. The next time he comes around the block, it's 'Two hundred dollars for the first pair of tickets, two hundred, two...'

As soon as it's dark and Stevie goes on to do his final set, the kids and the cops get down. Bottles crash on the pavement, and the cops mount separate and furious charges into the mob. It's Budapest in summer of '57 as four thousand people break and run down Eighth Avenue with cops on horseback in pursuit.

In the dressing room, two gleaming stainless-steel bowls are filled to the brim with sweet, dark melted chocolate. Little bits of pineapple and skewered cherries await dipping. There's a big cake in the shape of America with little flags marking each of the tour cities, 'Chicago: Nice Place You Have Here, Hef,' and 'K.C. — Is that Jackie?' and 'Dallas - Ft. Worth: Trouby, Radish, Peter Turning On.'

'Ohhh,' the princess asks, 'is that me?'

All the S.T.P. regulars are wearing purple t-shirts tonight with their names and jobs listed on the back. They mass outside the dressing room for a graduation photo of unparalleled weirdness, thirty-eight people from various levels and places who almost certainly will never again be in the same physical space.

'Now,' Chip instructs them, 'you are all paired off in twos to one of the artists. You must block all throws so that none go into the audience. Repeat, none. The first person goes up to the artist, whopp whopp. The face is out of bounds but the head, neck, and chest are permissible targets. The second person then presents the artist with two pies. He must stand there until he has given over possession of the pies. The original first person then returns with two more and act as the original second person's second...' Only the Monck would have a procedure for so simple an act as throwing a pie. He also has 154 cream pies. When the Garden discovers this, they freak and make him remove them. Off the stage, Chip, off! Shame on you, you bad boy. Monck argues, then allows them to be taken away. He's angry and crestfallen, but playing his part perfectly since the pies the Garden confiscates are the ones they're supposed to find while there is a whole other load hidden in boxes behind the amps.

Backstage, New York City is making one final attempt to beat the rules. Four firemen in full uniform saunter in to inspect reports of overcrowding and it's only after twenty minutes that they're revealed to be full-blown hippies in costumes with their hair pinned up under their hats. They get thrown out.

'Y'know this camera crew?' Stan Moore asks Gary Stromberg. 'They say you okayed 'em.'

'Fuck no, throw them out.'

Five people wander in with fake red S.T.P. badges. 'And you know this Rudge fellow, do you?' Peter Rudge asks one of them.

'Oh yeah,' the guy says blithely, 'he runs the tour.'

'Nice guy is he?' Rudge asks, playing with the poseur, like a fish on the line. 'Handsome lookin? Throw 'em out.' The tour accountant is walking around with thirty thousand dollars in cash on him and two plainclothesmen shadow him, ready to fall to one knee and whip out their service revolvers at the slightest unexpected noise.

'STAN!' Rudge screams. 'Can I please have all the people on the other side of the stage?' Then he's off, on a dead run to the next crisis, with no time at all to watch the Stones hit the stage for the last time as a great roar comes up from a crowd that knows it will see rock history. Michael Philip is going to stand on his head, take off his pants, and go completely mad. It's all going to happen and it's going to be great... oh my yes, it's gonna be great, why this here's the greatest rock and roll band in the world, even *Newsweek* says so.

Right from the start, Mick is leading it, as Keith shouts, 'C'mon, let's get it,' as Bobby Keys jumps up and down on his side of the stage. The guitars' notes slide one into another like tightly coiled steel springs and the decibel count rises (six above the pain level, *The New York Times* will report). The crew are drinking up their farewell case of Dom Perignon; there are flowers; the light truss goes down and then up again and multicolored gels litter the back of the stage. Pure white light bathes the band for the final time and they finish up 'Street Fighting Man' and walk off with the Garden shaking, like a building in flames after a direct buzz-bomb hit.

Rudge steers one of the Garden heavies to the dressing room for a celebration drink and as soon as he's out of the way, the Stones go for an encore. Monck wheels out a tray with a birthday cake and glasses of champagne on it, and Bianca comes forward with a great panda and kisses Mick and whopppp Chip hits him with a pie.

There have been memos within the S.T.P. community as late as this afternoon to suggest that there be no pie-throwing on stage tonight, what with the threats on Mick's life and all, but the Monck will have his fun. The boxes come open, Jagger gets one whopp on the arm, throws one at Charlie Watts, who ducks. Stevie's horn player cracks an amy and flings one pie that wipes out Stevie's three chick singers with one creamy swoop.

'Goodness,' the princess says in the relative sanity of the dressing room, 'does this happen all the time?'

'Oh, yes,' Chris O'Dell says knowingly. 'Sometimes it goes on all night. Maybe it would be safer if you...' but the sentence is still in her mouth when the door swings open with a pie-smeared, hysterical Gary Stromberg running in and letting go with a pie aimed at someone's head. He ducks and the pie hits a pile of camera equipment and runs up the princess' leg and all over Andy Warhol's jacket. Chris O'Dell gets up and scurries out of the room.

Out front, they're singing happy birthday to Mick. If you're M.J. you get to celebrate your birthday in front of twenty thousand people. The stage is covered with a quarter-inch of cream; it's everywhere, oozing and sticking. Charlie sits behind the drum kit, unscathed, still playing. He does the final roll on 'Happy Birthday,' kicks in the final beat, hits the cymbal and is about to rise when Ian Stewart, who is so covered with pie he looks like Frosty the Snowman, plants one large pie on either side of Charlie's head. Whop!

Whop! they hang there for a second like pastry ear muffs, then slide slowly off, leaving great mounds of fluffy white stuff behind.

'Get Rudge,' someone screams and the madness continues into the backstage corridors and dressing rooms.

After it's over, Gary Stromberg—three quarters of an inch of meringue and cream streaking his beard and hair, sightless, his glasses having been broken and lost somewhere, smelling like a bakery—hails a cab to get back to his hotel. 'Sherry-Netherland,' he says climbing into the back seat just as the driver turns to get a good look at him. Gary is also barefoot, his boots having become so filled with pie slop they were unwearable. 'Awright,' the driver says calmly. 'Get the fuck out.'

As twenty thousand kids empty into the streets outside the Garden, taking over the sidewalks and gutters, one New York cop looks them over and shakes his head. He spits in the street and nudges his partner. 'Look at 'em,' he says, pointing out the best minds of the next generation. 'Gowan. Take a look. It's eerie I tell ya. Dey're in a... a state of euphoria.'

People in drag with white paint on their faces stand in the lobby of the St. Regis Hotel like pilgrims denied ascension to the inner sanctum. So near yet still so far away. The party that ends the tour is upstairs.

'The wildest craziest best party of the year—so far,' Suzy will report breathlessly in the *Daily News* the next morning, so that all the people riding and sweating their way to work on the D train can read about it.

What a guest list: Zsa Zsa Gabor exiting early (after having had her picture taken with Bob Dylan at his request) saying, 'Doll-ink, ven you're hot, you're hot.' Lord Hesketh of Easton Naston Castle, Isabel and Freddie Eberstadt (making their first New York appearance in years), Gianni Bulgari, Andrea de Portago, with nothing on underneath her white satin pants and open-to-the-waist satin jacket, Oscar and Francoise de la Renta, Graziella Lobo, Count Vega del Ren, Mrs. Walther Moreira-Salles, Ceezee and Winston Guest, Caterine Milinaire, Lady 'Slim' Keith, Nitia Guerini-Maldini, Clyde and Maggie Newhouse, and many, many others as Suzy herself says, '...too straight to mention.'

Woody Allen, Carly Simon, Sylvia Miles, Dick Cavett, Andy, Peter, Truman and the princess, Candy Darling, Pat Ast, Huntington Hartford, George Plimpton, Tennessee Williams, why it's the party of all time; it's the final mix on the seventies with the

Beautiful People getting a chance to hang out with the rockbiz, for one night only. Bill Graham has even gone to the trouble of putting on a suit and tie for the occasion. With entertainment by Count Basie and the Muddy Waters Blues Band on the Starlight Roof of the St. Regis Hotel.

It makes Charlie Watts want to cry. Not the guest list, the fact that the Count himself is playing at a party in *his* honor. Markus, who has recovered from his Bowery phase and is now at the very opposite end of the New York social spectrum, goes right over to him sits down on the piano bench and says, 'You Count Basie?' The Count leans back nice and easy and says, 'Thass me,' and Markus says, 'M-M-M-Man, I just wanted a chance to see you before you got dead.' The Count digs that then nods in the downbeat and lets fly and the band has got to be together tonight because Bobby Keys checked in with them between sets.

Starfucker heaven. I'm somebody and you're somebody and she's somebody and there are so many somebodies a-jumble on the dancefloor it's goosebumps time. It's impossible to tell who's having and who's being had, which is of course what makes it so thrilling. Castes away, dear. It's certain that most of these people were not present at the party that ended Chuck Berry's last tour, so there must be something more involved here. 'The party is an Ertegt n affair,' Capote says. 'Ahmet and Mica... it has little relationship to the Stones.'

The New York Times reporter asks Bob Dylan what he thinks of it all. In a straw hat, flannel shirt, and dark shades, the poet-prophet of the sixties smiles and says, 'It's encompassing... it's the beginning of cosmic consciousness.'

How right you are, Bob. It is precisely that, a coming together of people from all levels that is perfectly diffracted, with no mixing or interaction at all, and a thousand separate parties going on at the same time. Everyone is there to see and be seen and honor their own egos. And aren't you, ah, wait a minute, I'll get it in a second. Mario the Big M says, 'I see this cat I know I know so I'm tryin to remember the motherfucker's name. I didn't think it could be Dylan, not in a big straw hat and raggedy glasses. Who the fuck is that I keep sayin to myself. That mother *must* know somebody 'cause when he go over to Mick all these people step back. So I walk up an say, "Hey boy, what's your name? I know you from somewhere." And he says, "Hey, how you doin?"'

He's the nicest motherfucker but he admires the Stones too. I know it. He tole me.'

Chris O'Dell is at the first table with Mick and Keith where it's Rabbit City. That's what Chris calls it. Like where's and who's and this and that. All these people rabbiting like crazy and wondering who's rabbiting about them. There's nothing to do but get high and drink as much as possible. Andy Warhol is snapping Polaroids. There's a table full of ghouls in the corner with washed-out muslin faces that glow blue and eerie in the half-light. The whole *mise en scene* cries out for von Stroheim to shoot it at foot-fetish level or for Dietrich to slink out on the dance floor and destroy Emil Jannings once and for all.

Instead, a naked girl with dark skin and heavy silicon-filled breasts comes out of a fake white cake and rotates tassles fastened to her nipples. She jerks, bumps, and grinds, flexes her tits, then goes back into the cake.

Bill Wyman's ten-year-old son, Stephen, is sitting with his father. He's having as rough a tour as anyone, having had to ride out the porno film in the front of the plane. Now this. Bill explains to him that it's kinda funny the way she can shake them in opposite directions and Stephen can see that, so he laughs. 'See that girl over there?' Bill asks him, pointing out a slim girl with Jean Harlow features. 'That's a man.'

Well, Bill has never lied to him before, but how can a woman be a man? Even a father's credibility has limits. Later in the evening, Candy Darling, slim, blond, and a man, sits down at the Wymans' table and asks Stephen, 'Would you like to dance with me?' and all of a sudden, Stephen knows his father hasn't lied. 'No,' he says, 'oh, no.'

'Where are the pies now?' Rudge groans from around a drink. 'We could use 'em!' They need something. One of the S.T.P. boys is so pissed off with the whole thing, he establishes a new tour record by cutting eight phones into shreds at the party. Who are all these people, he wonders, and what do they have to do with rock and roll? He draws obscene messages on all the posters in the hallway. All these people should be covered with booze and pies and then thrown out the window, he says. That's what a real rocking band like the Faces would do.

'How obscene,' Rudge sighs, looking more tired and defeated than is possible for a person who has lived only twenty-five years.

'Our assistant electrician sitting next to Zsa Zsa Gabor. The only person not here is Cynthia Sagittarius... ah, whatever you try to do, they take over, I suppose.'

'This is a fucking thousand-dollar-a-plate campaign dinner,' one of the regulars complains. 'The Stones are fucking up. It makes me sick to see 'em here with these people. Is this who they've left the people who buy their records for?'

Four black dancers are hoofing now, shuffling off to Buffalo as though it were 1929 and Cond Nast had the good table by the pillar. 'I get dragged into it,' Jagger will say after it's over, 'for my sins. But it happens to everyone in New York from Bob Dylan on down. It's one of the things I should be able to avoid, but as a tourist I find it difficult. I don't know New York City... don't pretend to. I never lived there. That society thing is like livin within a fuckin spider's web.'

Muddy Waters replaces the black dancers. Muddy is an old man now, and he never has been the same since a bad auto accident laid him up for a long time some years back. 'Rolling Stone Blues,' his song, is where the five Englishmen being honored tonight got the name for their band ten years ago.

'It's so wonderful bein here playin for them Rollin Stones,' Muddy says, 'and especially Marshall Chess. I worked for his father for twenty-five years an I wanna dedicate this next song to him.... Muddy goes into "Seventh Son" as Marshall smiles proudly. Here's Muddy taking time out to remember his father, one of the original rock and rollers, a hustling hard-working Jewish businessman who would have fit in no better tonight than the stage crew.

But no one listens as Muddy sings. The party is not for Phil Chess or his son Marshall, not for the Rolling Stones nor the black musicians they love. It's not for the people who wait hours in the street to see them. It's a party for people who go to parties, for whom the world of music is an amusing, temporary, and bizarre source of pleasant conversation.

At 5:00 AM. on a hot July morning in New York City, the insomniac crowd waited in the street outside the St. Regis for a glimpse, a glance, a touch. Maybe Mick, maybe Keith, maybe Bill, Charlie or Mick Taylor. Michael Jagger was twenty-nine. The next day the newspapers would carry accounts of his birthday party, and people who were not there would ask those who were, 'Was it good? What happened? What was it like?'

But what the newspapers left out and what you could not tell anyone who asked and still have them believe you was the way it felt. Desperate and futile; with people going around in circles and getting nowhere except more confused; empty and direction-less, like a circus with no center ring; and very, very sad, like a wake where the mask of false gaiety hides the real grief. It felt like something had died. All that remained was to find someone who could identify the corpse.

Epilogue

AFTERMATH

Three days after the tour ended, Stan Moore, Mr. Security, was back in San Francisco, getting up at 4:30 in the morning in order to get to his government job by six. He did that for three weeks, then went on the night shift. None of the people he worked with had any idea how he'd spent the last two months of his life and only one or two of his friends had noticed his name in the paper, saying he'd been busted in Rhode Island, along with those crazy Rolling Stones.

If anyone asked him about it, he'd tell them, yeah, he'd been back East on personal business and had helped out a promoter friend by doing a little security for the Stones for a week or so. After all, a guy with five kids had to do something to bring in a little extra money.

Two months after the tour, Stan was solidly back into the rhythm of his quiet suburban life in a middle class neighborhood outside the city. When he talked about the tour, he had to get out the pictures of himself with Truman Capote and princess Lee Radziwill in order to confirm that it had all really happened.

The doctor lived in a 'singles' compound built around a swimming pool that looked like a Holiday Inn. Back on his regular rounds, he looked much the same but was very close mouthed when it came to discussing the tour for publication. He wondered if it would be possible to establish some kind of rock and roll practice, and when Bobby Keys and Jim Price worked on the West Coast, he went to see them in San Francisco, then flew on down to L.A. for the concert there. He'd had a serious taste.

'The ends of tours are the saddest things,' Peter Rudge would say afterward. 'There were guys on it for whom it was a lifetime of experience and then it was over. For people like me and Chip, we were going on, we were still in the business. I didn't have to go home to my neighbor and try to tell him about it. I could talk to Bill Graham or someone who had shared it with me.'

After the last concert, Chris O'Dell flew directly from New York to England where she stayed in George Harrison's house to rest for a while. Then she returned to Los Angeles, thinner than possible, sleeping away her days, unable to get back into the time schedule the world calls normal. Two months after the tour, she lost her job as Marshall Chess' secretary. Suddenly, without a power base in the rockbiz, she slept for a day and a half and got scared. 'I've seen too many sunrises,' she said, only half-kidding. 'I'm gonna start eating real food again and getting up in the morning.' She began collecting unemployment checks and waiting. She knew everyone in the business. She was the Pisces Apple lady. Soon enough, she'd be working again.

Gary Stromberg spent four days in Palm Springs after the tour where he reported he went from 'one hundred percent fucked up to thirty percent fucked-up.' Within a week, he was back on his couch at Gibson-Stromberg, answering phones, planning publicity for the T. Rex tour, secure in the knowledge that, along with Gibson, he had engineered the rock PR job of the year, if not the decade. He was thinner than he had ever been and he coughed a lot. Someone asked Gibson whether the tour had done much to change his business partner. 'Yeah,' Gibson said laconically, 'he doesn't laugh much anymore. Otherwise, he's the same... still a lousy lay.'

Willie the baggage man went to Monmouth Park after the tour for a few days to relax. He now works as personal assistant and driver for the biggest rock agent in New York City, who travels by white Rolls Royce. Stevie Wonder's horn player got cooking during a hot set one night after the Stones' tour, and fell off the stage, splitting open his head. BERSERKNESS. He recovered. Months later Stevie himself suffered a severe concussion in a car accident. He was unconscious for days and brain damage was feared. He began to mend during an enforced six-month vacation from the business. He had come to be recognized as perhaps the most brilliant performer-composer in rock.

After a month's vacation, Robert Frank began work on the feature film of the tour. Danny Seymour had gone sailing in the Caribbean to recuperate, so Frank was going to edit it all himself with Marshall taking care of the business end as producer. The live double album of the tour, featuring the Stones and Stevie Wonder, which Marshall put so much time and effort into recording, would never be released. A business dispute with Allen Klein over who owned the rights to songs like 'Bitch' and 'Brown Sugar' tied up the whole thing in litigation.

Cynthia Sagittarius continued hitching from concert to concert to see the people she liked perform. The last time I saw her, she was in Washington Square Park in Greenwich Village. She was staying with a friend in a seedy, dark welfare hotel. Jo-Anne, she said, was in New York's St. Vincent's Hospital mental ward. She'd been there since September and the only time she'd gotten out was when she sneaked away to see Sha-Na-Na. There'd be no more of that. The doctors told her if she did it again, they'd cut off her welfare check. I asked Cynthia whether there was anything she wanted to do besides concerts. 'Yes,' she smiled, 'I'd like to be Queen of England.'

Rolling Stone recouped its considerable investment in the tour by sending Andy Warhol to interview Truman Capote on why he decided not to write about it and other topics. The interview ran over seventeen pages, interspersed with some excellent Peter Beard tour pictures. Capote had some kind things to say to Warhol about Jagger and the Stones but still found the tour a subject which did not his 'excite his imagination.'

For some, the tour did not end. Bobby Keys flew directly to London and the next morning was playing the part of a saxophone player in a movie featuring Ringo Starr. He began working sessions, then flew to Detroit to go on the Joe Cocker tour with Jim Price. Both of them left the tour shortly before drug arrests were made in Australia.

The Stones themselves left the country within three days of the final concert. Jagger made a present to a friend of the two .38 police specials he had carried with him for two months and went to Ireland, as did Mick Taylor. Watts and Wyman returned to the South of France and Keith to Switzerland.

The first time they were to find themselves all together was nearly five months later in Jamaica just before Christmas. With England out of bounds for tax reasons and America impractical because of visa difficulties, they assembled in Kingston to record their new album, which would come to be called 'Goat's Head

Soup.' Ian Stewart was there to oversee the little things. Marshall Chess was writing checks and keeping accounts, and Chip Monck and Rudge flew in for consultation about the upcoming tour of the Far East.

Rudge had spent nearly a month in New York City after the tour, ordering finances, and as he sat and talked about it all in Jamaica he puffed on another cigarette and realized that it was still not over. Someone wanted to hear him tell it all again. The American tour had taken up nearly a year of his life.

The Stones and their people were staying in a hotel that had been a private mansion on the street that once housed Jamaica's great families. The thick, rich smell of flowers hung over everything and rain squalls interrupted the sunshine. Black john crows swooped low over the swimming pool, and during the day there was nothing to do but sit on the wide sweeping veranda, smoke cigarettes, drink rum punch and Red Stripe beer, and talk. Raindrops collected on the waxy green tropical leaves and, after a while, the black servants would lay out the white tablecloths and turn on the lamps, another day having slid away in a humid haze.

Although the recording was going well and the band was playing as tight as ever, it felt like the end of the road. It was as though all of it were a scene out of Somerset Maugham or Conrad, with a group of civilized people doing their best to hold their own against the tropical darkness.

A warrant for the arrest of Keith Richard and his lady, Anita, on drug charges had been issued in France. Although the charges were unprovable and based on hearsay, it meant a mass of legal hassling and haggling and would have to be accomplished before it could be laid to rest. Jagger, Wyman, Watts, and Taylor left the Jamaica sessions to fly to France to make personal statements before a magistrate. The Stones' advisors worried whether the warrant would be made international and Keith made plans to take up residence on the other side of the island for a while.

At stake was the future of the band. The tour of Hawaii, Japan, Australia, and New Zealand, which was scheduled for late February 1973, depended upon whether these countries would grant the Stones admission. Japan is one of the world's leading record markets and the Stones were to play four or five nights at a Tokyo arena and do everything possible to create goodwill and a lot of press. There were Japanese, as well as English and American reporters and photographers at the Jamaican sessions, and the Stones approached the matter with a mixture of tolerance and business awareness that has allowed them to outlast all the other bands of their time. But Japan refused to grant Mick Jagger a visa and Rudge worried whether the Hawaii concerts might not be cancelled too.

Then a disastrous earthquake struck Managua, Nicaragua's capital city. Jagger and his wife, Bianca, who was born there, flew to the city to find her mother, who was unhurt. A month later, the Stones came back to America to play a benefit for the Nicaraguan earth victims at the Los Angeles Forum. With ticket prices higher than they had ever been for any rock concert, the Stones sold the place out almost immediately. Then they went on to play Hawaii.

And it seemed as though Jamaica might have signalled nothing more than the passing of one year into another. In LA., Jagger sported a new, shorter haircut. He worked with a rhinestone mask in front of his face and appeared as if he'd been watching David Bowie a lot. After an abbreviated tour of Australia and New Zealand, the band returned to their various places of exile. At the end of June, while staying in their London townhouse, Keith and Anita were arrested and later found guilty of possession of drugs and ammunition. Six months later, the band worked in England and embarked on their first European tour in three years. Keith's good friend, songwriter-musician Gram Parsons died under suspicious circumstances in California. He was twenty-seven.

As this book went to press, faint rumors were already fluttering in the rockbiz about if and when the Stones might try it again—another tour of America.

Rudge, Chip Monck, and Marshall Chess continued to work for the Stones, as did Ian Stewart and Alan Dunn, who had become part of the extensive branch of the London office.

Only Jo Bergman was totally and finally through with it. After spending five years of her life with the band, she had walked out of the dressing room in New York City one night, desolate, and in tears, able to say only, 'It's been... it's been terribly strange.' Later, when it was all over, she'd say, 'New York... I guess you could say that was the end of innocence for me... I finally saw

that this was it, kid... It's over.' Better than anyone, she knew that
the Stones would continue. It was their nature. They had lived so
long and done so well in the chaos, they could not easily stop it
now. 'There will never be green-carpeted offices,' she'd say. 'They
will never be respectable. No matter how close they come, they
will always blow it. Albums will come out and tours will be made
and so will music, but it will never be right, completely. It's one
of their strengths. They are fragmented...'

The man who had the final say on everything, whose wishes
and desires would dictate what would or would not happen for
the Rolling Stones, Michael Jagger, would certainly continue.
Soon after the tour, it was reported that he had engaged a Hollywood agency to read prospective film scripts for him.

'Jagger is on that Sinatra-Presley plateau,' Gary Stromberg said
'He's invulnerable. He knows instinctively how never to give an
audience enough. Because they'll take as much as you give and
chew you up if they can. Jagger will give you a touch, a glim-
mer. The way he works on stage makes him seem vulnerable, but
he has a tremendous sense of himself. He knows what works for
him. He's got great, fantastic instincts. He ain't finished yet. I
know that. He has a lot of mindfucking left to do.'

No, certainly not. Michael Jagger had his whole life in front of
him, with several already left behind. The Stones would go on
for as long as he needed them to, and they would most certainly
tour America again if legal troubles did not make that an impos-
sibility.

For Jagger was a young man, just thirty. And congratulations
were not necessarily in order.

Helter Skelter Publishing

All Helter Skelter titles are available by mail order from the world famous
Helter Skelter bookshop.

You can either phone or fax your order to Helter Skelter on these numbers:
Telephone: +44 (0)20 7836 1151 or Fax: +44 (0)20 7240 9880

Office hours: Mon-Fri 10:00am - 7:00pm,

Sat: 10:00am - 6:00pm, Sun: closed.

Postage prices per book worldwide are as follows:

UK & Channel Islands	£1.50
Europe & Eire (air)	£2.95
USA, Canada (air)	£7.50
Australasia, Far East (air)	£9.00
Overseas (surface)	£2.50

You can also write enclosing a cheque, International Money Order, or registered cash. Please include postage. DO NOT send cash. DO NOT send foreign currency, or cheques drawn on an overseas bank. Send to:

Helter Skelter Bookshop,
4 Denmark Street, London, WC2H 8LL, United Kingdom.

If you are in London come and visit us, and browse the titles
in person!!

Email: helter@skelter.demon.co.uk
Website: http://www.skelter.demon.co.uk

Razor's Edge: Bob Dylan and the Never Ending Tour
by **Andrew Muir. ISBN 1 900924 13 7.**
256 pages illustrated. 156 x 234 mm. UK: £12.99   US: $18.95
Since 1986, Bob Dylan has been permanently on tour! Dylan
expert Muir documents the ups and downs of this unprecedented
trek, and tries to get to grips with what it means: both for Dylan
and for his dedicated fans.

Get Back: The Beatles' Let It Be Disaster
by **Doug Sulpy & Ray Schweighardt. ISBN 1 900924 12 9**
160 pages – 156 x 234 mm, illustrated. UK: £14.95 US: $20.00
No-holds barred, hour-by-hour account of the Beatles self-
destruction in the studio.
"One of the most poignant Beatles books ever." **Mojo**

Bob Dylan: A Biography
by **Anthony Scaduto. ISBN 1 900924 23 4**
288 pages – 129 x 198 mm, illustrated. UK: £9.99 US: $17.95
Definitive biography covering Dylan's rise from Woody Guthrie
acolyte, through the Greenwich folk days to rock super-stardom.
Drawing exclusively on first hand interviews with Dylan.